Baseball in the Classroom

Baseball in the Classroom

Essays on Teaching the National Pastime

Edited by EDWARD J. RIELLY

McFarland & Company, Inc., Publishers
Jefferson, North Carolina, and London

All photographs courtesy of the National Archives.

LIBRARY OF CONGRESS CATALOGUING-IN-PUBLICATION DATA

Baseball in the classroom : essays on teaching the national pastime / edited by Edward J. Rielly.
    p.   cm.
Includes bibliographical references and index.

ISBN-13: 978-0-7864-2779-6
(softcover : 50# alkaline paper) ∞

1. College teaching—United States—Anecdotes. 2. Baseball—United States—Anecdotes. 3. Baseball—Study and teaching (Higher)—United States. I. Rielly, Edward J.
LB2331.B375   2006
378.1'7—dc22   2006029829

British Library cataloguing data are available

©2006 Edward J. Rielly. All rights reserved

No part of this book may be reproduced or transmitted in any form or by any means, electronic or mechanical, including photocopying or recording, or by any information storage and retrieval system, without permission in writing from the publisher.

Cover photograph ©2006 Image Source; baseball ©2006 PhotoSpin

Manufactured in the United States of America

McFarland & Company, Inc., Publishers
  Box 611, Jefferson, North Carolina 28640
  www.mcfarlandpub.com

To my sister, Mary Flanagan,
who "played school" with me
when I was very young
and then went on to become an outstanding teacher.
In both of these ways, she helped direct me
into a life spent in education,
a career choice that I have never
(or at least seldom) regretted.

Acknowledgments

Many people contributed to this volume. I appreciate the help of various individuals and organizations in distributing the call for submissions, especially James Gates, Library Director of the National Baseball Hall of Fame and Museum, who graciously included my call for submissions in a large Hall of Fame mailing, and the editors of *The SABR Bulletin* and the H-PCAACA list. This volume would not exist without the contributions of the outstanding faculty whose essays grace the following pages. I also am indebted to the faculty who offered to contribute what undoubtedly would have been valuable essays but whom I could not invite to submit because of previous commitments to essays in their areas. Finally, I acknowledge two constants in my life: the support of my college, Saint Joseph's College of Maine, where good teaching is valued and where popular culture studies is treated with the respect it deserves, and, most importantly, the support of my family, including my wife, Jeanne, and my children, Brendan and Brigid.

Contents

Acknowledgments	vi
Introduction by Edward J. Rielly	1
Archival Research: Using Documentary Records to Touch All the Bases *(John A. Vernon)*	3
Business: Applying Modern Financial Principles to the Babe Ruth Purchase *(Michael Haupert, Kenneth Winter and Lise Graham)*	19
Cultural Studies: Baseball in American Culture: A Sociocultural History of Baseball *(Alar Lipping)*	27
Educational Partnerships: Times, Traditions, and Technology—Teaching the Negro Leagues *(Raymond Doswell, Gerald D. Bailey and Dan Lumley)*	33
Experiential Learning: Journal of a Journey—Teaching Baseball on the Road *(E. Michael Brady)*	40
Film: O'Brien to Ryan to Goldberg—Fact, Fiction, and Cultural Stereotyping in Baseball Films *(Rob Edelman)*	51
Film: Baseball Cinema in the Classroom *(George Grella)*	61
History: Using Baseball to Teach U.S. History Since the Civil War *(Jerry Rodnitzky)*	69
History: Baseball and American Culture—A Seminar *(William M. Simons)*	77
Labor Relations: As Many Strikes as It Takes—Using Baseball to Teach Labor Relations *(Karen S. Koziara)*	87
Law: Even the Best Lawyers Must Know Baseball *(Roger I. Abrams)*	95
Law: "Legal Baseball" in the Law School Curriculum—The Contracts Example *(C. Paul Rogers III)*	104

Literature: Baseball Literature for General Education
 (Gary Gray and Gary Land) 113

Literature and Grammar: Baseball in the English
 Curriculum *(Edward J. Rielly)* 125

Native American History: More than a Game—Teaching
 American Indian History through Baseball *(C. Richard King)* 131

Philosophy: Baseball and Philosophy? "Let's Go to the
 Video Tape!" *(Eric Bronson)* 137

Public Speaking: The Rhetoric of Baseball—Citizenship and
 the Public Speaking Classroom *(Michael L. Butterworth)* 145

Race Studies: Redefining the Narrative—Effa Manley,
 Jackie Robinson, and the Integration of Baseball
 (Robert Cvornyek) 151

Race Studies: Teaching Social Justice by Examining the
 Desegregation of Baseball *(Joe Marren)* 159

Social History: American Vice and Teaching Baseball
 History *(Kevin Grace)* 169

About the Contributors 179

Index 185

Introduction
EDWARD J. RIELLY

Baseball has long been recognized as America's national pastime. That title is neither an accident nor an arbitrary designation. The history of baseball, in its earlier rounders and townball forms as well as in its more modern versions, chronologically parallels the history of our nation. Further, baseball reflects virtually every aspect of American society, both good and bad. Literature and the arts, race relations, business, labor-management conflicts, gender issues, war, religion and myth, and the media are just a few of the areas in which the sport intersects with American culture in a symbiotic relationship. Readers who wish to explore the wide range of these intersections are invited to consult this author's *Baseball: An Encyclopedia of Popular Culture* (2000; Lincoln: University of Nebraska Press, 2005).

So would anyone exempt education from the areas of social relevance to America's national pastime? Certainly not those college and university professors who have contributed essays to this volume. Baseball appears often in higher-education courses, both as the subject itself and as a teaching method. The focus in the essays that follow usually is on baseball as a pedagogical tool to teach specific disciplines. The academic range is wide: business, cultural studies, film, history, labor relations, law, literature (along with writing and grammar), Native American history, philosophy, public speaking, race studies, and social history. Essays also relate to archival research for pedagogical purposes, the formation of educational partnerships to facilitate instruction, and the use of experiential learning through a traveling summer course. Yet, as broad as this spectrum is, baseball is taught in other disciplines as well; regrettably, it was not possible to acquire essays in every academic area.

A number of high school teachers wrote concerning this volume when it was in its early stages. As worthwhile as essays regarding secondary education would have been, the decision was to maintain the higher-education focus in order to cover as many areas of college instruction as possible while keeping the size of the volume under control. Perhaps a second volume relating to secondary education would be a valuable future endeavor.

The essays are arranged by types of courses to help faculty quickly find the essays most relevant to their own teaching. It is important to remember, though, that most essays include pedagogical insights valuable for faculty in a range of courses; the initial headings merely guide rather than attempt to pigeonhole essays within one discipline each. Good teaching usually involves garnering ideas from many places, so readers are encouraged to read all of the essays.

Information on the contributors can be found at the end of the book. Readers will be impressed with the diversity and substantial accomplishments of the contributors.

It is the hope of all those involved in creating this collection of essays that readers will find the volume enjoyable, intellectually stimulating, and of practical value as they turn to their own teaching. Readers may find the origins of their own future courses within these pages, or they may discover ways, large and small, to enrich their current teaching.

Archival Research

Using Documentary Records to Touch All the Bases

JOHN A. VERNON

What could the "National Pastime" and the "National Archives and Records Administration" (NARA) have in common to describe them other than the word "national," one being a specialized recreational pursuit enjoyed by the many, the other a public institution enjoyed by the relatively few interested in the history of the federal government? In the popular mind that probably equates to baseball, YAY; archives, YAWN—and never the twain shall meet! Yet, in fact, the National Archives contain numerous baseball-related documents reflecting the intersection of key governmental functions with this peculiarly hardy sport. Further, these records lend themselves especially well to teaching about baseball because they are intellectually provocative, visually arresting, and can be photocopied and distributed for classroom purposes.

A short explanation of "archives" may be helpful here; these are merely organizational records retained by part of an organization for their long-term value. Although outsiders tend to assume that such documents will invariably be "old," "boring," or "irrelevant," that assuredly does not have to be the case; and any medium with imbedded information in it—whether photograph, computerized record, videotape, textual record, or something else—can qualify as archival records.

In the case of NARA and the Library of Congress, not only are all such media represented in their respective archival holdings, but so also is almost every realm of human activity, including baseball, that has ever attracted the national government's attention. Most records, at least those created and maintained by government employees, are not copyrighted. Others, of proprietary value because they originate from private sources such as a business or commercial firm, can usually still be photocopied and made available for academic purposes if "fair use" guidelines are followed.

Facsimiles of several baseball-related records are reproduced with this article. For each document, there is a section on its historical context and suggested instructional strategies for facilitating student comprehension,

U.S. NATIONAL ARCHIVES & RECORDS ADMINISTRATION
www.archives.gov

Photo Analysis Worksheet

Step 1. Observation

A. Study the photograph for 2 minutes. Form an overall impression of the photograph and then examine individual items. Next, divide the photo into quadrants and study each section to see what new details become visible.

B. Use the chart below to list people, objects, and activities in the photograph.

People	Objects	Activities

Step 2. Inference
Based on what you have observed above, list three things you might infer from this photograph.

Step 3. Questions

A. What questions does this photograph raise in your mind?

B. Where could you find answers to them?

Reproduced at the National Archives

discussion, and analyses. The records selected reflect the author's interest in racial attitudes and cultural biases in baseball. Teachers who prefer to focus on other aspects of the game can find a wealth of document alternatives within NARA (http://www.archives.gov) or Library of Congress records (http://www.loc.gov).

Also provided are two basic forms, one for use with photographs, the

U.S. NATIONAL ARCHIVES & RECORDS ADMINISTRATION

www.archives.gov

Written Document Analysis Worksheet

1. TYPE OF DOCUMENT (Check one):

   ___ Newspaper   ___ Map   ___ Advertisement
   ___ Letter   ___ Telegram   ___ Congressional record
   ___ Patent   ___ Press release
   ___ Memorandum   ___ Census report
                        ___ Report   ___ Other

2. UNIQUE PHYSICAL QUALITIES OF THE DOCUMENT (Check one or more):

   ___ Interesting letterhead   ___ Notations
   ___ Handwritten   ___ "RECEIVED" stamp
   ___ Typed   ___ Other
   ___ Seals

3. DATE(S) OF DOCUMENT: _____

4. AUTHOR (OR CREATOR) OF THE DOCUMENT: _____

   POSITION (TITLE): _____

5. FOR WHAT AUDIENCE WAS THE DOCUMENT WRITTEN? _____

6. DOCUMENT INFORMATION (There are many possible ways to answer A-E.)

   A. List three things the author said that you think are important:
   _____
   _____
   _____

   B. Why do you think this document was written?
   _____
   _____

   C. What evidence in the document helps you know why it was written? Quote from the document.
   _____
   _____

   D. List two things the document tells you about life in the United States at the time it was written:
   _____
   _____

   E. Write a question to the author that is left unanswered by the document:
   _____
   _____

Reproduced at the National Archives

Opposite and above: **The Photo Analysis Worksheet encourages detailed study of photographs. A worksheet approach can lead to greater understanding of archival documents.**

Japanese boys play baseball at a War Relocation Authority compound.

other for written documents. These forms are designed to help students concentrate their attention on information to be conveyed, its organization, and the physical form and format of the document. Forms can be modified by the instructor as instructional needs dictate.

Japanese Boys Playing Baseball

Historical Context

Organized Japanese baseball dates back to the 1870s, having been introduced by American sailors in 1853 when Commodore Matthew Perry arrived in Tokyo Bay. Since then, its practitioners in the Land of the Rising Sun have played at all levels, amateur and professional, and the game's hold on the hearts and minds of its populace has proved to be every bit as impassioned and sustained as the original American model. Soon after the Pearl Harbor attack ushered U.S. entry into World War II, an executive order called for the "evacuation" of most Japanese-American residents (both those born in America and those later naturalized) from the West Coast, where most had been working as farmers, fishermen, or small business owners. Altogether, by the war's end, more than 120,000 people—

Roy Campanella instructs members of the Tokyo Giants.

two-thirds of whom had been born in the United States—had been moved inland to several westernmost states and detained within ten barbed wired centers. Until 1943 Japan seemed almost militarily invincible in the Pacific, even driving American forces from a supposedly impregnable Philippine stronghold. Thus, grudging respect for Japanese martial prowess abroad fed ever-rising fears at home. If there were Italian-Americans and German-Americans during that same period actively working to subvert their adopted country's war interests, they were not as physically recognizable as a group, as recently emigrated, or as obvious in retaining their language as were Japanese-Americans.

Instructional Suggestions

One good vehicle for sharpening students' critical thinking skills is to have them describe and carefully scrutinize what they see in historic photographs. NARA maintains millions of photographs (see http://www.archives.gov/research/formats/photographs-dc.html#photos) in its agency collections. Document One shows boys of clearly Asian extraction playing baseball in a Japanese-American relocation camp situated in Owens Valley, California, later named the Manzanar Relocation Center. With journalism's "5 W's and 1 H" (Who, What, When, Where, Why, and How) in mind, instructors might ask students to discern factual information (such things as number of people depicted, assumed ethnicity, activity engaged in, approximate period when the photograph was taken, etc.) versus what might be inferred. Examples of the latter might include noting the apparently barren terrain, large-scale institutional setting, modest buildings within, assumed purpose of the buildings (dwellings or something else), perceived attitudes, and the like. Students find they may have different or even conflicting perceptions about the nature of the photograph, helping them to grasp the elusive nature of "historical truth," even when examining a document scarcely sixty years old. Instructors might also challenge students to speculate about why this photograph came to exist (that this takes place in a federal installation called a War Relocation Authority [WRA] compound) and what that connotes to them. For example, is the term "relocation center" employed as a euphemism for a concentration camp, facility for forced incarceration, or place for internment?

Educators might also encourage students to conduct an internet search of the word "Manzanar." Doing so results in a wide range of Web resources, including another striking and somewhat different shot of baseball at Manzanar taken by famous photographer Ansel Adams as part of an "American Memory" electronic exhibit created by the Library of Congress (see http://www.memory.loc.gov/ammem/aamhtml/aamhome.html). Ask students to compare the Adams photo to Document One. The instructor may seek to explain how it reinforces an increasing sense of irony in the situation represented, further opening the door to probing questions. For example, after the teacher mentions what the terms "Nikkei" (Japanese American), "Issei" (first generation), or "Nisei"(second generation) mean, the students might consider the audience and participants in the Adams photograph, and whether distinctions should have been made based on whether they were Issei or Nisei, young or old, male or female. A related assignment could be to learn more about Manzanar and other such facilities, the circumstances by which they were established, and their similarities and differences.

Historical Context

The long-standing Japanese fascination with baseball has contributed toward the sport's increasingly international dimension. The first Japanese player to break into our big leagues was left-handed pitcher Masanori Murakami, who performed for the San Francisco Giants in 1964 and 1965. Since then, Hideki Irabu, Hideki Matsui, Hideo Nomo, Ichiro Suzuki, and

CITIZENS COMMITTEE TO END DISCRIMINATION IN BASEBALL

44 WEST 125th STREET
NEW YORK CITY
LEhigh 4-0989

WILLIAM T. ANDREWS
Chairman

GOLDA HUNTMAN
Secretary

Sept. 9, 1942

SPONSORS

W. T. ANDREWS
State Assemblyman of N. Y.
REV. A. CLAYTON POWELL
New York Councilman
STANLEY ISAACS
New York Councilman
PETER CACCHIONE
New York Councilman
MAX YERGAN
National Negro Congress
WALTER WHITE
N. A. A. C. P.
HENRY POPE
Citizens Comm. of Harlem
ALGERNON BLACK
Ethical Culture School
SAUL MILLS
N. Y. C.I.O. Council
FREDERICK MYERS
National Maritime Union
LEON STRAUSS
Fur Floor Boys Union
EFFA MANLEY
Newark Eagles Baseball Club
JOE CUMMISKEY
PM
DAN PARKER
Daily Mirror
HY TURKIN
Daily News
JOE BOSTIC
Peoples Voice
WENDELL SMITH
Pittsburgh Courier
DAN BURLY
Amsterdam News
CHAPPIE GARDNER
HUGH BRADLEY
Writer and Author
HAROLD SCHACTER
Young Fraternalists
GOLDA HUNTMAN
Book & Magazine Guild

Mr. Harold Ickes, Sec.
Dept. of Interior
Washington,
D. C.

Dear Mr. Ickes:

    National unity of the American people is the most essential need today, to guarantee victory for our country. To achieve this national unity all discrimination against any section of the American people must be eliminated.

    One of the most flagrant discriminatory practices against the Negro people is the exclusion of Negro ball players from the major league teams. Two months ago, Judge Kenesaw M. Landis, Commissioner of Baseball, publicly stated that there are no bars against the hiring of Negro ball players. Yet to date, not one has been hired or given a tryout.

    America today needs team play and unity to defeat the Fascist Axis. Baseball is our national game, a symbol of American democracy. As a symbol of American democracy, baseball must end discrimination by choosing All-Americans from all Americans as its contribution to the building of unity.

    A group of prominent public officials, trade unionists and sports writers have gotten together to organize a nation-wide citizens committee to end discrimination in baseball. Your interest in the democratic rights of all peoples has prompted us to write asking you to become part of this committee.

    We urge you to join with us and that you indicate your consent by signing and returning enclosed postal card.

    Very truly yours,

WILLIAM T. ANDREWS,
State Assemblyman of N. Y.

WALTER WHITE,
N. A. A. C. P.

STANLEY ISAACS,
New York Councilman

Reproduced at the National Archives

Concerned citizens urge the Secretary of the Interior to help integrate baseball.

other recent Japanese émigrés left their own leagues to demonstrate playing proficiency in this country's majors.

Instructional Suggestions

    Speaking of "Giants," Document Two features the always affable Brooklyn Dodgers receiver, Roy Campanella, discussing the fine points of catching with the Tokyo Giants' manager and one of the manager's charges.

An instructor could use this photograph to see how much students can deduce from careful examination. Do they recognize Campanella, and can they guess how, when, and where the encounter likely took place? (March 1957 at the club's Vero Beach training facility after the Dodgers' goodwill trip to Japan in the Fall of 1956 shortly after their World Series loss to the Yankees.) What about the wristwatch? Are watches normally worn here in professional circles, even among managers? Are the gloves likely to be Japanese-produced and does sport—in this case, baseball—constitute such a universal language that, linguistic differences aside, all parties can make themselves understood? Is there really anything uniquely American about the game of baseball? If so, students may do some research to compare and contrast traditions, styles of play, and other pertinent cultural factors.

Facsimile: Appeal to Integrate Baseball

Historical Context

A landmark race-relations study, *An American Dilemma: the Negro Problem and American Democracy*, directed by Swedish sociologist Gunnar Myrdal, came out during World War II. The published work, based on a six-year study of prevailing racial attitudes and practices in the United States, utilized the findings of forty-eight writers and researchers, including noted African-American scholars Kenneth B. Clark and Ralph Bunche. The demands of global warfare, especially in a struggle represented as a necessary crusade against political repression and racial intolerance abroad, required total utilization and mobilization of all natural resources, human and other. As the war wore on, U.S. governmental leaders were forced to let various minorities play a more expanded role than ever before, in both military and civilian sectors within the overall war effort. Set in motion during World War II, such a dramatic shift in thinking continued after the war, contributing heavily to the advancement of civil rights in the United States and thereby planting the seeds of destruction for "Jim Crow" America.

During the early part of the conflict, the segregated Negro Leagues (the highest-level black teams affiliated into two leagues) enjoyed their high-water mark in popularity. Many African-American factory and other defense industry workers attracted to job opportunities in the city attended their games. At the same time, many critics, white and black, disapproved of continuing segregated play since the arrangement was involuntary and appeared to contradict any notion that white baseball could legitimately call itself "the national pastime" if skin color alone could be used to deny capable black aspirants the right to compete for jobs within that realm.

The letter to Department of the Interior Secretary Harold Ickes explicitly centers on the discrepancy between democratic ideals fought for by American servicemen and service women all over the globe and the prolonged resistance within "organized baseball" to allowing African Americans to participate on an equal basis. Ickes, one of the most liberal New Deal appointees, as early as 1933 had instituted a Department of the Interior agency-wide policy against racial discrimination, even creating an Office of Negro Affairs within which Robert Weaver (later, under President John F. Kennedy, the first African-American Cabinet member) worked against segregated employment policies both inside and outside government.

Instructional Suggestions

Few present-day college students have personally experienced this country's earlier advocacy of segregation as an official policy. As a consciousness-raising activity, ask students to learn more about one or more of the organizations represented on the letterhead. Similarly, ask them to find biographical material about the individuals named as spokespersons. Working individually or collectively, students might frame a proposed reply for Ickes. One aspect to investigate is whether the Interior Department of that time had any jurisdiction over recreational facilities where baseball was played. Based on this document or related information, students might speculate as to whether Ickes was contacted solely because of his reputation for open-mindedness.

Students could also probe the reference in the second paragraph to Judge Landis's statement by locating newspaper articles detailing that statement. They could locate biographical information on Landis and try to ascertain whether the people listed on the letterhead and at the bottom as sponsors were regarded as politically radical, and whether the opinions expressed represented those of New York City's broader population.

Did anything come of this plea? Ask one or more students to inquire into baseball's existing hiring practices and whether comparable "gentleman's agreements" in other areas of work existed to discriminate against particular groups or classes of job seekers. A student assigned to research the topic could discuss President Franklin D. Roosevelt's "green light letter" (urging the major leagues to continue playing during the war) and its intended parameters. Students should be able to discover independently, if the teacher has not broached it already, that the allegation of segregation in employment was justified, with the practice caused by the white establishment's de facto, if not de jure, adherence to such a practice. On the basis of fairly simple research, students could report that the war had made

Jackie Robinson gives batting tips to Latin-American players.

possible professional leagues for white women partially financed by major league owners and other figures associated with organized baseball. And in the white majors, teams were hiring teenagers, over-aged veterans, and even physically disabled players (such as Monte Stratton of the White Sox, Pete Grey of the St Louis Browns, and Burt Shepard of the Washington Senators) to play in preference to blacks. Ask a student to consult Brad Snyder's *Beyond the Shadow of the Senators* to determine what Homestead Grays sluggers Josh Gibson and Buck Leonard might have contributed to that Negro league team's counterpart in the American League: the perennially bad Washington Senators.

Students could also be challenged to evaluate whether so-called symbols (in this case, baseball as "a symbol of American democracy") ever make a difference in public opinion, and, if so, to identify the conditions under which they alter public opinion.

Jackie Robinson with Latin-American Baseball Players

Historical Context

Branch Rickey, as St. Louis Cardinals general manager, invented the highly successful and much-emulated minor league farm system for the Cardinals in the 1920s and 1930s and moved on to lead the Brooklyn Dodgers after that club's general manager, Larry MacPhail, accepted an Army commission at the end of 1942. Rickey quickly decided that he needed previously untapped talent if he were to field a Dodger team to compete on equal footing with the two other, more handsomely financed New York area teams, the Yankees and the Giants. Thus, for several years afterward Rickey had authorized the secret scouting of players from the Negro Leagues and Latin America. Once the war wound down, the man referred to in baseball circles as the "Mahatma," for a rare combination of erudition, religiosity, and political cunning, met secretly with Jackie Robinson in August 1945. Shortly afterwards the Dodgers announced Robinson's signing by its top farm team, the Montreal Royals of the International League. In that, relatively speaking, racial oasis, the newcomer played so well in 1946 that he was named the league's batting champion and was named Most Valuable Player in the minor league "Little World Series" post-season competition when the Royals triumphed over the Louisville Colonels.

The Brooklyn team, after Jackie's coming to the parent club in 1947, won six pennants in ten years, narrowly missed out on two more, and won a World Series over the hated Yankees. Four Rookie of the Year awards went to African-American Dodgers as did five seasonal league MVP's; and ultimately the first two black Dodger signees, Robinson and Campanella, were elected to the National Baseball Hall of Fame.

A September 1949 photograph taken at Ebbets Field of that year's eventual National League batting champion and MVP, Dodger second-baseman Jackie Robinson, shows him with three players from Venezuelan leagues. His image serves as a reminder not only of his pioneering status as the century's first acknowledged African-American major league player but also of the Dodgers' ability, by virtue of having signed Robinson, to attract the interest of many racial minorities.

Since the first Venezuelan entered the major league ranks in 1939, almost two hundred countrymen have joined the ranks, many of them as All-Stars, and one (Luis Aparicio) as a Hall of Fame member. At the shortstop position alone, baseball has been distinguished through the years by the play of such stellar performers as Aparicio, Alfonso "Chico" Carrasquel, Dave Concepcion, Ozzie Guillen (later manager of the 2005 World Series champion White Sox), and many others who came later. "Beisbol's" grip on Venezuela is so fierce that the country has not only won a U.S Little League Championship and an Amateur Baseball World Series in Havana, but also has had American Negro League luminaries such as Josh Gibson and later major leaguers, including Greg Maddox and Barry Bonds, join native-born stars such as Bobby Area, Magglio Ordonez, Melvin Mora, and others in spirited Venezuelan winter-league play. The quality of competition between teams has been so high that it is worth noting that the

Caracas Lions, champions of 1986–1987, included on its roster Andres Galarraga, Tony Armas, Bo Diaz, and Omar Vizquel, all Venezuelan and all either then or later named major league all-stars.

Instructional Suggestions

Ask students to compile a list of minority (in this case Latino) players signed through the years as big leaguers and to compare those teams' won-loss records with other teams in their leagues. They also could chart Caribbean-rim countries that have produced the most players historically, and determine whether traditional patterns of origin have changed, and, if so, seek to explain why. Additionally, they may offer opinions as to where and why the photograph came to be taken (since there is no copyright or caption given), and whether the appearance of comfortable rapport among the four men is merely something staged or a valid expression of mutual like and respect. Having students be generally conversant with the history of Latin American involvement in baseball can make for meaningful dialogue. Instructors could also address the issue of "race" (and how it may be differently defined in the U.S. and elsewhere in the hemisphere), the possibility of different cultural values in different countries, and whether there exist discernible differences in styles of play, and, if so, to what these differences are attributable. Could we be guilty of ethnic stereotyping based on simplistic cultural or racial assumptions? Finally, ask students to develop Latin American player rosters based on country of origin and have them consider whether one or more of these nations might have a realistic chance to beat United States teams.

A Letter to Jackie Robinson

Historical Context

During the twenty-year period from 1947 through 1966, thirteen African-American players won the National League MVP awards. The influx of U.S. and Caribbean black talent has undeniably raised the overall quality of play, and with Japanese and Koreans lately competing, too, it should be boosted even more. With or without steroids, the modern baseball player performs at a level unanticipated fifty or sixty years ago. Soon other talent will emerge from additional geographic areas, and that infusion should serve to make our professional game both better played and better understood elsewhere in the world.

Using Documentary Records 15

BASEBALL CLUB

February 11, 1971

Mr. Jackie Robinson
Cascade Road
Stamford, Connecticut

Dear Jackie:

    I am writing the Commissioner today with regard to my reactions to his new policy pertaining to the Hall of Fame.

    I, for one, feel that men such as Sachel Paige, Josch Gibson, etc., belong in the Hall of Fame. There should be no restrictions whatsoever. It seems to me that we are asking them to "sit in the back of the bus" again. Baseball itself has come a long way and I hate to see it do anything to affect the fine relationship we have with the minority groups.

    Perhaps I am wrong but in my simple way I have to feel that if Sachel and the other players are invited to share a house with Babe Ruth and Lou Gehrig, then they should not be asked to segregate themselves from the other members of the house.

    Perhaps you do not feel this way, Jackie, but I feel this way very strongly. If you have a chance, I would like to hear your views on this subject.

    With all best wishes, I am

Very truly yours,

Buzzie

E. J. Bavasi

[Handwritten reply:]

Dear Buzzie,
your letter of the 11th was sincerely appreciated. I not only agree with your sentiments but have expressed myself on the subject. 1971 is no time to go backwards and frankly I personally would refuse this dubious honor. you know I feel strongly about this matter. I am pleased you are expressing yourself about the way you feel. your action justifies the way I thought of you before the 1957 M.s understanding. I know baseball feels it is honestly doing its part to bring better understanding. I think it has failed miserably but your attitude and the action of Mike Burke of the Yankees is encouraging. I am sure this is only the start. hope there is much more to be done.

Jackie Robinson responds to E. J. Bavasi's letter regarding admission of Negro league players to the Hall of Fame.

Instructional Suggestions

    Have students analyze this letter from Buzzie Bavasi, one-time Dodger executive, to Jackie Robinson and the latter's annotated reply. Ask them to note the misspellings of Paige's and Gibson's names and solicit their views on what the errors mean. Are the misspellings unconscious but unmistakable slurs, are they due merely to a failure to proofread, or do they exist as broad evidence of "jock world" academic ineptitude? What does Bavasi mean when he states that blacks in the Hall will "sit in the back of the bus?" How should this be assessed in light of another Bavasi bon mot offered when asked how major league baseball was run: "We live by the Golden Rule. Those who have the gold make the rules."

Ask students to explain what Satchel Paige meant when responding to a reporter's question as to how he regarded being elected to the Hall of Fame: "The only change is that baseball has turned Paige from a second-class citizen to a second-class immortal." How does that statement square with the usual image of Paige circulated by the baseball press?

What about Robinson's reply to Bavasi when he indicates that "1971 is no time to go backward"? What is "the 1957 misunderstanding"? Why does Robinson regard baseball as having "failed miserably" thus far with "so much more to be done"? What has Robinson done already to try to goad baseball into doing more, and what will he do in the near future? Consider how he might have responded to onetime Montreal Royals teammate Al Campanis's statement made in 1987: "The reason baseball has no black managers is that I truly believe that they may not have some of the necessities to be, let's say, a field manager." Could it not be argued that Jackie Robinson should have been selected as the first black manager, black general manager, black league president, or even the first black commissioner? Would not the best tribute to the fiery Robinson in 1997 on the fiftieth anniversary of his breaking the major league color line have been to allow each team annually to award his number 42 to the player that best exemplified his fighting spirit, exemplary values, and sense of public service rather than to permanently retire that number on every team? Have students debate these points.

Ask students to address what seems a contradiction: the dearth of black fans, especially since they once attended games so gladly when Robinson and other early black players entered the majors. Students should know about rumors circulating since at least the early 1950s that teams quietly establish unspoken quotas as to numbers and positions that non-white players are allowed to play. And it has often been charged that endorsement opportunities are modest for players who are black. Correspondingly, the values of baseball-player card values appear to differ fairly consistently by race. Can they offer an explanation why, for example, Mickey Mantle's cards should be so much more expensive than Hank Aaron's when the latter's career statistics are so much better? Do blacks and Latinos rightfully occupy their fair share of field manager positions and high-level executive job slots? Are the positions of leadership and the salaries that go with them fully integrated? These are questions that students should consider important enough to search for answers no matter how tentative their answers may have to be.

This essay includes just a few sample document facsimiles with suggestions as to how they might be employed to facilitate student learning. Since most students will likely never take a historical methods or historiography course, open discussion and debate about what these and other primary sources really "say" or "mean" when so many interpretations are possible should be instructive.

Examining primary sources about baseball will help students comprehend the organic whole—how one piece fits into a larger puzzle—and gain greater historical understanding. They will be more apt to recognize that useful historical antecedents often exist for solving contemporary or future problems. Once given the direct exposure to primary sources relevant for dealing with real-life issues and current social problems, and the opportunity to dissect them for logic and persuasiveness, students can come away with a personalized sense of history impossible to gain from secondary sources alone.

Panning for Baseball and Archival Gold

What about the needs of instructors should they wish to search out archival sources beyond those presented here? What kind of preparation is necessary? At the very least, they can preliminarily browse the National Archives, Library of Congress, and National Baseball Hall of Fame (http://www.baseballhalloffame.org/library) Web sites for useful information. All of these institutions have finding aids for their collections, reference personnel who can help researchers, and experienced educational and curatorial staffs working toward broader public outreach beyond the narrowly traditional.

Probably most useful to the prospective user is recognition of the importance of developing a viable research strategy to identify and investigate promising collections, groups, and smaller clusters of records. These records will reflect the overall work of the organization and also contain baseball-related nuggets if that organization's activities involved baseball in some way. Thus, within the National Archives system (including regional archival centers and presidential libraries), a researcher could discover player-related civil suits pursued in federal courts, military service recreational activities, a surveyor's sketch and notes for a proposed new stadium in D.C., equipment patent drawings, a political cartoonist's pen-and-ink rendering of a harried president trying manfully to field a barrage of congressional amendments, published antitrust hearing findings, a restraint-of-trade action filed by one bubble gum company against another over issuance of player cards, a charming image of Yankees Babe Ruth and Lou Gehrig posing at West Point before playing the school's cadet team, and numerous photographic scenes that were shot of amateur and professional players for foreign propaganda and cultural purposes. All exist as legitimate documentary evidence of federal program activity.

What a baseball researcher needs to do in assessing archival records for their potential is to recognize that particular organizational roles and duties have to cut across baseball-related activities in some way for there to be any likelihood of success. Thus, to be successful in the archival environment involves looking for relevant documents by function rather than the usual "library" way we all know, by subject. For example, if a person wanted to know Satchel Paige's "real" age, he or she should look in federal census records; similarly, if one wanted to know whether Ty Cobb ever served in the armed services, or whether Charlie Lau was involved in baseball card litigation, one should look for pertinent military records for the former, and Federal Trade Commission records for the latter. It is as if a contract between the researcher and the reference archivist exists. The researcher brings deep content area expertise; the archivist brings broad knowledge about which record groupings, if any, lend themselves to the proposed topic.

In their relatively undiscovered state, an unexploited gold mine of archival sources parallels the untapped wellspring of Negro Leagues talent from long ago. Certainly, many buried archival documents potentially useful for teaching about baseball exist beyond what has been discussed within this essay. The scouting process for locating such records is similar to that employed in baseball for scouting player prospects. It takes determination, strategy, resourcefulness, planning, and an open mind to discover can't-miss prospects in either area. Both explorations are labor-intensive, so patience is a must. And in both these separate areas, when the scout comes up with a bona fide keeper, the satisfaction is immense. But in attempting to compare the quest for locating and utilizing archival records valuable for teaching purposes to the much more publicized hunt for blue-chip baseball talent, the reader would be wise to remember Branch Rickey's oft-quoted observation, "Luck is the residue of design."

In this case that means having a well-thought-out yet flexible search strategy. The seeker of historical treasures in an archival setting would be well advised to acknowledge that no one has complete foreknowledge when venturing into a situation for the first time. So the intrepid archival adventurer ought to maintain a resolute determination to have fun in the exploratory experience itself, even if what was found along the way was not exactly what had been originally anticipated. After all, no one said that getting to the big leagues was easy, all modes of transportation comfortable, all the fields along the way smooth and well lighted, and that all tutelary information from managers and coaches could be immediately assimilated. It is in the pursuit of the unknown that greatness as a player, researcher, educator, or learner lies.

Business

Applying Modern Financial Principles to the Babe Ruth Purchase

MICHAEL HAUPERT, KENNETH WINTER, AND LISE GRAHAM

Baseball may be "America's game" but it is also a business. One of the benefits of using baseball to teach economic and financial concepts is that it is a business with which students are relatively familiar. As with any other business, team owners and financial managers need to make sound financial decisions to ensure the long-term prosperity of the team. While there has previously been little or no detailed financial information available on any club, recent research provided the opportunity to create a case about the most famous baseball business decision ever made.

The decision we refer to is the sale of Babe Ruth from the Red Sox to the Yankees in January of 1920. The case, described below, is written from the perspective of the Yankee director of finance. The student or student group must convince the Yankee ownership that Ruth is worth the price. Until recently, even the purchase price for Ruth, $100,000, was widely disputed. Even now a few details about the purchase are uncertain. Was the mortgage on Fenway Park a condition of the sale? How much of Ruth's salary did the Red Sox pay after the trade and for how long? However, the authors' access to extensive financial data on the Yankees from 1915 through 1919 and beyond enabled them to provide foundation data to students.

In order to analyze the case, students must know specialized economics to forecast the incremental (additional) cash flows from acquiring Babe Ruth. They must compare the cash flows that occur over an uncertain number of years using tools of financial analysis. Finally, they need knowledge of accounting to understand the financial statements presented and how the acquisition of Ruth will impact those statements.

Faculty interest allowed us to create student groups with the full set of skills to analyze the case. In the fall of 2004, students from three classes, Intermediate Accounting I, Economics of Sports and Entertainment, and Problems and Cases in Finance (capstone), at a Midwestern comprehensive university were combined into groups where each group included at least one member from each class. The case accounted for approximately 5 percent of the grade for each course. Each project received one grade based on the input of all three faculty members.

The authors had two primary objectives in writing the case and assigning it to groups of students. The first objective was to increase student skills in the application of forecasting and financial analysis tools. We wanted them to make connections between this decision and similar types of problems they had seen in their foundation classes. The second objective was to simulate the increasing trend in business of forming short-term teams to solve a particular problem, after which the team dissolves.

The remainder of the paper is divided into five parts. The first section provides some historical context for the Ruth sale. The second section outlines the case. The third section provides the economics needed for predicting baseball outcomes. The fourth section discusses what instructors could look for in a solution to the case. The last section examines student response to the case and has concluding comments on how to use the case in different environments.

A Little Historical Context

The business and the game of baseball have both changed since the sale of Babe Ruth. The availability of data on baseball has changed, too. Web sites like baseball-reference.com and baseballlibrary.com provide a wealth of information. There are five relevant areas about which students and faculty might be uninformed: the reserve clause, home runs, World War I, the Black Sox, and baseball revenue streams.

Prior to 1919 and for decades after, baseball operated under the reserve clause. The reserve clause meant that a team owned a player as far as baseball was concerned. A baseball player could not even leave to coach a college team unless his current owner allowed it. The reserve clause meant that the Yankees did not need to worry about Babe Ruth becoming a free agent. If the Yankees bought Ruth then they had complete control of his baseball career. Babe could hold out but he could not play for anyone else.

Home runs were rare in (MLB) Major League Baseball through 1919. When Ruth hit 29 home runs to establish the single season record in 1919, only five of the fifteen other teams hit more home runs than he did. Ruth was the first major league home run leader to hit more homers than the major league triples leader accumulated triples. That pattern has never been reversed. In 2004, the New York Yankees hit 242 home runs in 162 games. That is more than either eight-team league hit in 1919 in approximately 1,100 games.

Serious fans know that the Black Sox scandal occurred when members of the White Sox conspired with gamblers to let Cincinnati win the 1919 World Series. The events of the Black Sox scandal happened in the 1919 World Series but the story did not break until September 1920, so there was no knowledge of the scandal when the Yankees were making a decision about Ruth.

The United States entered World War I on April 6, 1917, and remained in the war until the armistice on November 11, 1918. Because of the military demands for manpower the baseball season in 1918 was shortened and the entire 1919 season was in doubt. When the armistice was signed MLB decided on a slightly shortened season for 1919. The Yankees played 123 games in 1918 and 139 the next year. In 1920 MLB would play a full season of 154 games. The conclusion of the war in the fall of 1918 led to expanded attendance in 1919 at almost every venue.

Revenue streams in 1919 were much different than they are now. There was no television or radio and many cities had blue laws prohibiting, among other things, the playing of baseball on Sunday. One of the big events in New York in 1919 was the legalization of Sunday baseball. The ability of the Yankees to play at home on Sunday contributed to the doubling of their attendance in 1919. The other two New York franchises, Brooklyn and the Giants, also showed attendance surges in 1919. Sunday baseball was still not legal in Boston.

There was also no dispute over who should get the revenue from sales of Babe Ruth jerseys because there were no names or numbers on the backs of uniforms in 1919. Although there were earlier experiments, the Yankees and the Indians became the first teams to adopt numbered uniforms in 1929. In 1960 the White Sox became the first team to put players' names on the back of the jersey.

One revenue stream that was available to most teams but essentially unavailable to the Yankees was concessions. The Yankees rented the Polo Grounds from the New York Giants. As the appendix shows, they received from $4,000 to $8,000 in concession revenue, called Park Privileges, from the Giants. Concessions revenue would skyrocket to over $100,000 per year when the Yankees opened their stadium in 1923.

The Yankees' roster has some interesting stories now that we know how the stories played out. George Halas, a founding father of the NFL and member of the pro football Hall of Fame, played sparingly for the Yankees in 1919. Wally Pipp, whom Lou Gehrig would replace to start his then record 2,130 consecutive-games-played streak, was the first baseman. Gehrig first joined the Yankees in 1923 and became the regular first baseman in 1925.

An interesting perspective on the cost of players is provided by the answer to the following question: what Boston left-hander was sold to New York and led them to pennants and World Series glory in 1921 and 1922? The answer is Art Nehf, who was sold by the Boston Braves to the New York Giants for $55,000. Art once pitched a 21-inning complete game but lost 2–0.

The Case

The case makes it possible to teach both business history and baseball history. The key to creating a realistic case is the financial history of the New York Yankees. Appendix 1 shows the financial statements for the Yankees from 1915 through 1919. The assignment was to analyze the proposed purchase of Babe Ruth from the Boston Red Sox and determine if it was a financially viable purchase. The students were then to write their answer in memo form to the owners of the Yankees with a recommendation either to accept or to reject the offer, along with the financial rationale for their decision. They were to include an opinion on the proper accounting for the transaction and how it would impact the financial statements of the Yankees.

Much of the historical context described above is woven into the case. In particular, the reserve clause makes the financial considerations less complex. Under the circumstances in 1919, the Red Sox and later the Yankees would own Ruth. His three-year contract is not significant in determining the returns the Yankees could get on the purchase price. Ruth was a good negotiator but his only leverage was not playing baseball. Ruth would lose much more than the team by not playing baseball. The reserve clause simplifies the case because there is no problem in determining how long the Yankees will get returns from Ruth. They will get returns as long as he plays.

In order to examine the financial impact Babe Ruth will have on the Yankee organization and to determine whether the Ruth purchase is likely to be profitable, some projections will have to be made. Key questions include:

1. How long will Babe Ruth play?
2. How well will he perform?
3. In what way does Ruth add to the total revenue of the Yankees?
4. How will his salary change over his career?
5. How will the operating costs of the Yankees change as a result of Ruth?

This is where the economics models are useful. These models can be employed to predict the financial impact an individual player will have on his team.

Predicting Baseball Outcomes

Baseball is a great source for business cases because of the predictability of outcomes. The long history of baseball and the extensive statistics gathered on every player and team provide data that has been successful in predicting outcomes such as wins and attendance. On the other hand, quantitative analysis has had limited success in predicting business outcomes in a complex environment.

There has been a wealth of research on the demand for major league baseball. Most of it has centered on using attendance as the dependent variable because of the lack of financial data. Attendance is then transformed into a dollar amount by using average ticket prices. This is a reasonable approach, since it can be argued that most of the fluctuation in team revenue will occur in the area of gate revenue in a given year. In modern baseball, television and radio revenues are usually determined by multi-year contracts, so that the fluctuation of their revenues in a single year is really independent of the demand for the team product. Media revenue is not even an issue in the Ruth case since there was none. Television did not exist, and regular radio broadcasts of Yankees games did not take place until long after Ruth had retired. Therefore, attendance serves as a very reasonable proxy for demand.

Research has shown that the variables affecting the demand for MLB tickets include team won-lost record during the current and previous years, games behind, new stadiums and additional teams in the same town, hometown population, and income per capita of the hometown. The only variable that an individual player can directly affect is the won-lost record.

Research by members of the Society for American Baseball Research has identified very specific measures of the relationship between player performance and team won-lost records. There are many variables that can measure these relationships. In order to save time, we provided students with a brief reading list of good models, with instructions to use those models to project performance. Alternatively, students could be told to find their own models, and use them to make their projections, rationalizing their choice.

Either way, the students do not have to create their own models, as that is not the point of this exercise. Rather, they are using the models to plug in their own data, get estimates of financial returns, and make a recommendation as to whether or not the purchase of Ruth is a good investment.

What to Look for in an Answer

Students were expected to address the issues of Babe Ruth's career length, performance over that career, and the impact of that performance on the Yankees' revenues and costs, including the expense of Ruth's salary. It was also important that they consider the impact of Babe Ruth separately from the increases in revenues and costs that could have been expected anyway. That is, they needed to compare the incremental benefits and costs of acquiring Babe Ruth.

By 1919 Ruth was already in the sixth year of his career and was twenty-four years old. Any reasonable projection of additional career length will be for at least ten years, and even twenty years would not be out of line. Comparison to other players' ages and career lengths are reasonable ways to make this projection.

Projecting Ruth's performance is more difficult. Indeed, it is the magic elixir sought by all general managers over all time—to predict future player performance. However, research backs up casual observation in that the average player's career follows a hyperbolic path of production over time. As a player ages he becomes more productive up to a point and then his productivity begins to fall off. The simplest way to answer this question is to compare Ruth to other players and assume his career progress will follow the pattern of the average player. One simple, yet acceptable, example is to use the model illustrated by Knowles, et al. A projection of his performance is necessary to project Ruth's impact on the Yankees' revenues.

Ruth's impact on Yankees' revenues is largely a function of his on-field performance and its impact on the Yankees' won-lost record. The economic models discussed in the previous section are useful for predicting the impact of Ruth's on-field performance on Yankees' revenues. There are primarily two ways a player impacts the revenue his team earns: through his impact on the quality of the team and through his impact as a spectacle himself. The former is a component identified as significant in numerous demand functions for professional sports: the winning percentage of the team. The latter is called the "Superstar Effect."

A player impacts winning percentage through his contribution to team performance. In this regard, baseball researchers have produced numerous measures. The most straightforward is called "win shares," created by Bill James. This is a measure which calculates the number of a team's wins for which an individual player is responsible. Using this win shares measure for Ruth, it is easy to then calculate the winning percentage the team would have had without Ruth. The difference in the actual and calculated winning percentages can then be used in a demand function to estimate the impact of Ruth on team revenues.

A second way in which a player affects team revenue is the superstar effect. A model to capture this effect can be gleaned from another article, Hausman and Leonard's "Superstars in the National Basketball Association: Economic Value and Policy." This study essentially says that some players will draw fans simply for who they are. The article we refer the students to studies the impact of a few NBA players, such as Michael Jordan, on their team's revenues independent of the impact on their winning percentage. We do not expect the students to recompute these equations, just to use the coefficients and apply them to Ruth. It is then up to the student to make the case that Ruth is to the Yankees what Jordan is to the Bulls.

Students are provided enough salary information to give them a good idea how player salaries progressed with experience during the period 1915–20. A reasonable projection of Ruth's salary will show it increasing through the peak years of his career (about ages twenty-eight to thirty-two) and declining after that. This pattern is similar to the pattern of career output noted above. It should be noted that single-year contracts with ten-day release clauses were the norm, so the downside risk to the team of Ruth having an unexpectedly early diminution of his skills is essentially zero. In other words, if the team determined that Ruth was no longer of value to them, they were obligated only for ten days of his salary before they released him.

The students also need to consider the impact of higher attendance on team operating costs. Not just revenues will increase, but also the cost of security, maintenance, etc. Linear extrapolations based on actual and expected attendance data are reasonable here.

Since the outcomes are known, students must be cautioned against using the actual results. Babe did the unreasonable and became the first MLB player to reach 30, 40, and 50 home runs all in the single year of 1920, but that information was not available at the end of 1919. Students must argue from the facts known to the Yankees in 1919 rather than report the actual outcomes.

Teaching Outcomes

There was great involvement in the case. Of course, there were exceptions. For example, one Eastern European student did not know what a home run was. Other students were frustrated because they felt some team members did not fully participate. Since each student was supposed to contribute specialized knowledge from his or her discipline, when one team member's participation was low the other team members were concerned they did not know enough to adequately complete that part of the analysis. This, of course, gave us an opportunity to talk about the "real world" and the problems free riders (those not actively contributing) present for a business.

Some students had difficulty handling the uncertainty in the case. They were accustomed to having all the information they needed to solve a particular problem. Thus, many asked us to tell them what values to use in computing the cash flows. For example: How many years should we forecast cash flows for? What should we use as the estimate of attendance growth? Should we assume any increase in ticket prices? Through this we were able to illustrate that the difficulty in forecasting and financial analysis is actually not in the arithmetic, but rather in estimating the values to use in the model.

We also had the opportunity to talk about how the business of baseball has changed since the 1920s. The salaries are an obvious difference, but the biggest difference for the case is the reserve clause. It is hard to imagine that Ruth was a highly paid ballplayer at $10,000 per year. The reserve clause is an important issue to discuss but it also simplifies the case. Today, when a player is acquired a team must estimate how long the player will stay with the team. In 1919 the answer was easy: as long as the team wanted him.

In a senior or graduate class, students should have all the skills to fully respond to the case. The forecasting tools and discussion are the heart of the case, so if an instructor chooses to cut back on the case, the areas to cut back on are in the accounting (first) and finance (second) areas. The benefit of the case from a teaching standpoint is that it affords the opportunity to use tools of analysis in a nontraditional setting that is relatively familiar and interesting to many students.

APPENDIX: NEW YORK YANKEES
INCOME STATEMENTS AND RELATED DATA

	1915	1916	1917	1918	1919
Home Receipts	$ 121,395	$ 231,965	$ 156,848	$ 142,241	$ 338,298
Road Receipts	58,670	81,336	72,841	42,907	92,485
Exhibition & Training	6,839	9,131	7,374	4,648	9,258
Park Privilege	6,200	4,000	8,000	4,000	6,000
Other Revenue	2,525		1,511	18	
Total Revenue	$ 195,629	$ 326,432	$ 246,574	$ 193,814	$ 446,041
Expenses					
Player Salary & Bonus	$ 114,375	$ 130,525	$ 117,456	$ 72,791	$ 115,625
Player Purchased/Sold	4,000		35,190	31,150	
Ground Rent	55,000	55,000	40,000	35,000	65,000
Training Trip	11,559	16,531	14,920	11,796	14,089
Other Expenses	84,057	83,685	97,144	89,728	144,355
Total Expenses	$(268,991)	$(285,741)	$(304,710)	$(240,465)	$(339,069)
Net Income (loss)	$ (73,362)	$ 40,691	$ (58,136)	$ (46,651)	$ 106,972

	1915	*1916*	*1917*	*1918*	*1919*
Attendance	256,035	469,211	330,294	282,047	619,164
Revenue per ticket	$ 0.47	$ 0.49	$ 0.47	$ 0.50	$ 0.55
Games	152	154	153	123	139

Works Cited

Domazlicky, Bruce R., and Peter M. Kerr. "Baseball Attendance and the Designated Hitter." *American Economist* 34.1 (1990): 62–68.

Greenstein, Theodore N., and John P. Marcum. "Factors Affecting Attendance of Major League Baseball: I. Team Performance." *Review of Sport and Leisure* 6.2 (1981): 21–34.

Hausman, Jerry A., and Gregory K. Leonard. "Superstars in the National Basketball Association: Economic Value and Policy." *Journal of Labor Economics* 15.4 (1997): 586–624.

James, Bill. *The Baseball Abstract*. Various volumes.

Knowles, G., J. Murray, K. Sherony, and M. Haupert. "Shirking in Major League Baseball in the Era of the Reserve Clause." *NINE: A Journal of Baseball History & Culture* 12.1 (2003): 59–71.

Schofield, John A. "Performance and Attendance at Professional Team Sports." *Journal of Sport Behavior* 6.4 (1983): 196–206.

Sherony, Keith. "A Topology of Baseball Player Behavior." *NINE: A Journal of Baseball History & Culture* 10.2 (2002): 144–56.

Whitney, James D. "Winning Games Versus Winning Championships: The Economics of Fan Interest and Team Performance." *Economic Inquiry* (October 1988): 703–724.

Winter, Kenneth, and Michael J. Haupert. "Yankee Profits and Promise: The Purchase of Babe Ruth and the Building of Yankee Stadium." *The Cooperstown Symposium on Baseball and American Culture*, 2003–04 (forthcoming).

Cultural Studies

Baseball in American Culture: A Sociocultural History of Baseball

Alar Lipping

In 1998 I offered a new course entitled Baseball in American Culture: A Sociocultural History of Baseball. The course was originally designed as an elective course in the popular culture studies degree program at Northern Kentucky University, but it is open to all students regardless of their major. The popular culture studies program is an interdisciplinary degree program that includes faculty from a number of disciplines; I am a member of the popular culture studies faculty association and my discipline is in the area of sport history and sociology. The baseball course that I teach is offered during a three-week summer session that meets every weekday for three hours.

The course is designed to expose students to the study of baseball from two perspectives: a popular culture studies approach and an academic sport history studies perspective. Popular culture is "the way of life in which and by which most people in any society live" (Browne et al., 3). The popular culture approach takes into consideration the many aspects of the world that we inhabit, e.g., sports, music, fads, foods. In regard to the popular culture approach the course reviews the various contributive factors that have become part of baseball: players, teams, events, records, traditions, as well as the material features such as stadiums, uniforms, equipment and nonmaterial features such as rules, behaviors, and criteria for evaluating icons in baseball. The academic sport history approach deals with the perspective of reviewing the social context in which baseball developed. Considerable attention is given to the social forces such as urbanization, industrialization, immigration, technological developments, and political and labor movements that related to the development of baseball in American culture.

The following are specific objectives for the course: (1) to develop operational definitions of popular culture, sports, games, play, and levels of sport engagement; (2) to examine the historiography of sport history; (3) to provide a historical context of the social, political, and economic forces that influenced the development of baseball; (4) to analyze issues of race and gender in baseball; (5) to become familiar with electronic searches to conduct literature reviews on baseball history.

Since the course meets daily for three-hour sessions, there is considerable opportunity to utilize audiovisual presentations. A major component in the instructional process for this course includes the 18½ hour Ken Burns series entitled *Baseball* and the attendant text, *Baseball: An Illustrated History,* by Geoffrey Ward and Ken Burns. The popularity of the Burns epic and the textbook are effective in arousing the interest of students to explore the many contributive factors associated with baseball history.

The epic baseball video presentation by Ken Burns has not been free from criticisms from academicians studying baseball history. In reviewing the coverage of Jackie Robinson and the integration of baseball, historian Jules Tygiel comments on a number of inaccuracies in the treatment by Burns of the integration of Major League Baseball (69–71). Reviewing the early innings of the Burns epic, historian Steven Riess states that the video cannot be considered as "cutting edge" scholarship on the topic of baseball history (68). However, Riess admits that he is in "awe of the exhaustive research and the great visual images that were uncovered for *Baseball*" (68). In addition, he intends to use segments of the video in his classes. In reviewing the final three innings of the video, Gerlach examines a number of mistakes that were included in the video ("The Final Three Innings," 72–77). Despite the erroneous information, Gerlach comments that "for all his shortcomings, Ken Burns accomplished what legions of baseball historians have failed to do—impart to millions an appreciation for and understanding of baseball as the National Pastime and the ways in which sport is an integral part of American history" (77).

To provide balance for the popularization of baseball history as presented by Ken Burns in his video and the accompanying textbook, the course at Northern Kentucky utilizes required readings from academic sources. Many of the readings are available via online sources. Readings from the *Journal of Sport History* are available online in full text form (http://www.aafla.org) as are articles from the journal *Nine: A Journal of Baseball History and Culture* (http://www.muse.jhu.edu). These readings provide a means to analyze the historical accuracy of some of the popular topics depicted in Ken Burns's popular account of baseball. In essence, the course attempts to provide a synthesis of understanding popular appeal and historical accuracy of accounts in baseball.

Three main themes are threaded, as opposed to treating them as separate topics, throughout the video: race in baseball, labor and management relations, and athlete as hero. Within the framework of these three themes, there is considerable attention given during the course to analyzing the broader societal context in which these three themes develop. For example, race relations in baseball are discussed with relation to social forces such as social Darwinism, the eugenics movement, and Jim Crow legislation; labor relations in baseball are contrasted with the rise of labor unions and collective bargaining in American society; and in promoting understanding the popularity of baseball athletes as icons, attention is given to the zeitgeist in which athletes played and the criteria that prevailed for being a hero or an antihero.

The following is an outline of some of the topics that are covered in the course and a sample of the attendant readings for the course introduction and innings five and six. Ken Burns's series is segmented into nine cassettes (each cassette identifying one of nine innings) that cover baseball from the mythological development of baseball in Cooperstown, New York, to the early 1990s. In viewing each inning, students are provided with a handout that includes a series of questions that they need to answer while viewing the video. These are short-answer questions and are intended for students to become familiar with some of the specifics of baseball history. The following are samples of questions for the fifth inning:

1. Black baseball stars played their white counterparts in 438 exhibition games. How many did the black teams win?
2. How did the Great Depression affect Major League Baseball and the Negro Leagues?
3. When was the first major league all-star game staged? What brought on the idea of an all-star game?
4. What sparked the development of professional baseball in Japan in 1936?
5. What teams dominated the Negro Leagues?
6. When did the National Baseball Hall of Fame come into existence? Who were the first inductees?
7. What were some of the innovations that were created by Larry MacPhail?

The course outline follows:

Introduction:Popular Culture Studies, The Study of Sport History, Sociological Theories of Sport, Community History and Sport (baseball in nineteenth century Cincinnati)

Readings:
Ray B. Browne and Pat Browne, ed. *The Guide to United States Popular Culture*, chapter 1.
Jay Coakley, *Sports in Society: Issues and Controversies,* chapter 2.
John A. Lucas and Ronald A. Smith, *Saga of American Sport,* chapter 11, "The National Pastime: A Game for the Masses."
Larry R. Gerlach, "Not Quite Ready for Prime Time Baseball History, 1983–1993."
Darryl Brock, "The Journey to Find the 1869 Cincinnati Red Stockings."

Documentaries : Negro League Baseball and Community:
Negro League Baseball in Cincinnati: Cincinnati Tigers, Cincinnati Crescents, Cincinnati Browns, and Cincinnati Clowns (newspaper clippings).
Black Diamonds, Blues City: Stories of the Memphis Red Sox, video about community, race relations, power politics, music, and Negro League Baseball.
Kings On the Hill: Baseball's Forgotten Men, video about Negro League Baseball players and the teams they played on.
Readings and Video: The Integration of Major League Baseball
John A. Lucas and Ronald A. Smith, *Saga of American Sport,* chapter 16, "The Nadir of Blacks in American Sport"; chapter 21, "Blacks in Sport: From Jim Crow toward Integration."
Chris Lamb, "I Never Want to Take Another Trip Like This One: Jackie Robinson's Journey to Integrate Baseball."
William Simons, "Jackie Robinson and the American Mind: Journalistic Perceptions of the Reintegration of Baseball."
David K. Wiggins, "Wendell Smith, *The Pittsburgh Courier-Journal* and Campaign to Include Blacks in Organized Baseball, 1933–1945."
Gerald Early, "Performance and Reality: Race, Sports and the Modern World."

Soul of the Game, HBO video dealing with the integration of Major League Baseball.

Students are evaluated according to a point system on the following student activities: two exams, 100 points; biography assignment on a major league and Negro League Hall of Fame player, 20 points; attendance and group participation in-class activities, 10 points. The first exam is a take-home exam that deals with essay questions in which students have to reference sources from the textbook, handouts, and readings that are available online as well as on reserve in the library. The second exam includes a take-home part that includes two essay questions in which students have to make reference to sources. In addition, the final exam includes an in class part that consists of twenty true and false questions taken from the handouts distributed to students prior to viewing each Ken Burns video. Each exam is accompanied with specific instructions dealing with knowledge of content, expression of content, and organization of content. After grading the student responses to exam number one, I allow students to make revisions to achieve a higher grade, but I do not inform them of this opportunity while reviewing the instructions for the first exam. The following are sample questions from exam number one:

1. Defend or refute the following statement: "Abner Doubleday invented baseball in 1839 in Cooperstown, New York." (If you defend this statement then you must provide substantial documentation.) Discuss the origin of American baseball. Where did the game become organized and rules codified? Who was instrumental in organizing the game? What was the circumstance surrounding the association of Doubleday with baseball?
2. What is the historical background of the National League and the American League? How did these two leagues develop? Who was responsible in the development of each league? When did each league come into prominence?
3. The post-Civil War era was a period of extreme racial segregation in American society. Jim Crowism resulted in separate black and white societies in America. How did racial segregation affect baseball? Who were the first African-American professional baseball players during the nineteenth century? How did the Negro Leagues of baseball develop?
4. What evidence is there of women in baseball (amateur and professional)?
5. A continuous topic in baseball history is the confrontation between capital and labor. Provide a historical review of capital and labor during the first three innings. What is the reserve clause? What attempts were made by players to organize against owners? What was the outcome?

The final exam includes two essay questions. The first question is worth 20 points and the second question has a 10-point value:

1. Baseball, as was the case with other American institutions, remained segregated until Jackie Robinson was signed by the Brooklyn Dodgers. Discuss the significance of Robinson's entry into Major League Baseball. Your answer needs to include the following: (1) provide an interpretation of the social forces that influenced segregation in American society; (2) who was responsible for signing Robinson, when, for what purpose; (3) when did Robinson play his first major league game; (4) how was Robinson received by players, fans, and African Americans; (5) what was the agreement that Robinson made regarding his behavior for the first three seasons; (6) was the experiment of integration successful, how so?
2. Describe the history of the development of baseball in America. Your answer should include the following details: (1) how did Doubleday get credit as being the inventor of baseball; (2) how did baseball evolve, who was responsible, where did baseball develop, and when; (3) what was the purpose of organized baseball prior to 1869; (4) what happened in 1869 to change the objective of organized baseball?

In addition to the exams, each student selects randomly a player who is in the Hall of Fame and a Negro League Hall of Fame player. Students are to conduct a biographical review of each player by utilizing baseball encyclopedias that are available on reserve at the library and Internet sites that are reviewed in class (Lipping 79–85). To augment the popular culture studies approach, each student is to utilize the *New York Times* microfilm to review headlines, movies, television shows, and box scores of the major league player during a year in the middle of his career for one week, the last week in July. The biographical assignments are reported in class.

A final class project consists of a team activity to continue the Ken Burns series from 1994 to 2004. Students are organized into teams to research the players, teams, events, issues, and controversies that occurred in baseball during the 1994–2004 period.

In conclusion, students enjoy the Ken Burns series, as well as the accompanying textbook. (The bookstore has reported that there has not been a single copy resold to the bookstore.) The readings from the *Journal of Sport History* seem to be somewhat tedious for students, due to the length and academic nature of these readings. Several students who major in popular culture studies have continued to conduct their culminating project for their degree on a topic dealing with baseball. Overall, the course makes for a pleasurable three weeks in May.

Works Cited

Brock, Darryl. "The Journey to Find the 1869 Cincinnati Red Stockings." *NINE: A Journal of Baseball History and Culture* 9 (2000): 23–34. 12 June 2005 <http://www.muse.jhu.edu>.

Browne, Ray B., and Pat Browne, eds. *The Guide to United States Popular Culture*. Bowling Green, OH: Bowling Green State University Popular Press, 2001.

Early, Gerald. "Performance and Reality: Race, Sports and the Modern World." *The Nation* (August 10/17, 1998).12 June 2005 <http://www.ferris.edu/isar/archives/early/homepage.htm>.

Gerlach, Larry R. "Not Quite Ready for Prime Time: Baseball History, 1983–1993." *Journal of Sport History* 21 (1994): 103–137. 12 June 2005 <http://www.aafla.org>.

———. "The Final Three Innings." *Journal of Sport History* 23 (1996): 72–77. 12 June 2005 <http://www.aafla.org>.

Lamb, Chris. "I Never Want to Take Another Trip Like This One: Jackie Robinson's Journey to Integrate Baseball." *Journal of Sport History* 24 (1997): 177–191. 12 June 2005 <http://www.aafla.org>.

Lipping, Alar. "The Internet and the Popularization of the Negro Leagues." *Baseball and American Culture: Across the Diamond*. Ed. Edward J. Rielly. New York: Haworth Press, 2003. 79–86.

Lucas, John A., and Ronald A. Smith. *Saga of American Sport*. Philadelphia: Lea and Febiger, 1978.

Riess, Steven A. "The Early Innings." *Journal of Sport History* 23 (1996): 63–68. 12 June 2005 < http://www.aafla.org>.

Simons, William. "Jackie Robinson and the American Mind: Journalistic Perceptions of the Reintegration of Baseball." *Journal of Sport History* 12 (1985): 39–64. 12 June 2005 <http://www.aafla.org>.

Tygiel, Jules. "Ken Burns Meets Jackie Robinson." *Journal of Sport History* 25 (1996): 69–71. 12 June 2005 <http://www.aafla.org>.

Wiggins, David K. "Wendell Smith, the Pittsburgh Courier-Journal and the Campaign to Include Blacks in Organized Baseball, 1933–1945." *Journal of Sport History* 10 (1983): 5–29. 12 June 2005 <http://www.aafla.org>.

Educational Partnerships

Times, Traditions, and Technology— Teaching the Negro Leagues

(RAYMOND DOSWELL, GERALD D. BAILEY, AND DAN LUMLEY)

Great alliances that spark change in education are often forged between scholars at the finest institutions of higher learning. Rarely have they been cemented on road trips to Denver. Yet, in 1999, one such alliance was born. A convention in Colorado brought several regional Kansas and Missouri school board members, teachers, administrators, and faculty from Kansas State University (KSU) together. While on the road, sharing ideas in a general conversation, one of the board members mentioned that he volunteered for the new Negro Leagues Baseball Museum (NLBM) in Kansas City, Missouri. A collective response from his fellow travelers was: "What is the Negro Leagues Baseball Museum?" with an even more compelling question lingering, "What are the Negro Leagues?"

Negro Leagues baseball, so named in its historical context, generally consisted of the highest level of professional baseball available to African-Americans from the late 1880s to the 1960s. African Americans began to excel professionally at the game by the 1880s and, in spite of segregation laws in many communities, played briefly, in small numbers, on teams comprised mostly of white players. However, by 1900, racial attitudes and threats forced those players from the white teams, although no written rules were instituted to bar black players. Undeterred, black players and enthusiasts organized their own teams and leagues with various levels of success. Urged to action by members of the African American press, independent team owners in the Midwest met to formalize a league structure in 1920. Rival leagues and teams would soon join the newly formed Negro National League. Each brought entertaining, fast-paced play to several major urban centers across North America and Latin America. The complete story is thoroughly chronicled at the Negro Leagues Baseball Museum in Kansas City, Missouri.

Founded in 1990, the Negro Leagues Baseball Museum (NLBM) is a privately funded, nonprofit organization dedicated to preserving the rich history of African-American baseball. Located at 18th and Vine in the heart of Kansas City, it sits just a few blocks away from the Paseo YMCA building, where in 1920 the historic meeting was held to form the Negro National League. The permanent facility opened in 1997, permitting visitors to experience the full scope of black baseball history against the backdrop of post-Reconstruction America, the Great Migration, the Harlem Renaissance, the Great Depression, the World Wars, and the beginning of the Civil Rights Movement. Hundreds of photographs as well as artifacts and computer information kiosks highlight this 10,000 square foot multimedia exhibit complete with film theaters and life-sized bronze sculptures of important Negro Leagues players. Various outreach programs, lectures and public events, many of which target teachers and schools, supplement these exhibits (See http://www.nlbm.com/).

Intrigued by this information, key members of the group, led by KSU faculty, visited the NLBM, where friendships have developed and "what if" ideas have become commonplace. Out of a simple conversation on a road trip, a dream was born: "What can school districts and Kansas State University do to bring this extraordinary story to students and teachers throughout the United States?"

The Negro Leagues Education Partnership was subsequently created between three educational organizations: NLBM; Lee's Summit, Missouri, School District (a large suburban district); and the College of Education at KSU. Faculties from Lee's Summit School District and KSU are working with archivists, administrators, scholars, and former baseball players to create unique curriculum materials for K-12 classroom teachers as well as for university faculty. This partnership demonstrates how public schools and universities can work together with museums and other public history institutions to explore issues of diversity while creating dynamic educational tools to serve millions of students, teachers, and leaders in higher education throughout the United States.

The partnership has sought to explore basic concepts for understanding the "Times," and "Traditions" of the Negro Leagues and present them with the support of emerging technologies to the modern teacher and student:

1. Times—The history of the Negro Leagues is saturated with stories of phenomenal athletes and leaders who overcame almost insurmountable odds of racial discrimination to make a positive social, political, and economic impact on society. This history stands parallel to the larger history of baseball in America, although it had been largely misunderstood or ignored by the mainstream.
2. Traditions—Negro Leagues Baseball is a story rooted in African-American history that reflects in several ways the traditions of the culture, including folklore, art, and political and economic strivings. The history of the Negro Leagues also reflects connections with and contributions of women as well as the Latin community in America.
3. Technology—The partners committed themselves to bringing this story to students and teachers using twenty-first century technology, including computers, personal digital assistants (handheld computers), and the Internet.

Early Stages of the Partnership

An early strategy of the partnership was simple: bring faculties from Kansas State University and Lee's Summit to the NLBM. It was believed that awareness of the NLBM and personal relationships among faculties were essential to building a strong foundation for the partnership. A common reaction among the faculty and teachers was that "the NLBM was a phenomenal museum with unbelievable potential for bringing a different story to students." Personalized tours for various school district faculties were provided. An important step in the partnership was holding roundtable discussions that focused on the possibilities of a formalized partnership. Reactions were rich and varied. Lee's Summit faculty and Kansas State University professors agreed that the partnership's potential was limited only by the collective imagination of the participants.

Specific observations from the roundtable discussions included the following major points:

1. The story of baseball—especially the story of the Negro Leagues—from statistics to players' accomplishments provides highly interesting topics to educators at every level.
2. "Untold, motivational stories" need to be presented to students in both public schools and higher education. Inherent in the game of African-American baseball are stories that deal with the social, political, economic, and leadership issues in American history.
3. The story of the Negro Leagues goes far beyond one subject matter or one discipline. The story cuts across all subject areas, including history (social studies), math, science, reading, art, English, and special education.
4. Opportunities still exist to discover new material on the Negro Leagues, especially as it relates to biographical information on players. Much of the published history has focused on the exploits of major players and teams in the sports arena. However, more of the social, political, and economic story remains untapped but available from still living former Negro League players. Useful material may also remain in documents located in attics or basements of players, relatives, collectors or other regional institutions.

The Partnership Projects

From these roundtable conversations, several projects emerged:

Project # 1: The Players Videotape Project involved interviewing Negro Leagues players and relatives and friends of deceased players. With cooperation of the NLBM staff, both KSU and Lee's Summit faculties conducted a small number of interviews with players, as well as with their spouses and children. Specific videotapes were produced and made accessible to college faculty and teachers for classroom viewing. In addition, a multimedia presentation was developed for faculty and student use (see http://www.coe.ksu.edu/nlbm/).

Project # 2: The Personal Digital Assistant (Handheld Computer) and the Negro Leagues Baseball Project involved bringing faculties from Lee's Summit and KSU together to create new software for curricular use. Handheld computers were used to collect, organize, and display the story of Negro Leagues Baseball. Teachers and college faculty were trained in the use of handheld computers, while the NLBM supplied materials (print, pictures, audio, video, etc.) that were placed on handheld computers. Classroom teachers and college faculty used these materials in their respective classrooms to expand the regular curriculum.

Project # 3: The NLBM Teacher's Field Trip Guide Project (see http://www.coe.ksu.edu/nlbm/) involved partners developing a comprehensive teacher's guide for touring the museum (see http://www.coe.ksu.edu/nlbm/). The guide is a complete overview of the entire field trip experience for teachers to relay to their students. Everything is covered, from the bus ride to the museum, tours of the surrounding neighborhood, and all the exhibits inside. The guide also provides valuable research information to supplement classroom lesson plans.

Project # 4: The Buck O'Neil Research Center and e-Library Project is the next project that the partnership will undertake. In 2006, new plans are being made to create additional K-12 curriculum lesson plans and place them on the Internet, providing unlimited access to teachers and educators in teacher-training programs. Part of this project involves the expansion of the museum to the historic Paseo YMCA located a short distance from the NLBM. In spite of its significance to Negro Leagues history, the over eighty-year-old building has sat abandoned for over thirty years. The museum plans a renovation and reuse of the structure that will include the development of an e-library and discovery center to house lesson plans and materials.

An ongoing component of this project will be student interviews of community members historically connected to the Paseo YMCA. Students under the direction of Lee's Summit School District teachers will be conducting interviews of community members who used the historic building. The interviews and materials will help create a permanent display on the history of the building.

Roadblocks and Opportunities

University-public schools-nonprofit organization partnerships have their share of roadblocks. Blending three organizational cultures is never easy. Partnerships require patience, listening skills, and immense social-emotional skills.

These difficulties are further complicated by the fact that not all people at Kansas State and Lee's Summit (e.g., administrators, board members, and teachers) see the value of public school-university-nonprofit organization partnerships. Generating and sustaining the vision of this partnership will continue to be problematic without continuous discussion and involvement by all parties. Fortunately, the dean of education at KSU and the superintendent of Lee's Summit School District have generously supported the project with their time and monies. Still, funding of the partnership has always been a nagging problem. Exciting, bold ideas require money. The search for funds continues to be one of the biggest challenges.

Classroom teachers have needed released time, and resources for releasing teachers have not always been available. Hiring substitute teachers is becoming cost prohibitive. Rewarding faculties for participation at the university level has been and will continue to be a challenge as well, although small stipends have been provided periodically. However, the real reward often comes from the inherent motivation of hearing and learning about an inspiring story of African-Americans under conditions that were not always pleasant.

The physical locations of the NLBM and KSU have always presented a challenge to the partnership. Kansas State faculty has had to travel over two hundred miles roundtrip from Manhattan, Kansas, to Kansas City. Likewise, restrictive school scheduling practices limit the amount of time spent by classroom teachers at the museum. In addition, the time required to coordinate the partnership by the NLBM staff has been daunting. Basically, the NLBM (as well as KSU and Lee's Summit School District) is understaffed as it relates to the scope of the project. As a result, not all projects and products from the partnership have been equal in benefit or quality.

All partners agree, however, that the rewards far outweigh the roadblocks encountered thus far, and that each partner in the collaborative venture has enjoyed unique benefits from the endeavor.

Benefit and Outcomes

The Negro Leagues Baseball Museum benefits from its partners bringing "new eyes" to the role and mission of the museum. As a consequence, multiple educational perspectives are considered when developing the long-term agenda of the NLBM. The partnership also allowed the NLBM to undertake projects that were not normally covered by its limited budget. As a result, the museum has the ability to reach wider numbers of educators with its history. Locally and nationally, teachers and students are visiting the NLBM with more frequency. Furthermore, the partnership has helped the museum focus on the untold story of the Negro Leagues—its social, political, economic, and leadership impact on American and world history.

In the Lee's Summit School District, teachers have gained insight in how to develop highly motivational materials while still focusing on subject-or discipline-related standards (required outcomes). In addition, dialogue among faculty members from several different disciplines has been extremely beneficial to those teaching with a multidisciplinary approach. Also, dialogue with university faculty has been healthy from the perspective of problem solving and building trust and friendship between vastly different cultures.

Since Kansas State University has had a long historical commitment to cultural diversity, the partnership has become a twenty-first-century curriculum centerpiece for multiculturalism in the university community. KSU faculty have gained new insights and information about an exciting and unique part of American history. The faculties participating in the project have gained new insights into how to incorporate the story of baseball across different disciplines and have introduced the story of Negro Leagues baseball into several courses. Graduate students in Educational Leadership and Curriculum Development, for example, have designed lesson plans and units featuring Negro Leagues history. Another graduate course, Educational Leadership and Technology, has incorporated new technology into lesson plans and units featuring Negro Leagues history. Each course uses the current National Social Studies and National Technology standards for secondary education. In addition, several graduate students, including one graduate teaching assistant, are part of a newly formed Negro Leagues Scholars group with the intent of extending the members' study and work to the proposed Negro Leagues Research and Education Center currently under development by the NLBM. Dissertations and internships by KSU graduate students have become unexpected benefits to students who would not normally be afforded these opportunities. Finally, since the NLBM is located some distance from KSU, "car time" has allowed faculty to share with each other their insights about teaching and learning philosophies. These trips have become a form of staff development or faculty enhancement.

Conclusion and Recommendations

The partnership has a solid foundation and a bold new vision for the future. Here are some recommendations for faculty at colleges and universities to consider:

1. Schedule a visit to the NLBM. It an exciting story that will grip your imagination and broaden your perspective of leadership in the broadest possible interpretation.
2. If you cannot visit the NLBM in person, visit and review the Web site.
3. Assign students to study and report on the Negro Leagues if you are teaching a course in which that assignment would fit.
4. If you are located in an area that has former Negro League Baseball players, have your students contact and interview them. Invite them to speak to your classes.
5. If you are interested in learning how teachers are using classroom materials in conjunction with the museum, download The Teacher's Field Trip Guide (see http://www.coe.ksu.edu/nlbm/).
6. If you are interested in visiting or finding out information about the NLBM, write, call or e-mail Raymond Doswell, Curator/Education Director, Negro Baseball Leagues Museum, 1616 East 18th, Kansas City, Missouri 64108; rdoswell@nlbm.com; 816–221–1920.
7. If you are interested in learning how universities can establish exciting partnerships with nonprofit organizations, write, call, or e-mail Gerald D. Bailey, Professor of Education, Bluemont Hall, College of Education, Kansas State University, Manhattan, Kansas 66506; jbailey@ksu.edu; 785–532–5847.
8. If you are interested in learning how public schools can establish exciting partnerships with nonprofit organizations, write, call, or e-mail Dan Lumley, Curriculum Director, Lee's Summit-NLBM Liaison, 600 Southeast Miller, Lee's Summit School District, Lee's Summit, Missouri 64063; Dan.lumley@leesummit.k12mo.us; 816–986–1006.

Experiential Learning

Journal of a Journey—Teaching Baseball on the Road

(E. MICHAEL BRADY)

In the summer of 1996 the University of Southern Maine launched a course that aimed, while traveling by motor coach, to teach baseball and its relationship to American culture. "Baseball and American Society: A Journey" attracted 40 students, some taking the course for three undergraduate credits and others auditing. Locations visited that inaugural year included Norwich, Utica, Cooperstown, Scranton, Philadelphia, Baltimore, New York City, and Pawtucket. Along the way, our group read and discussed baseball literature, viewed and debriefed films, discussed observations made at ballparks, and interviewed people who had richly diverse experiences in baseball. Among these were Rob Fowler (owner and general manager of New York-Penn League franchise), Jim Gates (librarian at the National Baseball Hall of Fame), Gene Benson (former Negro League all-star), Rex Barney (teammate of Jackie Robinson and long-time public address announcer of the Baltimore Orioles), Larry Doby (later to be inducted into the National Baseball Hall of Fame), and Bill Monbouquette (former major league player and minor league pitching coach).

Based on rave student reviews, strong interest on the part of the press, and enthusiastic encouragement from the university, a second baseball journey was planned for the summer of 1997. That year brought its own set of highlights (including a group interview with Bob Feller and an afternoon spent with six former players from the All American Girls Professional Baseball League.) From then on, "Baseball and American Society: A Journey" took on a life of its own. In the summer of 2005, when this essay was written, faculty were preparing to board a bus with another forty students for the course's tenth season.

During the 2004 road trip that will serve as the basis of this essay, as with every other iteration of "Baseball and American Society: A Journey," all participants—credit students and auditors—were expected to read three core texts. The books for 2004 were *Baseball and American Culture: Across the Diamond,* edited by Edward J. Rielly; *I Had A Hammer,* by Hank Aaron and Lonnie Wheeler; and *Moneyball,* by Michael Lewis. Students taking the course for three undergraduate credits also read a fourth book of their choice (selected from a ten-page bibliography mailed in advance), and wrote a three- to five-page reflection essay on each of the four books. The purpose of the essay was to summarize the main ideas in the book, provide a critique, and examine ways the author(s) connected the game of baseball with American society. An oral report of the individually selected book was given on the bus during the journey. Additionally, two weeks after we arrived home from the trip, credit students submitted a final essay that summarized their thinking about the relationship between baseball and American society.

Students also were required to keep a journal of ideas and observations throughout the journey and submit five pages of her or his best journal entries to faculty along with the final course essay two weeks after the completion of the journey. As one of two faculty members who co-teach this course, I believe it is important to model this writing activity. Therefore, since the initial 1996 odyssey, I have kept detailed observations and reflections about our many and varied experiences. What follows is a selection of journal entries written during the 2004 course. These reflections will give the reader a feel for what "Baseball and American Society: A Journey" is about, some of the logistics, a sample of topics that are addressed, and challenges that present themselves along the way to those teaching on the road. Since my long-term journal writing practice (over thirty-five years) is to write early in the morning, I continue to adhere to this schedule while on the annual baseball travel course. Each of the following entries represents a retrospective of the previous day's events.

Sunday, August 8

We began this year's course, as we often do, with an initial visit to our "home team," the Portland Sea Dogs and Hadlock Field. Chris Cameron, a double alumnus of this course and the director of public relations for the Sea Dogs, provided a tour of the ball park and answered students' questions about minor league baseball. One new piece of information for me related to community appearances by Sea Dogs players. Somehow I had been under the impression that making visits to schools or hospitals were nonpaid activities that were part of players' contracts. Portland Sea Dogs players are paid for community appearances they make, autograph sessions with the public, etc. However, they are not paid in cash. Instead they are given gift certificates to the team store, which apparently are welcome because players often like to pick up team merchandise to send to family and friends. Chris commented that this arrangement seems to work well both for the players and organization.

We finished our two hours at Hadlock Field under cover in the right field picnic area with Maine author Edward J. Rielly. Since one of the core textbooks we are using this year is *Baseball and American Culture: Across the Diamond*, edited by Professor Rielly, who teaches at St. Joseph College in Standish, we scheduled an educational session with him. Ed began by telling us the story of his own roots in baseball, which go back to rural Wisconsin in the 1950s. There were only thirteen kids in his school, so boys and girls played ball together. Professor Rielly went on to describe some of his teaching and writing projects, including the two years of work that resulted in *Baseball and American Culture*. This talk helped set the stage for students' questions.

We discussed a broad range of topics, including whether Pete Rose deserves to be in the Hall of Fame, steroid use, the financial inequities in today's game, and details about the development of Ed's book. An interesting issue arose when Dr. Kay Yung, a psychiatrist who is taking the course for non-credit, asked a question that, in my memory, has never come up before. "Why is it that baseball players—apparently at every level—always appear to be chewing something: tobacco, gum, sunflower seeds?" The group quickly engaged this question and we heard a number of opinions that included oral fixation (whatever that means) and tradition. My own take on Kay's question, and I shared this during our discussion, is that baseball is especially stressful because players are not physically moving all the time. Constant running (like players do in basketball, soccer, and other sports) helps reduce tension. Chewing something can help to take the edge off.

In the bus on our way to New Britain we began with a journal writing assignment ("Write a reflection on an early baseball memory") and personal introductions. As usual, we have a solid core of returning people—ten or twelve—and a healthy mix of those taking the course for credit and audit. I'm happy we made the decision years ago that every student, whether taking the course for three undergraduate credits or not, would read the core books. This way we have a common basis for discussion. We have obtained our average of about 20 percent women. I'd like to see this ratio increase in the future but am not quite sure how to do it. It would be interesting to learn from other professors who teach courses on baseball if a substantial proportion of their students are female. The most we have ever had on this course has been nine (out of forty) and this year seven.

Our educational session with Bill Dowling, principal owner and general manager of the New Britain Rock Cats, held in box seats along the third base line in New Britain Stadium ninety minutes before the game, was fascinating. Bill used to be the executive vice president and general counsel to the New York Yankees. "George Steinbrenner is tough to work for. He is very detail-oriented and works his staff hard. When I was with the Yankees I had almost no personal life. I think I had three days off in three years." In 2000 Bill and a partner bought the New Britain Eastern League franchise.

Bill stressed how minor league baseball is primarily about family entertainment. The key is to sell an alternative to a night out at the movies or an amusement park. They have created a jingle that is helping to sell interest in Rock Cats baseball: "These cats rock!" The trick, says Mr. Dowling, is to get wives and children to want to go to baseball games. Additionally, Bill feels that one of his best friends is Major League Baseball. With high ticket prices (especially in the two closest major league cities to New Britain—New York and Boston), parking, expensive concessions, etc., minor league ball is perceived as a real bargain to many baseball fans.

Monday, August 9

We spent yesterday in Baltimore. Although our original plan was to have a session with co-general manager Jim Beattie (an old friend of my teaching partner, Al Bean) after the afternoon game, Jim is away this weekend and sent a pinch-hitter, Dave Ritterpusch. Dave has a long history in baseball (including being a scout) and has also served as a colonel in the U.S. Army and as an assistant secretary of labor. He is currently director of Baseball Information Systems with the Orioles. We met in the organization's executive boardroom.

The Orioles do not employ a pure "Money Ball" approach to scouting and player development but prefer to use a blend of tools. They do use statistics—Bill James's "win shares" is an important instrument for this organization. But Dave and his fellow Oriole senior administrators place a great deal of trust in a personality profile that is given to every ballplayer (across baseball) each year during spring training. The profile is available both in English and Spanish. Evidently these data are offered to all baseball organizations through the Major League Scouting Bureau, but only a few teams take advantage. "Certainly no other team has the thirty-one years of experience working with this profile that the Orioles do." The instrument itself is a paper and pencil test involving 130 questions that measure a variety of traits: drive, determination, composure, trust, self-confidence, coachability and so on. According to Mr. Ritterpusch, "We've taken our scouts pretty much away from the intangibles. This profile handles those. What the scout can concentrate on are baseball skills. Is this guy a baseball player? We're after talent and it is an art to find it."

Tuesday, August 10

The course seems to be going well thus far. There is healthy energy and a developing sense of community on the bus. We had our first three student book reports yesterday (on the book selected from the large bibliography people are sent in advance that is in addition to our three core texts.) Because students make such a wide range of choices it's hard to group these in any meaningful way. Yesterday we had reports on Dan Shaughnessy's *The Curse of the Bambino*, Harvey Rosenfeld's *Iron Man* (which is about Cal Ripken, Jr.), and a classic in the baseball literature, Ring Lardner's *You Know Me Al*. Over the course of the week we try to have some of these reports on the bus and others in a motel conference room that we rent specifically for this purpose. While giving the report itself works fine on the bus (the student comes to the front and uses the microphone), it's hard to facilitate a discussion with bus seating the way it is.

Typically, however, three or four people will come forward to comment about the content in the book report or ask a question. So while it's not the ideal environment, we still achieve substantial learning while cruising at sixty-five mph along the interstate.

On our way from Baltimore to Durham we had to—naturally—view the film *Bull Durham*. This film was shot on location at the old Durham Bulls Athletic Park, which is several miles away from where the Bulls currently play. One of the reasons why we do not want children on this course (we set the lower age limit at 14—if that person has a parent or guardian along) is because of R-rated films such as this. And even then there have been times when we've gotten into trouble. I remember once, five or six years ago, after we showed this film (we do not show *Bull Durham* or any other particular baseball film every year) one of our students came up to the microphone during the debriefing and castigated the faculty for "showing such filth in the presence of children!" After this embarrassing situation we now make a concerted effort, when we know that an adolescent will be accompanying a parent or grandparent on the course, to advise the family ahead of time that not all baseball films are "Disney-like" and, in the least, the language is not what one would usually hear in church. While discussing this caveat on the telephone I have, without exception (at least up until now), only heard responses such as "We understand;" "This is not a problem for us;" or even "Don't worry. We have plenty of experience with sex and foul language in this house!"

While we met with several Durham Bulls front office personnel prior to game, a highlight was spending thirty minutes with field manager Bill Evers. This is Bill's seventh season with Durham and he is the only field manager the AAA Bulls have had. (While this franchise has had a long and colorful minor league history, it has been affiliated with the AAA-level International League only since 1998.) Bill has led Durham to back-to-back International League championships and has more wins than any other manager in franchise history (471). All totaled, Evers has managed for twenty-eight years and has over 1,200 victories (fourth among active minor league managers).

Bill spoke with us about a wide range of issues, including team travel (the Bulls fly to away games), pitch counts in the Devil Rays organization (90 for the first five starts; 105 after that), the difficulty of making it all the way to the majors ("Of all the guys who are drafted, only three percent make it"), and drugs ("Yes—drug use does take place here. It exists at all levels of the game. Players at the AAA level are tested four times a year"). Bill feels that minor leaguers are rushed too quickly today and consequently are not as sound fundamentally as they were ten and twenty years ago. Clubs are in a hurry to move prospects up the organizational ladder because of the large signing bonuses many young players receive. Finally, Bill is not a believer in the philosophy espoused by Michael Lewis's recent best-selling book. "I'm not a *Moneyball* guy. Intangibles are important, especially heart."

Wednesday, August 11

We did something highly unusual for a college course of any kind yesterday. On our way from Durham to Atlanta we held a memorial service on the bus for Ed Amos, who recently died. Ed was a double alumnus of this course and a number of people aboard the bus knew him, either from those two previous trips or Ed's near-constant presence at Hadlock Field. We held a similar service for Larry Epstein several years ago. When, at the age of 86, Larry traveled with us for the second time (1997), he was then and remains the oldest person to have taken "Baseball and American Society: A Journey."

There was nothing religious, at least in the formal sense, about either of these memorial services. In Ed's case, I began by telling the group a little about him and read the obituary that was in the newspaper. I knew that Bob Paskal and Paul Marshall were close to Ed (mostly by way of Sea Dogs games) and asked them in advance to prepare brief statements about their friend. Then we opened up the microphone to anyone else who may have known Ed and wanted to share a story. I have been to many church funerals and believe that what happened on the bus yesterday was no less sacred than any of those rituals, albeit with the name of God never once being invoked. To have done this, and to have had it work so nicely, says something about the special nature of the community we have built over the years through this course.

Yesterday was supposed to have been our day to meet with Hank Aaron. I had worked at arranging this meeting for several months. I still have the e-mail message that I received from Susan Bailey, Mr. Aaron's personal secretary, on June 8: "Dear Dr. Brady—Mr. Aaron is pleased to address your group on Tuesday, August 10 at 3:00 PM at Turner Field...." Indeed, this was among the happiest moments I have had in planning the hundreds of events we have experienced in nine years of running this course. And then the e-mail message I received from Ms. Bailey only twenty-four hours before the bus departed last weekend: "I just left you a voice mail as well.... I am sorry to tell you that Mr. Aaron has to travel to Mobile tomorrow to be with his mother and get her to the doctor on Monday. She is in her mid-90s and since Mr. Aaron's sister passed away (she lived in Mobile very near Mrs. Aaron and was her caretaker) a few months ago Mr. Aaron has had to spend more time with his ailing mother...."

How can one argue with this? Hank Aaron is not only a legendary ballplayer but is a good son. When I told the class about this disappointing news several hours before arriving in Atlanta yesterday, there was an audible group sigh. People were respectful enough of my obvious disappointment and of the circumstances Mr. Aaron faced that nobody openly complained. But the depletion of spirit and energy was palpable. I chided myself about having told everyone, by way of the final itinerary we traditionally mail to students several weeks prior to departure, that we were going to be meeting with Hank Aaron to discuss his memoir, *I Had A Hammer* (written with Lonnie Wheeler). "Better to surprise everyone with good news" was my self-talk. But how could one have anticipated this turn of events? It's nobody's fault. Just one of those things that happens on occasion and with which we all have to live.

I like *I Had A Hammer* and consider it one of the better baseball memoirs. We have used it once before in this course without any plans to meet with the author or even come within 500 miles of Atlanta. The end of Susan Bailey's e-mail message held out the promise that we could plan to arrange such a session again the next time we are in Atlanta. But who knows when that will be, if ever?

It would be nice to return to Atlanta, however, with or without an educational session with baseball's all-time home run leader. The people there were gracious. The Braves bent over backwards to compensate for our not having the conference with Hank Aaron. For example, they provided us with a free tour of Turner Field and also complimentary passes to the impressive "History of the Braves" museum that is located inside the ballpark. Our group was even impressed by the civility of the public address announcer moments before the first pitch: "Ladies and gentlemen, the Atlanta Braves would like to welcome the Milwaukee Brewers and their fans to Turner Field." As one of our students said to me during the game, "Can you imagine such a welcome at Fenway Park or Yankee Stadium? It would be more like 'Welcome to Fenway Park where we hope to beat the brains out of the Yankees!'"

Thursday, August 12

Baseball was first played in Asheville in 1866. The famous American writer Thomas Wolfe was a batboy here in 1915. Decades later Cal Ripken, Jr., had the same job. Up until now nearly 500 players (the actual number is 499) came through Asheville on their way to the major leagues. *Baseball America* rates this small city in the western mountains of North Carolina as one of the top five places to watch a baseball game.

As we planned our first itinerary in nine seasons that would take us south of Virginia I wanted to visit three locations: Durham, Atlanta, and Asheville. All are legendary in their own right in the annals of American baseball. Meeting yesterday afternoon with Chris Smith, assistant general manager and local baseball historian, and Ron McKee, co-owner, general manager, and former president of the South Atlantic League, made our visit even more worthwhile. As we sat in the grandstands two hours before game time, watching the grounds crew roll tarp onto the infield and then roll it off once a fast-moving storm moved through, we learned a good deal about the history of this fabled city and franchise. What is more important than the facts and traditions we learned, however, was to take the measure of these men who represent their ball club and are willing to spend time with our class when so many other responsibilities call. For the most part I have observed over the years that, although not well paid at the minor league level, people in this game love their work and take pride in the cities and franchises they represent. Smith and McKee beamed with enthusiasm when they spoke about the Asheville Tourists, the old and beautiful McCormick Field, and the details of their day-to-day activities running a team in the SALLY [South Atlantic] League. It was an honor to have spent time with these generous and passionate folk. I hope some year we shall travel south again on this course and, if not all the way to Atlanta, at least make it as far as Asheville.

Friday, August 13

Thursday night's game in Charleston, West Virginia, was rained out. It was only the second time in nine years (approximately 90 games) that we have lost a ball game to rain. Fortunately, because of another Maine contact, Alley Cats field manager Kenny Joyce, we were at least able to have an "up close and personal" educational program despite the disappointing rain-out. I say "up close and personal" because we actually had our interview and discussion in the club house and his office.

Kenny grew up in Portland and played for coach Ed Flaherty at the University of Southern Maine. He later coached with Ed. He was a grammar school teacher in South Portland when the new Eastern League franchise, the Sea Dogs, came to Portland in 1994. Kenny volunteered his services to the organization as a hitting coach. Carlos Tosca, who was Portland's manager at the time, took notice of his teaching talent and became Kenny's mentor and advocate. "Most coaches need someone to open doors. But once the door is open you're on your own to work hard and show your talent. So, like, I suppose, in many businesses, in baseball it's who you know that gets you a job, but what you know keeps you in."

Over the years Kenny has coached in Utica, Glens Falls, Bangor (Independent), Medicine Hat, Alberta, and most recently here in Charleston. Up until this year he had been able to keep his teaching job because his baseball coaching involved short-season leagues that begin play in mid-June and end by the start of the new school year. "There is no security in baseball and last year I had to make the tough choice to give up my full-time teaching position." Kenny and his family understand the risks. But he enjoys working in baseball and thus far has no regrets about this decision to give up the security and roots provided by a public school teaching position in order to both continue and further develop his coaching career

Saturday, August 14

I think folks are getting tired. I know I am. I slept all the way to wake-up call (6:00) this morning, which is very unusual.

We got lucky yesterday with the weather. We were rained out in Charleston Thursday night and all indicators were that we would be traveling east and north with this low pressure front to Philadelphia. It rained much of the way from Charleston across West Virginia and into Maryland yesterday while we kept busy on the bus debriefing the Kenny Joyce experience, engaging book reports, and viewing and discussing films. To our delight and surprise the sun actually greeted us late in the day as we approached Philadelphia. However, with two hurricanes having struck Florida within the past forty-eight hours and now on their way up the East Coast, we may have weather problems tomorrow and the rest of the way home.

As one student said last night at the ballpark, feeling the tension and observing the fans' incessant and intense heckling of the Giants (especially Barry Bonds): "You can tell we're back in the North!" There was a palpably different "feel" to this game as compared with Durham, Atlanta, or Asheville. An edge, an intensity, even a sense of anger. Our psychiatrist colleague, Kay Yung, whom we have endearingly come to call "Moonlight" (after Dr. "Moonlight" Graham in *Field of Dreams*), and I had a conversation about sport as catharsis. Catharsis used to be an outcome of theater in Ancient Greece. It was a way of letting go of deep feelings. Apparently sporting events have assumed some of this role in contemporary society. There is an anonymity in large venues such as these baseball parks that may give permission to people to "let it out." Another thought related to the psychology of sport: Is heckling a kind of displaced envy? A way of drawing attention to oneself?

Sunday, August 15

For the ninth year in a row we have included Cooperstown in our course itinerary. And once again this quaint and lovely town in out-of-the-way Otsego County, New York, did not disappoint. A highlight of our visit to Cooperstown, as always, was a conference with the senior librarian at the National Baseball Hall of Fame and Museum. Jim Gates has been a constant in this course and, in fact, the only person besides myself who has participated in all nine runnings of "Baseball and American Society: A Journey."

While he calls his talk "Hall of Fame 101," the information that Jim shares with us changes from year to year. Yesterday he talked about the work of the library, the myth of baseball's beginnings, rules changes over time, use and abuse of statistics, new "electronic educational programs" that have been developed by the Hall of Fame, and little-known facts. (For example, the only U.S. Navy chief petty officer enshrined is Bob Feller, Lou Gehrig never had an induction ceremony, and the accounting firm Ernst and Young actually counts the Hall of Fame election ballots.) Having Jim speak to the class before we individually tour the museum helps many people derive more insight and meaning from exploring the National Baseball Hall of Fame. In academic terms this is called an advance-organizer. This approach is effective in traditional classroom-based courses as well as with this more experientially based model of education.

Summary Reflection on the 2004 Experience—Monday, August 16

We spent our final afternoon on this year's trip in Boston watching the Red Sox lose a heartbreaker to the Chicago White Sox. Before the game, our class was invited to stand in the New England Sports Network television studio to watch the pregame show. In doing so we got a chance to meet Jim Rice, and a number of our students received autographs.

We had a terrific group of people this year. Everyone arrived on time for all our rendezvous points, was respectful of the educational mission of this journey, and worked hard to build a learning community. We have not always had such cooperation in the past. (Although the above-mentioned attributes describe the vast majority of people we take on the road every summer, all you need are one or two discourteous people to change the dynamics of the entire group. Gratefully, we had none this time.)

There are characteristics of this course that I do not find in any of my other teaching. It would be difficult, if not impossible, to replicate the experiential nature of this learning in any traditional campus-based course. The education engaged here represents, in my view, the action-reflection cycle at its best. Also, in no other educational setting that I have observed does one find the vast range of ages that interact meaningfully with each other. Some day I would like to write a paper about the myriad meanings that derive from sixteen-year-olds spending hours sitting on a bus or in a ballpark next to seventy-six-year-olds and learning from each other. And where else do people have so much fun learning? I have been teaching more than thirty years, and only with "Baseball and American Society: A Journey" have I received course evaluations that read "This was the best week of my life" and "I hope heaven ends up like this trip."

I am grateful for the opportunity to have been part of this annual baseball learning journey these past nine years. During the nine road trips we have undertaken since the inaugural 1996 season, we have logged tens of thousands of miles, experienced nearly one thousand innings in ballparks both grand and modest, engaged hundreds of eager and thoughtful students, and met scores of knowledgeable people inside the game of baseball. I hope my teaching partner, Al Bean, and I shall continue to enjoy the university's support and have the health, energy, and overall good fortune to keep "Baseball and American Society: A Journey" alive long into the future.

Works Cited

Aaron, Hank, with Lonnie Wheeler. *I Had a Hammer: The Hank Aaron Story*. New York: HarperCollins, 1991.
Bull Durham. Dir. Ron Shelton. Orion, 1988.
Field of Dreams. Dir. Phil Alden Robinson. Universal, 1989.
Lardner, Ring. *You Know Me Al*. New York: Scribner, 1925.
Lewis, Michael. *Moneyball: The Art of Winning an Unfair Game*. New York: Norton, 2003.
Rielly, Edward J., ed. *Baseball and American Culture: Across the Diamond*. New York: Haworth, 2003.
Rosenfeld, Harvey. *Iron Man: The Cal Ripken, Jr., Story*. New York: St. Martin's, 1995.
Shaughnessy, Dan. *The Curse of the Bambino*. New York: Dutton, 1990.

Film

O'Brien to Ryan to Goldberg— Fact, Fiction, and Cultural Stereotyping in Baseball Films

(ROB EDELMAN)

"There are very few Jewish ballplayers. You'll never hear, 'Ground ball to short. Flo Ziegfeld moves to his right, scoops it to Leonard Bernstein at second, who fires to first. George Gershwin stretches. Double play.' It's not gonna happen."

This bit of dialogue, excerpted from Barry Levinson's screenplay for *Liberty Heights* (1999), epitomizes the characterization of Jews as mild and meek, and inherently unphysical. According to this stereotype, Jews are scholars, creative artists and movers in business. They work behind counters and desks. They employ their brains, but never their brawn.

Yet not all major league ballplayers have been named Jackson, Johnson or Jones—or, for that matter, Mazzilli, Morales and McGwire. Some have such unmistakably Jewish surnames as Holtzman, Epstein and Ginsberg. A few—perhaps you've heard of Sandy Koufax and Hank Greenberg—even are enshrined in the National Baseball Hall of Fame.

On August 29 and 30, 2004, the Hall of Fame, in conjunction with Jewish Major Leaguers, Inc., and the American Jewish Historical Society, offered a program titled "A Celebration of 143 American Jews in the National Pastime, 1871–2004." The event spotlighted the careers of Jewish big leaguers from Koufax and Greenberg to those who sipped glasses of Manischewitz in the majors.

Jewish major leaguers date from Nate Berkenstock and Lip Pike, outfielders who debuted in 1871, and include such one-game wonders as Joe Bennett, a third baseman born Joseph Rosenblum Bennett, and Jesse Baker, a shortstop born Michael Myron Silverman: the Moonlight Grahams of Jewish ballplayers. Jews have been twenty-game winners (Erskine Mayer, who earned twenty-one victories each for the 1914 and 1915 Philadelphia Phillies and, more recently, Ken Holtzman and Steve Stone). They are career .300 hitters (infielder Buddy Myer, who began his seventeen years in the majors in 1925) and World Series heroes (relief pitcher Larry Sherry, who starred in the 1959 Fall Classic). Al Rosen, a third baseman, won a couple of home run and RBI titles for the Cleveland Indians in the 1950s. Presently, Shawn Green, whose family name originally was Greenberg, is a marquee major league flychaser.

Other noteworthy Jewish ballplayers include Moe Berg, the catcher-who-was-a-spy, and Ron Blomberg, who in 1973 became the American League's first designated hitter. Greg Goossen, an early New York Met backstop, has appeared in movies since the late 1980s, and often is Gene Hackman's stand-in. Celebrity New York Yankees fan Billy Crystal might be intrigued by Bill "Lefty" Cristall, who pitched in six games for the 1901 Cleveland Blues. Then there is outfielder Mose Solomon, nicknamed "The Rabbi of Swat," who sports a .375 lifetime batting average. Only problem is, Solomon's .375 translates into three hits in eight at-bats, all for the 1923 New York Giants. None was a home run, leaving Solomon 714 behind Babe

Ruth, the bona fide "Sultan of Swat," who then was bashing dingers for the rival New York Yankees.

For younger Jews in the U.S.—first, second and third generation Americans who never realized their dreams of playing pro ball, let alone becoming the next Greenberg or Koufax—baseball has been a conduit for blending into the mainstream. When not studying Torah in Hebrew school, pre-teen boys have collected and traded baseball cards. Shortstops named Schwartz, second basemen called Steinberg, and first basemen named Feldman have played the game in urban playgrounds and on suburban ball fields.

A one-sentence summation of the life of Izzy Goldstein reflects the union between baseball, American dreams and the American immigrant Jewish experience: Goldstein was born in 1908 in Odessa in the Ukraine, pitched in sixteen games for the 1932 Detroit Tigers, and died in 1993 in Delray Beach, Florida.

In my film history courses, I emphasize that motion pictures serve as reflections of the era in which they were made. They offer information about the prevailing culture, popular and otherwise; they mirror the politics and social norms of their times. One can study films of all types and explore how they serve as historical and cultural barometers.

Similarly, it must be acknowledged that there is a cinema aesthetic, that a film may be appreciated for its artistry: how the choices made by its creators before, during, and after the shoot are reflected on-screen and impact the movie-going experience. Yet it is essential to recognize that most films—and certainly those produced in Hollywood—are not envisioned as works of art. They are not purposefully fashioned to mirror popular culture or comment on the state of society. Hollywood is, at its core, a factory town, with the production of motion pictures and television programs paralleling the manufacture of automobiles in Detroit and beer in Milwaukee. The films produced at MGM, Universal, or Warner Bros. are commercial entities; they are placed on the market to attract enough of an audience to earn a profit. This explains why the term "product" is employed to describe the output of a motion picture studio.

In my study of baseball films, I have observed that the typical script highlighting ball-playing characters usually focuses on wooing the heroine, thwarting the villains (who often are gamblers or others who would corrupt the sanctity of the sport), and overcoming obstacles to win the Big Game, most often with a clutch ninth-inning hit or dramatic stint on the mound. Such scenarios are formulaic—and, throughout motion picture history, the major studios rarely bankroll films that are innovative. They prefer not to deviate from the tried-and-true, the cookie-cutter storylines that audiences favor and that most likely will guarantee box office profits.

The formulaic nature of baseball films even extends to the names chosen for fictional celluloid ballplayers. Many feature colorful nicknames: Battling Bill Cosgrove; Specs White; Bee Line Tulliver; Dutch Holland; Long John Willoughby; Wacky Walters; Swat Anderson; Bingo Long; Crash Davis; Nuke LaLoosh. Plenty are generically Irish: Mike Xavier Aloysious Casey, Jim Dolan, Frank X. Farrell, Frank Maguire, Jimmy Dugan, Eddie O'Brien, Dennis Ryan, Tom, Jim and Larry Kelly—not to mention Truck Hogan, Spike Nolan, Monk Lanigan, and Guffy McGovern. Nicknamed ball playing characters may reflect the monikers of real major leaguers from Choo Choo Coleman to Wildfire Schulte, but there is no explanation as to why so many are sons of Erin. Nonetheless, a few—but not all—ball playing Irishmen are stereotypes: Mike Casey (Wallace Beery), the title character in *Casey at the Bat* (1927), is a boisterous, beer-guzzling Ruthian slugger; Guffy McGovern (Paul Douglas), the Pittsburgh Pirates' manager in *Angels in the Outfield* (1951), is comically stubborn and gruff; Jimmy Dugan (Tom Hanks), the Rockford Peaches' manager in *A League of Their Own* (1992), is a fall-down drunk.

Conversely, just about all the relatively few celluloid Jewish ballplayers found in pre-1950s movies are manifestations of the sentiment expressed in the dialogue from *Liberty Heights*. The manner in which these characters are rendered has evolved into a lecture titled "O'Brien to Ryan to Goldberg: Jews, Baseball and Celluloid Stereotypes." I have presented this program, which is illustrated with film clips, at venues ranging from the University at Albany (SUNY) and the National Yiddish Book Center, located on the campus of Hampshire College in Amherst, Massachusetts, to Jewish centers and cultural festivals.

To understand why Jewish athletes (and Jewish characters in general) were depicted as unphysical and anti-athletic, such characterizations must be placed within the framework of the era. During the first half of the twentieth century, millions of U.S. moviegoers were European immigrants, or their offspring. Countless films were fashioned to appeal directly to this viewership, and it is for this reason that so many films are crammed with characters who wear their ethnicity on their sleeves.

One stock character—the celluloid sibling of Mike Kelly and Guffy McGovern—is the ruddy-faced Irish New York City cop. He always is friendly; he becomes teary-eyed whenever he bursts into a chorus of "When Irish Eyes Are Smiling" or "Mother Machree"; but he can be stern when the situation warrants. Being that he is Irish-Catholic, he usually has sired quite a few children. If any are boys, you can bet your tickets to the policeman's ball that they, too, will grow up to become members of New York's Finest.

Until his death in 1945, character actor Henry Armetta fashioned a career playing comical, Italian-accented waiters, restaurateurs and shopkeepers. Armetta acted these characters in a manner that our current culture might dismiss as politically incorrect. But 60, 70, 80 years ago, broadly-played Italian waiters and blarney-soaked Irish cops were readily accepted, and were welcomed by moviegoers. If you were Italian or Irish, you were not offended by these characters. They were familiar to you, and you relished seeing them on-screen.

At the time, Hollywood producers did not consider black or Asian moviegoers as sources of box office revenue. So African-American characters were consistently stereotyped negatively as lazy, stupid, and all-too-easily frightened, and often as maids and Pullman porters who desecrated the English language. The films in which they appeared were fashioned for Caucasian audiences and, in that pre-Civil Rights era, such characterizations were acceptable to the American mainstream.

It was pretty much the same for Asian characters. Charlie Chan, novelist-playwright Earl Derr Biggers's celebrated detective, was the hero of a series of films released between the late 1920s and late 1940s. Even though Chan was a sharp fellow who employed his wits to solve murder mysteries, his on-screen characterization was largely stereotypical. Primarily, he spoke in broken English, and he was not played by an Asian-born or Asian-American actor. Three non-Asians—Warner Oland, Sidney Toler and Roland Winters—were cast as the detective in the bulk of the Charlie Chan films.

This is not to say that Asian actors were absent from Hollywood. From 1922 until his death twenty-three years later (Canton) China-born Willie Fung played small and supporting roles in almost 120 films. His stock character was a loud, comical, monosyllabic houseboy, cabin boy, cook, laundryman, waiter, valet or servant. Fung's characterizations were acceptable, because his films were intended for Caucasians.

All this racial and ethnic stereotyping parallels the manner in which Jews in general—and Jewish athletes in particular—were portrayed on-screen. Beyond the physical representations of Jews, Hollywood movies featured such cookie-cutter characters as pawnbrokers, grocery store owners and tailors: Lower East Side workingmen who looked Jewish, moved Jewish, and spoke Jewish. An occasional screenplay centered on the offspring of immigrants who abandon their downtown tenement roots for uptown Manhattan Towers assimilation. In *The Younger Generation* (1929), a Jewish family suffers because of one son's determination to disown his lineage and break into New York City society; in *Counsellor-at-Law* (1933), an adaptation of the Elmer Rice play, a successful uptown lawyer must deal with his humble downtown roots.

In a number of Hollywood films, Yiddish—the language of the Eastern European Jewish immigrant—may be heard on the sound track. Even non-Jewish New Yorkers spoke the language. In *Taxi* (1932), James Cagney stars as Matt Nolan, an Irish cab driver. He smilingly looks on as an Irish cop haplessly attempts to communicate with a comically flustered, Yiddish-speaking Jew seeking directions to Ellis Island. Nolan intercedes and converses with the man—in Yiddish!

Another Cagney film, *The Mayor of Hell* (1933), spotlights several youngsters who are a United Nations of the Lower East Side. There is the Italian kid, the Irish kid and the Jewish kid; all have joined a street gang and, after robbing a candy store, they appear before a judge empowered to send them to reform school. The Jew is Isadore Horowitz (Sidney Miller), a lanky youngster who is nicknamed "Schnoz." Isadore and his shopkeeper father are comical ethnic stereotypes. The father is amenable to dispatching Isadore to the school only after learning that it is not a prison—and that there is no tuition! But the father's love for his son clearly is displayed as he speaks emotionally to the boy in Yiddish.

Isadore's Jewishness lingers after he is dispatched to the school. At one point, he attempts to trade his portion of bacon for some eggs in the school dining room. Cagney's character is the center's new administrator, and he announces that the school will operate like a democracy, with officials elected by the boys. Upon mention of the treasurer position, Isadore, in a reaction shot, attempts to appear businesslike by solemnly buttoning the top of his shirt.

Back in 1933, Jewish audiences could relate to these sequences—and find them entertaining. The actions of Isadore and his father are inoffensive within the context of the film. A character like Isadore Horowitz exists as a reference point for Jewish moviegoers.

While the celluloid Jewish athletes of the period primarily are sweetly comical, there is another, more insidious stereotype: the Jew who is fearful and unphysical, who cowers in the face of confrontation and is incapable of being a fighting hero. A classic example of the bullied Jew is found in *Cimarron* (1931), a Best Picture Academy Award winner based on the novel by Edna Ferber—the daughter of a Hungarian-born Jewish shopkeeper. Much of the film is set in a dusty Oklahoma town in the late 1880s. Sol Levy (George E. Stone), one of the supporting characters, is a diminutive young would-be R.H. Macy, who, in one sequence, trudges down a muddy street hawking safety pins, needles, and thread from a pushcart. First, Sol is verbally abused by a group of hooligans. Then he is lassoed, like a calf in a rodeo. He begs to be left alone as Lon Yountis, the head thug, force-feeds him liquor and fires a gun at his feet. Sol runs away, stumbles, and ends up dangling from a wooden cross in a Christ-like pose. The "little Jew" then is rescued by Yancey Cravat, the tall, sturdy hero.

In a Western, a character named Sol Levy could not be a sheriff or a gunslinger, a hero or a villain. He is a business entrepreneur, and he cannot be a "physical" character: a man who is well-built, and who can handle himself in a fight. Instead, he is a victim. (Ever so typically, Sol eventually opens a Macys and Gimbels-style department store. The *Cimarron* scenario concludes in 1929, with an aged Sol Levy presiding over his business empire.

A character like Sol Levy plays into the stereotype of the Jew as victim, and negates the fact that real-world Jews of the period were athletes, soldiers and gangsters as well as pushcart vendors and business entrepreneurs.

In the realm of athletics, Jews not only were baseball players, but scores of Benny Leonard, Barney Ross, and "Slapsie" Maxie Rosenbloom wannabes attempted to slug their way to fame between the ropes. So it is appropriate that the most notable on-screen Jewish athlete of the pre-1950s Hollywood cinema is a boxer. Charlie Davis (John Garfield), the main character in *Body and Soul* (1947), may not have a generically Jewish surname, but he exudes New York Jewishness. The son of a Lower East Side shopkeeper, Davis is a child of the Depression; his robust knockout punch allows him entrée into the uptown upper classes. As he mingles with the well-heeled sharpies in a Park Avenue dream world, Charlie is corrupted. Eventually, he is humbled, and can reset his moral compass only when he struggles with his conscience and rediscovers his tenement roots. Garfield played similar (albeit nonathletic) characters in *Humoresque* (1946), in which he was cast as a concert violinist, and *Force of Evil* (1948), in which he played a lawyer. All three films explore a dilemma faced by the children of immigrants: How does one maintain one's roots and one's sense of self while assimilating into the American mainstream and rising in American society?

Charlie Davis is a fictional character whose conflicts are culled from real life. But as a representative celluloid Jewish athlete, his ferociousness and physical dexterity are the exception rather than the rule.

Similarly, the athleticism that is present when a real-life Jewish ballplayer appears in a Hollywood movie is undeniable. By 1949, Hall of Fame slugger Hank Greenberg had retired as an active player and was employed by the Cleveland Indians. That year, *The Kid from Cleveland*—the story of a troubled orphan (Rusty Tamblyn) who is a die-hard Cleveland Indians fan—came to movie theaters. Practically the entire Cleveland organization appeared in the film, from players Bob Feller, Satchel Paige, Bob Lemon, Larry Doby, Gene Bearden and Mickey Vernon to Greenberg, team owner Bill Veeck, player-manager Lou Boudreau, and Hall of Famer Tris Speaker.

In *The Kid from Cleveland,* Greenberg is not seen shagging flies or swatting homers. But in his scenes, in which he interacts with his fellow baseball professionals and the actors in the cast, he looks the part of a recently retired jock. He is tall and well-built, and he towers over Boudreau, Veeck and actor George Brent. Greenberg is not a movie star who has bulked up to believably impersonate an athlete. He is a real ballplayer who happens to be Jewish.

Greenberg's appearance in *The Kid from Cleveland* may be contrasted to the era's fictional celluloid Jewish athletes. With the exception of Garfield's Charlie Davis, all are fashioned to tickle the audiences' collective funny bone—and all may be viewed as cultural stereotypes.

One is a supporting character in *The Shamrock Handicap* (1926), a horse-racing yarn in which director John Ford—as he often did in his films—liberally lays on the blarney. The film spotlights the affection between an Irish lass and a son of Erin who heads off to America to ride the ponies. One of the jockeys slated to compete in the climactic race is Bennie Ginsburg (George Harris), a son of Aaron. While real-life jockeys generally are diminutive, Bennie is a tad shorter than his fellow riders. Mostly, he is a comical character who is embarrassed when the heroine pins the stable colors to the back of his shirt. Then Bennie tumbles to the ground after mounting his horse and is unable to ride. The non-Jewish hero, who is on crutches, takes his place, but Bennie is not rankled that he has been denied the chance to compete in, and perhaps win, the Big Race. For after all, it is just an athletic competition.

As the race begins, Bennie is just another spectator. At one point, he comically *davens* (prays) for his replacement to emerge victorious. *The Shamrock Handicap* is a silent film, and Bennie's entreaties appear in the intertitles in Yiddish—a clever device that still evokes laughter all these decades later. Certainly, back in 1926, Jewish moviegoers were supposed to relate to, and be entertained by, the character of Bennie Ginsburg.

The Jewish athlete as nonathlete also is found in *Hot Curves* (1930), a baseball film. Benny Rubin, a veteran vaudeville and burlesque comic, stars as Benny Goldberg, a double-talking Jewish train employee who is signed by the Pittsburgh baseball club because he will "bring plenty of Jewish business through the gate in New York." During the course of the film, Goldberg befriends Jim Dolan (Rex Lease), a highly touted rookie pitcher. The Pittsburgh manager is named McGrew; supposedly, the story angle was culled from the real-life signing of Andy Cohen, a Jewish infielder, by New York Giants manager John McGraw. Cohen played for the Giants in 1926 and 1928–29.

In *Hot Curves,* Dolan is the handsome, traditional cinematic hero, while Goldberg is the comic relief. Near the beginning of the film, Benny is approached by a scout (Mike Donlin, an ex-major leaguer turned movie actor) and offered a contract. Benny brags about his baseball skills and then, in order to sign for more money, coyly plays hard-to-get with the scout. Today, an athlete who is as coveted as Benny likely would hire an agent to negotiate the highest possible salary. In 1930, when ballplayers mostly were blue-collar working stiffs, the depiction of Benny makes him an ethnic stereotype.

Benny signs with the team, and heads to spring training. But he is no Hank Greenberg. He is physically inept on the field, responding with terror as a line drive flies past him. Then a grounder haplessly bounces off his chest. Benny does get his athletic act together, however, and makes the team as a catcher. Here, the Jewish athlete actually gets to play in the Big Game—the deciding World Series game—but he is not the slugger who smashes the game-winning hit. These heroics are assigned to Jim Dolan. At the finale, Benny awkwardly slaps a single and jumps up and down at first base like a hyperactive grade-schooler. Then Dolan bashes an inside-the-park dinger. Benny contributes to the rally, but Dolan is the star. His hit is the one that will headline the following day's sports pages.

Another character named Goldberg is the most famous fictional celluloid Jewish ballplayer: Nat Goldberg (Jules Munshin), who appears in the musical *Take Me Out to the Ball Game* (1949). The setting is the early twentieth century and this Goldberg, a major league first baseman, is part of the famed, Tinker-to-Evers-to-Chance-inspired double play combination of O'Brien, Ryan and Goldberg.

Despite this billing, O'Brien and Ryan are the primary male characters and the romantic heroes. Gene Kelly's Eddie O'Brien is a brash, overconfident womanizer, and Frank Sinatra's Dennis Ryan is lovably sweet and shy; they are amorously linked to characters played by Esther Williams and Betty Garrett. Munshin's Nat Goldberg is the comical supporting character. Tellingly, he has no girlfriend, no wife, no on-screen romantic life. His sole purpose is to amuse the audience. This is evident in the opening sequence, as the ballplayers pose for a spring training group photo. The manager growls at Goldberg to douse his cigar. The first baseman responds by comically coughing and putting the still-lit stogie under his cap.

O'Brien and Ryan, off-season vaudeville performers, finally arrive at spring training. Goldberg effeminately pirouettes as he rushes up to greet them. He asks about their vaudeville tour, and the duo tells him about all the "girls" they met on the road. Here, O'Brien and Ryan have personalities. They have interests. They are the male centerpieces of the story. Goldberg, meanwhile, is little more than a sounding board. O'Brien and Ryan act, while Goldberg reacts.

Nat Goldberg does have one big moment in the film, which he predictably shares with O'Brien and Ryan. The trio performs a spirited song-and-dance number, "O'Brien to Ryan to Goldberg," in which they tout their on-field prowess. At a juncture in the routine, the three perform Irish jigs to celebrate the ethnicity of O'Brien and Ryan. Then they segue into an old-country Jewish-style dance to honor Goldberg. Tellingly, Goldberg observes that his mother would have preferred that he forsake swinging a Louisville Slugger for a more intellectual-cultural pursuit: playing the violin.

In "O'Brien to Ryan to Goldberg," the three performers share equal time. Once the number ends, Goldberg returns to the background. O'Brien and Ryan begin a conversation; Goldberg is an onlooker.

Liberty Heights was released in 1999, but it is set in the 1950s—and its baseball reference reflects a pre-1950s mindset: Jews make wonderful musicians, composers and show business impresarios but are athletically inept. Happily, other post-1950s films depict ballplaying Jews in a more realistic manner. One example is Ben Lewin (Michael Douglas), the recently retired major leaguer who is the male lead in *It's My Turn* (1980). Lewin is handsome, desirable and athletic; he commences a romance with a math professor (Jill Clayburgh) and attends a Yankee Stadium Old Timer's Day ceremony in the company of Mickey Mantle, Roger Maris, Whitey Ford, and other real-life legends. And with a name like Ben Lewin, how could he not be Jewish?

When one watches and analyzes baseball films, it becomes apparent that baseball-on-screen constantly has been employed as a symbol of Americana, of mom's apple pie patriotism. The association directly relates to immigrants of all backgrounds, as well as to the children of immigrants, for, after all, how do these new Americans come to feel at home in the United States? How do they become part of the fabric of America? For a male, the answer is by knowing and playing baseball as a youngster, and following the sport as an adult.

Baseball plays a pivotal role in the opening sequence in *The Chosen* (1981), based on the Chaim Potok novel. The setting is Brooklyn, the time is World War II, and the sequence spotlights a spirited schoolyard softball game between two groups of very different Jewish teenagers. One is made up of Americanized youngsters. The other consists of old-world-style Hasidic Jews. All the boys are linked as residents of New York City, and they express their Americanism by swinging baseball bats and scooting around bases.

Danny Saunders (Robby Benson), a Hasidic Jew, is the star player. He might be a junior Hank Greenberg as he grips a bat, confidently takes a practice swing, and promptly cracks a double. When he returns to the plate, Reuven Malter (Barry Miller, the son of Sidney Miller) is the new pitcher.

The two square off, and the at bat is tense and confrontational. It ends with Danny smashing a line drive that caroms off Reuven's face, breaking his glasses, cutting his eye and landing him in the hospital.

While narrating the sequence, Reuven notes that, at the time, young American Jews wished to repudiate Hitler by displaying their physical prowess to the rest of the world. One way to accomplish this was by playing baseball.

The characters in *The Chosen* are Jewish, but they are not stereotypically so. Even though they exist in a 1940s world, they are the polar opposites of the earlier fictional Jewish ballplayers. Danny Saunders and Reuven Malter may be adolescent boys batting and fielding in a school yard, but their athletic ability is more a reflection of the real Hank Greenberg and Sandy Koufax than the fictional Benny and Nat Goldberg.

Film

Baseball Cinema in the Classroom
(GEORGE GRELLA)

Anyone who doubts the validity, the popularity, or even the simple acceptance of courses in baseball need only examine a recent column by Ron Fimrite, entitled "Hardball Classics," in *Sports Illustrated* (June 20, 2005), which describes such a course at San Francisco State University. Taught by two well-known scholars, Professors Eric Solomon and Jules Tygiel, the course deals with the history and literature, both fiction and nonfiction, associated with the sport, as well as the cultural context that surrounds it. The most important conclusion for a reader, however, really involves the mere appearance of the piece: when a story about some perhaps unusual or noteworthy phenomenon makes the pages of a national magazine or newspaper, identified as something of a novel business or a new trend, one can generally be sure that, in fact, the practice has been around for years, if not decades. In a sense, then, the news item sanctifies, if only by the staleness of its perception of something "new," the subject of its story; baseball in the classroom dates back many years (nineteen at San Francisco State) and hardly seems either revolutionary or threatening to anyone inside or outside the academic establishment.

In these enlightened times, in fact, one would think that only the stuffiest of college and university humanities departments would deny the importance and usefulness of teaching some aspect of baseball in some accepted academic discipline. The most obvious scholarly areas in which to cover the subject include, of course, American history, American literature, and that amorphous field that often combines the two, American studies. Perhaps less obviously, other disciplines outside the humanities also employ baseball in one way or another—sociology, for example, or economics, which has inspired a number of important studies of the game, architecture, urban design, and, of course, statistics, which the game supplies in such plenitude and which so preoccupies a whole generation of number crunchers and computer nerds.

Although the sport occupies an undeniably important place in the culture, it generally (and surprisingly) appears only in minor ways in major American literature: a highly relevant allusion to the Black Sox scandal in *The Great Gatsby*, several brief references in Hemingway's works, most notably the important function of the fisherman's admiration for Joe DiMaggio in *The Old Man and the Sea*, a minor mention in Faulkner's *Sanctuary*, a rich set piece at the beginning of Don DeLillo's *Underworld*. Among the hundreds of baseball novels, only a few stand out as worthy of serious analysis: Mark Harris's Henry Wiggen tetralogy, Bernard Malamud's *The Natural*, Robert Coover's *Universal Baseball Association, J. Henry Waugh, Prop.*, Eric Rolfe Greenberg's *The Celebrant*. On the other hand, the cinema—specifically, a course in the baseball film, an area rich in potential for students of the game at all levels—has become a growing source of interest for scholars of both film and sport. While many courses in baseball literature, history, and economics appear in college and university curricula around the country, few exist that deal with the cinema of baseball.

A course in the baseball film inevitably encompasses a number of matters beyond its nominal subject; like baseball itself, the study constantly proliferates and expands, serving a truly interdisciplinary function and engendering additional material and concepts. Such a course at the University of Rochester, created by this writer, was last offered as recently as the spring semester of 2004; the substance of that course provides some sense of an approach to both the sport and the art that may interest instructors in other disciplines and areas of study. The syllabus, enhanced by a number of well-known baseball books, both fiction and nonfiction, employs a central text, *Reel Baseball* (Wood and Pincus). It follows a roughly chronological order in the listing and screening of films, but also organizes titles along generic lines, so that, for example, baseball biographies, with which the course begins, occur within a discrete unit; further, some of the more or less historical works, and those that attempt to capture the magical and mythic interpretations of the game, which chiefly preoccupy the present author, also fall roughly within separate clusters.

That first group of biographies includes some of the most famous and important earlier (at least to the students) baseball films—*The Pride of the Yankees* (1942), *The Babe Ruth Story* (1948), and *The Jackie Robinson Story* (1950). *The Pride of the Yankees*, the biopic devoted to Lou Gehrig which some scholars regard as the best baseball film ever made, provides considerable material for class discussion. Although it sticks relatively closely to the truth of Gehrig's life–not always standard procedure in Hollywood–the movie quite understandably glorifies its subject. Gehrig himself had died less than two years earlier and had, of course, attained a legendary status through his brilliant career, the perfect subject for poetic or even tragic treatment—the glorious athlete dying young and leaving the game with a graceful and moving gesture of farewell.

The movie shows the short life of perhaps one of the last acceptable specimens in popular art of a man with a significant Oedipus complex; for much of the story Gehrig struggles to convince his doting, domineering mother of the respectability and profitability of playing ball instead of continuing his studies in engineering at Columbia University. It also details, of course, the usual business of the gifted athlete developing his talent and honing his skills, the awkward rookie coping with unusual social situations, the triumphant years of his career, and his marriage to a young woman who learns to deal with the formidable Mrs. Gehrig. Perhaps more importantly, the film's admonitions and its story of stoic endurance in the face of disheartening illness directly address the situation of the United States in 1942, a nation suffering a string of defeats in a global conflict that began with the Japanese attack at Pearl Harbor. It is surely no accident that Gary Cooper, who played Gehrig, had most recently starred in *Sergeant York* (1941), essentially a propaganda flick urging Americans, whatever their beliefs, to support the draft and the war; in many ways *Pride of the Yankees* seems a companion film to *Sergeant York*, a baseball movie serving the war effort almost as obviously as its predecessor and almost as blatantly as all those Frank Capra *Why We Fight* shorts.

Although *The Babe Ruth Story* (1948) occupies a dishonored place among students of the baseball film, it demonstrates in the most fulsome manner the general hagiography of so many baseball biopics. Made when the Babe was dying of cancer, the movie also provides the initial proof of the sacerdotal possibilities of the baseball film and the sport itself, its tendency toward the supernatural, the spiritual, the religious. The bowdlerized and wildly inaccurate narrative shows the young boy emerging from the obscure origins of the mythic hero to become a great ballplayer, a national figure, and ultimately, a saint and savior. Babe Ruth not only hits a remarkable number of home runs but also cures the sick and makes the lame walk, and attains the first canonization as a true saint in the church of baseball.

Somewhat less worshipful and certainly more relevant to its time and place, *The Jackie Robinson Story* (1950), starring its subject as himself, exhibits a different kind of heroism, on and off the field, as its protagonist fights the familiar battle against segregation in his sport and racism in the country. The cultural context of the film, moreover, supplies additional material for discussion: the final sequence shows a version of Robinson's notorious appearance before a Congressional committee, speaking for the black citizens of the country, condemning communism, and upholding America. The picture dissolves into a shot of the flag, with appropriately patriotic music playing, revealing that *The Jackie Robinson Story* resembles *Pride of the Yankees* in its apparent mission as a propaganda film, in this instance a reaction to the internal political threats of communism and the external dangers of the USSR in the Cold War, and perhaps even a patronizing endorsement of the patriotism of African Americans. The film demonstrates the extent to which external political forces influence even a relatively straightforward and honest representation of the struggle of a living ballplayer to attain acceptance from fans and fellow players.

The next segment of the course deals with the instructor's ideas about the essential magic of baseball, which may initially grow out of its origins as a ritual endeavor back somewhere in the prehistoric past. The scientist's discovery of a substance that repels wood and thereby enables him to coat baseballs with it in *It Happens Every Spring* (1949) provides a lighthearted glimpse of the pure, inherent craziness of the game. Students also notice the movie's odd notions about academic life—Ray Milland dates one of his students, the daughter of the university president!—and cheating in sports, both perhaps more innocent back then and both perhaps merely examples of Hollywood's tendency to misrepresent certain areas of American life. Both versions of *Angels in the Outfield* (1951 and 1994) continue the aspect of the supernatural and the divine in the game (the original, by the way, is a much more satisfying and less sentimental picture than the remake); they also provide a useful opportunity for a written assignment in comparison and contrast, with the potential for a multitude of approaches and subjects—characters, effects, emotional complications, historical contexts, etc.

Another group of films deals with some cinematic versions of baseball history, employing, without any need for factitious political correctness, some honest inclusion of otherwise neglected components of the game. Assigning both Eliot Asinov's book *Eight Men Out* and John Sayles's movie of the same title (1988) allows the students to understand some solid history of the game, especially, of course, its darkest moment, the Black Sox scandal, which has haunted baseball since 1919. Although broadly comic at times and not always strictly accurate, *Bingo Long's Traveling All-Stars and Motor Kings* (1976) provides some insight into the conduct of the old, segregated game. The movie shows some insight into racial prejudice, the difficulties confronting players in the Negro Leagues, and some of the internal politicking of the owners.

As a kind of companion piece, in its account of a season with the Rockford Peaches of the All American Girls Professional Baseball League, *A League of Their Own* (1992) shows again the history of another side of the sport. Simply on its own, the theatrical release of the picture initially instructed a great many filmgoers on a little known but highly entertaining piece of baseball history. It also struck a few blows for gender equality, while enlightening students about some of the conditions in America during World War II. In the context of the course, it reflects the variety of approaches to the sport in film, and the bittersweet recollection of a time when some tough and talented women played their version of the game with enormous zest and commitment.

The next trio of films, all of them based on some well-known baseball novels, attempt to capture something of the powerfully mythic nature of the sport, a quality that distinguishes the best baseball literature. *Bang the Drum Slowly* (1973), adapted from the Mark Harris novel, the second in his Henry Wiggen trilogy, only hints at the cynicism, fakery, and hypocrisy that accompany playing in the major leagues, where profits count far more than people or even winning ball games. The movie also confronts with at least a modicum of honesty some of the book's atmosphere of loss, sadness, and regret in its treatment of the last season in the life of a dying catcher; despite its pervasive melancholy, the film also now and then stumbles into humor, partly through the work of its odd cast. Although moderately well reviewed and relatively successful at the box office, the movie looks rather flimsy and cheaply produced some thirty years later, and, perhaps because of those problems, exerted almost no influence on its form.

It took the appearance of *The Natural* in 1984 to put the baseball movie on the map; despite its several major departures from Bernard Malamud's brilliant novel, the picture's fine cast of character actors, and a couple of big stars, Robert Redford and Glenn Close, assisted in that successful errand in cartography. Filmed in the sepia light of the past, creating a kind of visual nostalgia, and accompanied by an evocative score, the story of Roy Hobbs's defeated promise and resurrected career falls into the sentimental and inspirational school of cinematic interpretation. Robert Redford's understated performance and graceful movement, along with a certain softness and sweetness, redeem the occasional mawkishness of *The*

Natural, however, and certainly account for its influence on the production of later films.

After *The Natural* proved that baseball movies could draw large audiences and not incidentally earn significant sums of money, a great many motion pictures on the subject, few of them of any lasting quality or importance, followed. An expanded course in baseball film might well deal with numerous variations on the genre, but, as in any course, the instructor must compromise with the material. Some works, however, simply must be included, and the most successful baseball film of them all, *Field of Dreams* (1989), belongs in that category; just about all the students in any course in the subject will know the movie, which enriches discussion beyond the level of many of the other, less familiar titles. Aside from its terrific lighting and cinematography and the perfectly adequate performances of Kevin Costner and Ray Liotta, the movie features one grand old man of Hollywood cinema, Burt Lancaster, and one individual growing rather consciously and obviously into that category, James Earl Jones.

As with *The Natural*, the picture makes an appropriate companion piece to the W. P. Kinsella novel, *Shoeless Joe*, which inspired it, enabling students to draw numerous instances of comparison and contrast and also instructing them in some of the ways in which the mechanics of the cinema differ from the process of fiction writing. Discussion of the whole supernatural basis of the film opens up a cornucopia of philosophical enigmas: does the voice of God speak to Ray Kinsella, and if not, then who utters the fateful words? If the players lived a reasonably natural span of years, why do they return from the dead in the prime of their youth? If they are dead, then where do they dwell? Both Shoeless Joe and Ray's father ask the same question, "Is this Heaven?" to which Ray replies, "No, it's Iowa." Is Iowa like Heaven, or is Iowa an even better place? (For anyone who's been there, by the way, Iowa does not particularly resemble any Heaven that most people would want to enter). Why can only certain people see the players? Why doesn't the Black Sox scandal itself figure strongly in the movie? What measure and degree of belief does the picture demand? The questions go on.

The film also further demonstrates some of the present writer's contentions about the origins of the game in ancient vegetation rites; as the players and, later, Moonlight Graham and Terrence Mann, melt into the cornfield, the connection between baseball and fertility ritual emerges with utter clarity. The players quite literally are corn gods, magically materializing from and dissolving into the corn, underlining the connection between the cornfield and the ball field, which Ray Kinsella carved out at the behest of that mysterious, disembodied voice. Whatever the defects of either *Shoeless Joe* or *Field of Dreams*, the vision of both suggests a closer relationship of the film to the novel, at least in spirit, than, for instance, the two versions of *The Natural*. Despite the brilliance of Malamud's novel and the generally pleasant adaptation, *Field of Dreams* allows for some richer analysis of the mythic nature of the sport and of its representations in literature and cinema.

The course deals, finally, with a few more lighthearted baseball movies, the fully comic *Major League* (1989) and the grittier *Bull Durham* (1988). The first movie reminds us all that the game exhibits numerous possibilities for fun. Its slight plot shows the hapless Cleveland Indians resolving to foil the plot of their devious owner by winning the American League pennant despite her best efforts to attain a losing record in order to move the team elsewhere. The film's most important contribution to the course and to discussion derives from its depiction of a not atypical baseball team as a collection of personalities as old as comedy itself. The team features such familiar comic characters as the *senex iratus* (Angry Old Man), *miles gloriosus* (Boastful Soldier), the Clever Servant, the Wise Old Man, etc., translated into baseball characters—the Crusty Manager, the Hot Dog, the Grizzled Veteran, the Lovable Goof, the Rookie, etc. The personnel of the Cleveland Indians, introduced in a lively montage at the beginning of the movie, a collection of misfits, has-beens, and eccentrics, constitute a brief and useful epitome of the characters of baseball.

Many of those characters return in a quite different way in *Bull Durham*, possibly the best baseball film of them all in terms of its understanding of the game, of some of the ways it should be played, and of the sociological context of the world outside the major leagues. Within its comic, sometimes satiric examination of the game, the movie may stand alone in showing some of the reality of playing in the low minor leagues or perhaps anywhere else. Starring one of the best athletes in Hollywood, Kevin Costner, who has convincingly played ball or impersonated a ballplayer in four movies, the film captures some of the inherent humor as well as the inherent heartbreak of a life in the minors. It shows the sadness of the perennial minor leaguer, the obnoxiousness of the gifted rookie, the attitudes of some of the fans, especially the primary Baseball Annie (Susan Sarandon), the ordinary business of simply playing the game on a far less glamorous level than the major leagues. It provides some sense of the kinds of things the players do and say when they are not on the field, the actions of a group of not terribly sophisticated young men far from home, on the loose and often lonely in a town that is not their town, working hard toward a distant dream of success.

In the process of its fun and satire and even in its bumpy and bawdy love story, the movie offers a salutary contrast to *Field of Dreams*, an unsentimental response to the earlier movie's sometimes mawkish and melodramatic dialogue and action. Just as Kevin Costner's character as the career minor league catcher, Crash Davis, provides a refreshing contrast to his role as Ray Kinsella in *Field of Dreams*, so Susan Sarandon's smart, earthy, unabashed sexuality provides a healthy alternative to Amy Madigan's soppy, perky cuteness. The differences in the roles and in the interpretation of baseball underline the chasm that separates the two movies and perhaps the two most dominant views of the sport, the romantic and the realistic.

The course ultimately explores a considerable amount of other territory in addition to the subjects of baseball, film, and the baseball film. It introduces students to some of the issues surrounding the history of baseball in the twentieth century—social, economic, racial, etc.—as well as to some of the history of the nation itself during that time. Perhaps more importantly, the films show something of the state of American society at particular times, the stages of the cultural contexts that surround the films, whether the charming innocence of the first *Angels in the Outfield*, the exuberant toughness of the black players in the rural South in *Bingo Long's Traveling All-Stars and Motor Kings*, or the state of the home front during World War II in *A League of Their Own*.

A final word about requirements: To begin with, a student need not know anything in particular about baseball, though naturally the course will attract fans. It is always a wonder that now and then someone who has grown up in America knows nothing about the game, but that really presents no problem. The students will learn everything they need to know as the course progresses and their knowledge and experience improve. Perhaps more urgent and important, they also need not know anything about film. Many instructors, drunk on theory, overwhelm their students with vocabulary and ponderous abstractions about film, most of which are incorrect, insensitive, and irrelevant. Many students either feel intimidated by the actual, useful vocabulary of film and the technical nature of the art or obsessed by the purely mechanical; geeks and nerds proliferate in every calling. All that students need to know about film they can learn through the evolution of the course: enough theory to conceptualize some larger issues in a particular film or films, enough technical knowledge to understand just how a particular shot or sequence made the journey from the fact or the imagination to the screen. Finally, they will learn some of the ways in which a writer, director, actor, camera operator, or any of the other hundreds of people needed to make this labor-intensive, highly collaborative art, managed to achieve the level and quality of emotion and intelligence in a particular shot or sequence or film—in short, how a movie creates its meanings.

Appendix

Sample Syllabi. Spring 2004
Wed. Jan. 14 Introduction, Organization, Background; Film: *The Pride of the Yankees*; Readings: *Reel Baseball*, Prefatory Material, pp. 102–146.
Wed. Jan. 21 *The Babe Ruth Story*
Wed. Jan. 28 *The Jackie Robinson Story;* Reading: *Reel Baseball*, pp. 63–88. Paper#1
Wed. Feb. 4 *It Happens Every Spring*
Wed. Feb. 11 *Angels in the Outfield* I
Wed. Feb. 18 *Angels in the Outfield* II; Reading: *Eight Men Out*
Wed. Feb. 25 *Eight Men Out.* Paper #2
Wed. Mar. 3 *Bingo Long's Traveling All-Stars and Motor Kings*

SPRING BREAK
Wed. Mar. 17 *A League of Their Own;* Reading: *Bang the Drum Slowly*
Wed. Mar. 24 *Bang the Drum Slowly;* Reading: *The Natural, Reel Baseball*, pp.20–35
Wed. Mar. 31 *The Natural*; Reading: *Shoeless Joe, Reel Baseball*, pp.52–63, 88–102
Wed. Apr. 7 *Field of Dreams*
Wed. Apr. 14 *Major League*
Wed. Apr. 21 *Bull Durham*; Reading: *Reel Baseball*, pp. 146–240
Wed. Apr. 28. To be announced.

Works Cited (Books)

Asinof, Eliot. *Eight Men Out.* New York: Pocket Books, 1979.
Harris, Mark. *Henry Wiggen's Books.* New York: Avon Books, 1977.
Kinsella, W. P. *Shoeless Joe.* New York: Houghton Mifflin, 1999.
Wood, Stephen C., and J. David Pincus. *Reel Baseball.* Jefferson, NC: McFarland, 2003.

History

Using Baseball to Teach U.S. History Since the Civil War

(JERRY RODNITZKY)

Six years ago I decided that baseball history offered several advantages and insights in teaching the second half of the American history survey to freshmen college students. I began by adding Robert Creamer's book, *Baseball in '41,* to the condensed textbook and reader I always used, along with two additional monographs on concentrated subjects. The monographs had ranged from Vietnam War books to those about the postwar Civil Rights Movement. Creamer's book was especially concentrated since it centered on only one year. However, its real innovation was correlating what happened in baseball in 1941 (for example, Joe DiMaggio's hitting streak) to what was happening in America and the world. Creamer's 1991 book was a very personal look at what he had experienced at age eighteen, in what on the title page he called "a celebration of the best baseball season ever in the year America went to war." In recreating the cultural climate of that year, from Hollywood films to clothing styles, he vividly brings back the times, but is so personal that sometimes the big historical picture is lost. I then alternately tried Jules Tygiel's *Baseball's Great Experiment: Jackie Robinson and His Legacy* as a substitute for my civil rights book.

Both these books worked fairly well in giving an offbeat, though narrow approach to the standard American history my students knew, and in holding their interest. In fact, the books worked so well in one small course segment that I decided to try using baseball history throughout the course, which stretched from 1865 through the 1990s. Since baseball history stretches from just before the Civil War to the present, it seemed a perfect chronological match. And since baseball was largely a cultural phenomenon, it seemed the perfect complement to the textbook, which stressed political, diplomatic, and military history.

After researching what was available in paperback, I decided to use Jules Tygiel's *Past Time: Baseball as History* (published in paperback in 2000). I have used it with increasing enthusiasm ever since. This book of Tygiel's essays covers aspects of baseball from the 1850s through the 1990s, and it views baseball as a classic American business as well as a sport. It also emphasizes some neglected subjects, such as the Negro Baseball League and the early development of baseball statistics. Its broad chronological sweep allows an instructor to constantly fill in the blanks and make his or her own connections between baseball and important developments and trends in American history. This essay suggests a number of developments in American history that can be highlighted by parallel trends in baseball. The basic teaching strategy is not to substitute baseball history for American history, but to use baseball history to show important patterns in American history. Students usually find popular culture history entertaining. However, the teacher should stress that he or she is not trying to entertain students but is trying to make history entertaining.

One of the first connections that struck me (early in the course) was baseball as a national metaphor for the reunification of North and South, long before the Spanish-American War brought the nation together under the flag. Baseball identified itself as a "national" game immediately after the Civil War. It had enthusiastic players and fans all over the nation, even though most of the famous professional teams remained in the East and Midwest for over a century. North-South sectionalism was clearly never a part of baseball, although local loyalty and rivalry clearly were. Americans took national pride in having invented and perfected this game and proclaimed this to the world as a nation.

As teachers move chronologically through late nineteenth-century history, they can easily draw instructive parallels between the new business tycoons such as Andrew Carnegie and John Rockefeller, who started modestly and became industrial giants, and pioneer baseball owners such as Charles Comiskey and Clark Griffith. The baseball tycoons did not build their empires until the early twentieth century, but Carnegie, Rockefeller and other innovative businessmen were their clear models. Like the early tycoons, baseball owners built monopolies, and indeed had more success in legally maintaining them. Whereas Carnegie's steel empire and Rockefeller's Standard Oil trust were steadily controlled and limited by government antitrust actions, baseball achieved and maintained a special status as the national pastime.

Moreover, individual baseball players now became the favored heroes of American youth. After the Civil War the new heroes were industrialists such as Carnegie and Rockefeller, who were born with few advantages and pulled themselves up by their own bootstraps. These new heroes replaced traditional self-made political heroes such as Andrew Jackson and Abraham Lincoln. Politics now seemed stodgy and corrupt. After 1900, with the rise of big-time sports in general and baseball in particular, baseball players such as Home Run Baker and Christy Mathewson replaced the tycoons. Business now seemed boring and corrupt to many youth. Our present students also usually see businessmen and politicians as largely stodgy and corrupt, so they can identify with this development. The twentieth century saw the steady rise of celebrities created by newspapers and magazines—for example, Nelly Bly, the young woman reporter sent around the world to report only on her experiences; Anna Held, the Ziegfeld chorus girl; and the many male and female early silent film stars who were all soon forgotten, though temporarily famous. Celebrities, however, were seldom real heroes. They were more likely famous for being famous. The baseball stars were usually real heroes, famous for their deeds on the field, and thus they had a special credibility. When Babe Ruth was chided in the 1920s for having a larger salary than President Hoover, he answered, "I had a better season than he did." There was more truth than whimsy in that comment.

Replacing heroes with celebrities was largely the result of the rise of a new journalism in which many newspapers and magazines competed for public attention. Most history texts talk about the "yellow press" exemplified by William Randolph Hearst and especially his use of his newspapers to stir up support for the Spanish-American War in 1896. They usually ignore the print media revolution that inexpensive magazines and newspapers fostered. Baseball was also an important facet of the new journalism. Increasingly in the twentieth century Americans turned to the sport section of their daily newspaper first, and for most of that century the top sports news concerned baseball, which has the longest season of any sport. The invention and selling of baseball statistics created steady daily news that many Americans found mesmerizing. Statistically, a family might not know how well they were doing economically compared to others, but they did know how their favorite team's pitchers and hitters were doing. Relative batting averages and pitchers' won-lost records became topics of everyday conversation. Indeed, baseball led the way toward the American romance with statistics of all kinds.

One can show students a clip from the 1996 film *The Mirror Has Two Faces* to demonstrate that baseball statistics are still a universal language. Jeff Bridges plays a stiff college math professor who bores his class to death. However, on the advice of Barbra Streisand, a lively professor, he connects with his students by using baseball batting averages and won-lost percentages to illustrate math principles.

In the 1920s, the media revolution took another turn with the spread of radio, and baseball was a natural subject for broadcasts. Our present students know just how profoundly new media can change their lives. They have gone from LPs to CDs, from TV to VCRs to DVDs, and from tape recorders to MP3s. Baseball game scores had long been relayed around the country by telegraph, with important games telegraphed play-by-play. Showing students a still photo of a pre-1920 crowd sitting in a hall listening to a ballgame by telegraph makes the point dramatically. The 1922 World Series was brought to the public via both radio and telegraph. Radio quickly made telegraphing baseball obsolete. Radio picked up the entire flavor of being present. One heard not only the play-by-play from the announcer but picked up the roar of the crowd and the umpire bellowing: "Play ball!"

Historians constantly argue about when contemporary America starts. However, the 1920s were clearly the start of modern America. Wide ownership of autos, a sexual revolution, a generation gap, and a media revolution of modern film and radio were perhaps the most striking modern aspects for our students, but sports also supplied a modern twist. Baseball and football obviously predated the twenties, but this was the first decade that America became sports crazy across the board. Horse racing, boxing, tennis, golf, and track all became big attractions even though baseball was clearly the most popular and widely followed sport. And students understand instinctively that an America that is not sports crazy is not modern America.

Heywood Hale Broun, the perceptive cultural critic, caught the newly fervent, almost religious attitude toward baseball in a way still striking to students. Broun dreamed that John Roach Stratton, a famous hellfire and brimstone preacher, had gone to heaven. Stratton asked God to rain fire on Yankee Stadium because the Yankees had attracted a crowd of forty thousand on a Sunday. But in Broun's dreams, as Babe Ruth came up to bat, God told Stratton, "Let's at least wait until the inning is over" (Carter, 22).

A more vivid way to connect baseball and the 1920s is with film clips from John Sayles' acclaimed 1988 film *Eight Men Out*. This exquisitely detailed film centers on the Black Sox scandal of 1919 and is based on Eliot Asinof's superbly researched 1963 book with the same title. Director Sayles used a number of little-known actors such as John Cusack and D. B. Sweeney to re-create both baseball and the dawn of the twenties. The portrayal of Charles Comiskey, the greedy White Sox owner, enforces the profile presented in *Past Time*, and Studs Terkel is superb as a Chicago sportswriter. Shoeless Joe Jackson, whom students know from the 1989 film *Field of Dreams*, is also highlighted.

Unfortunately, Hollywood has not yet really captured the charisma and mystique of Babe Ruth in the 1920s. Slightly paunchy unathletic actors such as William Bendix and John Goodman have diminished Babe in Hollywood film renditions. The closest we can get to the reality are clips from Ken Burns's eighteen-hour documentary on baseball. Ruth was the king among numerous sports heroes of the twenties such as football player Red Grange, tennis star Bill Tilden, golfer Bobby Jones, and boxer Jack Dempsey. These new-style heroes, along with the occasional nonsports hero such as pilot Charles Lindbergh, filled a public vacuum. They helped the public rise above the sordid gangsters, politicians, and business figures that permeated the 1920s. Sports heroes have never been held in such high esteem before or since. Babe Ruth was for many the antithesis of gangster Al Capone, and Ruth's baseball exploits washed away his own personal weaknesses, including his voracious appetite for food and women.

In the 1930s, sports, particularly baseball, represented an escape from the reality of The Depression. It played the same role as Hollywood's historical, musical, and fantasy films, which sought to escape or obliterate hard times. And baseball began to work to attract new ethnic immigrant fans. These groups had already been mobilized in the large cities by FDR's New Deal politics. Major league teams began to search out ethnic players, such as Detroit's Jewish slugger Hank Greenberg, and Italian players, including Joe DiMaggio and his two brothers, Vince and Dom.

For the early 1940s, baseball history can be used to highlight the social leveling and national solidarity that World War II sacrifices brought. Rich, famous baseball players such as Ted Williams and Joe DiMaggio joined

Hollywood movie stars and simple laborers in the armed forces. And no matter how cheap or expensive one's auto, everybody got the same gasoline ration. Baseball's role in ethnic solidarity and national patriotism can be presented dramatically and wittily in the little known song, "Moe Berg," written by Chuck Brodsky. Moe Berg was a Brooklyn Dodger reserve catcher in the 1930s. Brodsky's song suggests Berg was added to the roster to attract the many Jewish-Americans who lived in Brooklyn, the Bronx, and Yonkers. But Berg had another historical side that Brodsky dramatizes. He was highly educated, spoke several languages, and was recruited as a spy by the American Intelligence Services in the late 1930s. As Brodsky puts it, Moe's baseball card was the only one in the "CIA Museum" (*Radio*).

The post-World War II era presents an opportunity to use the racial integration of major league baseball to help students understand the beginning of the later Civil Rights Movement of the 1950s and 1960s. Jackie Robinson's breakthrough with the Brooklyn Dodgers can be seen as a catalyst for civil rights, and Branch Rickey, the Dodgers' general manager, should be credited for being ahead of his time. Rickey likely sensed what many civil rights advocates argued, that there is nothing so powerful as an idea whose time has come. It should be noted, however, that Robinson was not just an African American but a college graduate and World War II veteran. The large number of African Americans who served in World War II helped open the door for African-Americans in many fields besides baseball.

It was also true, but less fully understood, that segregation separated whites and blacks in the Negro baseball leagues as well as in the major leagues. The irony of this is presented superbly by Chuck Brodsky in one of his several songs about baseball—"The Ballad of Eddie Klepp" (*Letters*). The virtually unknown Klepp after World War II became the first white ballplayer to integrate the Negro Leagues. As the song notes, Klepp had problems similar to Robinson's. He could not eat in the same restaurants as his black teammates or sleep in the same hotels because they could not service "mixed clientele." And Klepp was heckled vigorously by black fans. Brodsky's artful song dramatically shows that segregation always cut both ways. It cut blacks off from whites but also cut whites off from blacks, both in baseball and the wider society.

Baseball not only exemplified the lifting of racial barriers but was a historical showcase for America's new multiethnic society in general. Following baseball's racial integration, there was a steadily increasing influx of Spanish-speaking ballplayers from Latin America, where baseball was very popular. By the 1990s some native Japanese players were on big league teams. Of course, these international players attracted an increasing international fan base and baseball became an early example of globalism. A hilarious scene from the 1973 film *Bang the Drum Slowly* shows the language problem among teammates, as a manager's pep talk has to be translated into Spanish by a bilingual teammate. *Bang the Drum Slowly* was the first Hollywood film to show that baseball films could be commercial successes by concentrating on plot and acting. It features a stellar performance by a young Robert DeNiro, and film clips resonate well with contemporary students.

Baseball history from 1953 through 1972 (when the Washington Senators became the Texas Rangers and ended two decades of franchise moves) can be used to show how America's increasingly corporate structure affected every facet of American life. Corporate growth and tactics had grown dramatically since the Civil War, but big business manipulation usually got little mass attention from the average American until recently. When a large corporation closed a factory in a large city and headed for cheaper labor, taxes, or other advantages, relatively few residents were affected. However, when a baseball team moved its franchise from New York or St. Louis, hundreds of thousands suddenly saw corporate America at work. This made Americans (and perhaps our students) more sympathetic to those displaced Americans who have lost their jobs, then and now, when a corporation closes a plant in a small or large city.

Major league baseball's move west and south and to Canada after 1950, through expansion teams as well as franchise changes, illustrates another constant in American history. Americans have always been quick to move wherever economic opportunity beckoned. And Americans traditionally refused to let local or family loyalties hold them back. Even today many foreigners do not understand how American college students can leave their families and relatives and travel three thousand miles away just for a better job. They consider it uncivilized, yet it has been peculiarly American. Americans moved west constantly in the nineteenth century for economic advantage. And northern "carpetbaggers" even moved south after the Civil War to take advantage of cheap land and labor in the depressed South. Indeed, it was usually economic advantage that drove the first Americans to leave Europe and settle in Colonial America. Local fans criticized baseball team owners for having no loyalty to those cities who had supported the team, but they themselves often had little loyalty to place.

Perhaps the most important way that baseball can contribute to a history course is to facilitate understanding of what is uniquely American about the nation's history. Films such as *The Natural* (1984), *Bull Durham* (1988), and *Field of Dreams* (1989) romanticized baseball, but they also showed how connected baseball was to both everyday life and peculiarly American ways, and the ways baseball cut across class and regional lines.

Hollywood finally learned that to gain an audience it had to center on the baseball game and not baseball stars. The films take us to small-town as well as metropolitan America and connect us to both everyday life and past decades. *Field of Dreams*, the most successful of these films, even explores the complicated 1960s and the generation gap. When James Earl Jones's character dramatically tells us near the film's end that "Baseball has marked the time ... and reminds us of all that was once good ... and that could be again," the statement resonates with Americans both young and old. The film has set us up to agree.

However, perhaps the quickest and most convincing way to show students how baseball is intertwined with American life is through baseball idioms. Idioms are the bane of anyone trying to learn American English as a second language. Yet they are essential for anyone trying to be American. Idioms have historically been used to identify with what is peculiarly American and prestigious. Thus, in the nineteenth century, Americans used Western idioms such as "loco" and "vamoose," because to appear Western was to appear more American. Since the 1920s, Americans have favored youthful idioms because Americans want increasingly to appear youthful. Before 1920, young people wanted to appear older and used adult idioms.

Baseball cuts across these trends. Both younger and older Americans use baseball idioms, often without realizing they are baseball idioms. Many students see themselves as basketball or football fans rather than baseball fans, but they are amazed to find how many baseball idioms they are familiar with and use. When Americans fail, we say they "strike out" or they "don't get to first base." Various state courts adopt either a "one strike you're out" or "three strikes you're out" penalty system. A good guess is called "a ballpark estimate," and a big achievement is described as "hitting a home run." If you cooperate you "play ball," and when you replace someone temporarily you "pinch-hit" for the person. Politicians "field" questions the way infielders handle ground balls. We have just scratched the surface of baseball idioms, but a teacher does not have to "touch all the bases" to convince students that baseball is more deeply embedded in American culture than they had imagined. The language is the best support for Jacques Barzun's often quoted comment, "Whoever wants to know the heart and mind of America had better learn baseball" (Tygiel, *Past Time,* ix).

Finally, using baseball history has a wider benefit. It widens the student's perception of history to include other types of cultural history — from music to clothing styles. However, whereas music, clothing, and other cultural aspects have changed constantly since 1900, baseball has provided much more continuity. As James Earl Jones intoned, "Baseball has marked the time." That continuity makes it an exceptionally good tool for teaching American history. Students need to know how America's past was similar to its present, and also how it was different, to draw any perspective or wisdom from their history.

Works Cited

Bang the Drum Slowly. Dir. John D. Hancock. Paramount, 1973.
Baseball: A Film by Ken Burns. Dir. Ken Burns. Public Broadcasting System, 1994.
Brodsky, Chuck. *Letters in the Dirt.* Red House Records, 1996.
———. *Radio.* Red House Records, 1998.
Bull Durham. Dir. Ron Shelton. Orion, 1988.
Carter, Paul A. *Another Part of the Twenties.* New York: Columbia University Press, 1973.
Creamer, Robert W. *Baseball in '41.* New York: Penguin Books, 1991.
Eight Men Out. Dir. John Sayles. Orion, 1988.
Field of Dreams. Dir. Phil Alden Robinson. Universal, 1989.
The Mirror Has Two Faces. Dir. Barbara Streisand. TriStar, 1996.
The Natural. Dir. Barry Levinson. TriStar, 1984.
Tygiel, Jules. *Baseball's Great Experiment: Jackie Robinson and His Legacy.* New York: Oxford University Press, 1983.
———. *Past Time: Baseball as History.* New York: Oxford University Press, 2000.

History

Baseball and American Culture—A Seminar
(WILLIAM M. SIMONS)

History 394: Baseball and American Culture is an undergraduate history seminar that I teach every fourth semester at State University of New York at Oneonta. Responsibility for teaching the History 394 seminar, a required course for majors, rotates among our faculty, and instructors shape content to reflect their own specialty. Regardless of instructor or content, however, the purpose of the seminar is always the same: to provide a capstone experience for our majors in historical research and writing. The course is limited to fifteen history majors, in their junior or senior years, with significant prior work in the discipline. Although History 394 carries the same credit, three semester hours, as other history offerings, the expectation and reality is that it calls for twice as much work as other courses in our department. When I teach History 394, it carries the title Baseball and American Culture. The pages that follow will examine the spring 2004 edition of Baseball and American Culture.

During the spring 2004 semester, Baseball and American Culture met weekly, for fifteen sessions, on Tuesday evenings for approximately two and one-half hours, leavened by a five-minute break at the midpoint. Discussion drove the seminar, and long sessions allowed discussions to gain momentum and nuance, creating the familiarity and trust that would transform a class into a community of learners. Although there was a range in abilities, the students in Baseball and American Culture were, as a group, capable and, more importantly, motivated. The ensemble included two nontraditional students—a working journalist and an army veteran—both intelligent iconoclasts who imbued class discussions with a distinctive energy, but, alas, only two women, who, despite the demographic inequity, ensured that the feminist perspective was heard. From the first meeting, students understood that although they would learn a good deal about baseball history and historiography in the course, the primary goals of the seminar were skills-oriented, the acquisition of facility with historical research and writing. This meant that Baseball and American Culture would be a writing-intensive course.

The syllabus outlined a sequence of writing assignments—three mini-papers based on narrow topics from the text, three article reviews, an essay exam, a research proposal in the form of an abstract, an outline of a research paper, a draft of a research paper, and a research paper. I provided a rationale for the numerous writing assignments, including a justification for their sequence in a series of related tasks that grow more demanding. As students enumerated the assignments, their anxiety was palpable; to ameliorate it, two pledges were made: Baseball and American Culture would prepare students for graduate seminars, and, if a commitment to work collaboratively was realized, they would all complete the course. Despite the demands, no one dropped the course.

For the common readings, students needed to acquire two books, both of which examine American society and culture from the perspective of baseball. *The Cooperstown Symposium on Baseball and American Culture: 2001*, which I edited, provided the ballast for a series of article reviews by students. An anthology consisting of twenty-three eclectic essays by various scholars, this volume *The Cooperstown Symposium* includes articles on such topics as baseball's relationship to biography, race, ethnicity, gender, myth, symbolic heroes, literature, cinema, business, labor, philosophy, science, statistics, and youth. Although historians constitute the largest contingent of contributors, *The Cooperstown Symposium* essays represent various disciplines. The essays introduced students to academic models of baseball writing that they were encouraged to emulate, and the notes accompanying each article provided a guide to the Chicago documentation style that they would need to master.

Prior to employing *The Cooperstown Symposium,* the class, in the early weeks of the course, read the second edition of Benjamin Rader's *Baseball: A History of America's Game.* Although most students had previously completed my "Athletics, Society, and History" course, which has a major component on baseball, it was essential that students possess a good general knowledge of the game's relationship to American history before conducting their own research, and the Rader book allowed for this. An excellent survey of the game from its antecedents to the present, the volume, by one of the leading students of sport, sets baseball within the context of the larger American history. Evaluated class discussions, facilitated by handouts featuring probe questions, encouraged students to master the content and analysis provided by *Baseball.*

During the three class sessions devoted to *Baseball,* students presented oral and written reports based on the volume. For the first class focusing on the Rader volume, each of the fifteen students was assigned a different topic from the following—the Baseball Fraternity, Knickerbocker Base Ball Club, impact of the Civil War on the game, Cincinnati Red Stockings, National Association of Base Ball Players, National Association of Professional Base Ball Players, William Hulbert, National League, American Association of Baseball Clubs, Players League, John Montgomery Ward, Albert Spalding, Adrian "Cap" Anson, Ban Johnson, and American League. During the next two weekly meetings, which paralleled the chronological organization of *Baseball,* students similarly reported on assigned topics from the Rader volume. Students were encouraged to comment on each other's oral reports.

Students also passed in written versions of their three oral reports on the Rader volume. These were fairly brief, 250–500 words. Beyond reinforcing empirical knowledge, these reports asked the students to think analytically by considering the significance of their subject to baseball and American history. Perhaps even more importantly, the three concise *Baseball* papers gave students writing experiences very early in the course. Particular attention was given to fashioning a thesis statement, topic sentences, and transitional sentences. In addition, students were expected to consider additional attributes of good writing in their Rader papers, including organization, clarity, grammar/syntax, balance between generalization and supporting evidence, creating interest in the topic, judicious use of a few direct quotes, and fashioning synthesis. Prior to the due date for the next *Baseball* essays, graded papers, with instructor's written comments, were available during my office hours. The Rader mini-papers were the pedagogical equivalent of playing pepper (a game that has one batter and at least one fielder separated by 10 to 15 feet, the fielder tossing the ball to the hitter, who uses a half-swing to hit the ball back to the fielder).

To ensure that students had a broad fundamental knowledge of baseball prior to more specialized work, the Rader component concluded with the course's only examination. To prepare for it, students were told to review their *Baseball* reports and their notes on class discussions of the Rader book. An entire two and one-half hour class session was devoted to the test, and, on the evening of the exam, students encountered, for the first time, the question: "Who/what were the ten most important people, events, decisions, phenomena, innovations, and/or institutions in baseball history? Provide a detailed rationale and explanation for your choices." Test instructions emphasized that simply providing the equivalent of ten loosely connected commentaries was insufficient. Exam construction was expected to incorporate what students had previously learned about threading a central thesis through a presentation linked by topic and transitional sentences. Although not all students succeeded in molding their essay exams into an organic whole, most, even at this early point in the course, appeared to understand that an effective presentation is not merely a collection of randomly assembled information. One student, for example, provided cohesion to the ten subtopics examined in her test essay by an integrating thesis that depicted baseball history as defined by recurring cycles of crisis and reform.

Article reviews provided the ballast for the next three writing assignments. As the objects of these critiques, articles trumped books since the former are briefer than the latter, thus facilitating multiple review assignments. Students learned that article reports and article reviews are not one and the same. A report is often no more than a summary of the contents of the work under consideration whereas a review is an interpretive evaluation. As part of their orientation, students examined several reviews of baseball books, which had appeared in the *Journal of Sport History*. In addition, students received in-class exhortation and a handout providing guidelines for crafting article reviews. The reviews were to be approximately 500–750 words in length and provide commentary concerning the following attributes of the article: (1) identification and description of the topic, thesis, and content; (2) evaluation of the analysis and conclusions; (3) assessment of writing style, methodology, and sources; (4) historiographic relationship to other literature on the topic, that is, similarities in methods of historical research and writing; (5) overall quality of the article; and (6) consideration of audiences, if any, for whom the article might be useful or interesting. For a number of students, this endeavor prompted their first in-depth scrutiny of endnotes. In discovering that most topics were covered in more than one article in their anthology, as well as in the Rader text, students learned how to establish historiographic context.

By writing reviews on three successive weeks, students had the opportunity to respond to peer and instructor feedback in subsequent article critiques. Although *The Cooperstown* anthology served as a common reading, each student was assigned three essays from the volume to review. Given class size, this meant that there was always more than one reviewer for each article and that students were familiar with articles critiqued by others. On the night that the first review assignment was due, the students responsible for particular essays orally shared, in sequence, their article critiques, followed by general discussion involving the entire class about the strengths and weaknesses of the various presentations. The next two classes also employed this format, and students, over time, grew more adept at offering and receiving criticism from peers. As for the written component, these were collected at the end of each session and typically returned, with instructor comments, during scheduled office hours prior to the next class, so that students could reflect upon evaluations of their work before completing their next article review.

Simultaneous with these early assignments, students were investigating potential topics for their culminating and defining project, a research paper due at semester's end. Indeed, during the first class meeting, expectations for the research paper were clarified. In length, the papers were to comprise twenty to twenty-five pages of text, plus endnotes, rendered in Chicago style. Sources had to include a variety of primary and secondary sources, at least one oral interview, and the resources of the National Baseball Hall of Fame Library. Topics for research papers, which had to relate baseball to the larger American history, needed to be narrow enough to allow for meaningful treatment in the allotted pagination yet broad enough not to be exercises in trivia. If not overused, direct quotes that were evocative or illustrative were welcome, keeping in mind that direct quotes that were overlong or merely informative detracted from the presentation. With discretion, limited use of telling anecdotes, vignettes, irony, stories, and humor would engage the reader. Save as a participant observer, use of the first person, singular ("I") or plural ("we"), was verboten. For verbs, the active voice trumped the passive. An evocative title and a descriptive subtitle ought to announce the text. The introduction of a clear thesis statement early in the paper and the systematic organization of the text around that thesis statement should provide an organic unity to the presentation. Employment of topic and transitional sentences would strengthen the framework. Students were cautioned that assertions necessitated support via analysis and appropriate evidence. By engaging in dialogue with previous commentators on the topic, historians could demonstrate an awareness of the relevant historiography. Grammar, syntax, spelling, and punctuation still mattered. Tenses, so far as possible, were to remain consistent. An effective conclusion ought to provide synthesis, reconfiguration of thesis, and closure. Finally, students were counseled that evaluative criteria for their research papers would encompass command of the relevant history and historiography, linkage between baseball and the larger American history, caliber and scope of documentation, significance/persuasiveness of thesis and interpretation, organizational framework, clarity, and quality of the writing.

Although students were provided with a copious list of possible subjects for their research papers, they could propose their own topics, subject to the instructor's approval, through in-office conference and then, about a third of the way into the course, by submission of a 500–750 word abstract. To facilitate the writing of student abstracts, I shared with the class a few that I had written. It was explained that an abstract is a concise proposal for a larger research paper and ought to identify and describe the following: (1) the topic: subject matter and scope; (2) methodology; (3) analytical questions to be investigated and a preliminary thesis; (4) significance of the topic to baseball history and to the larger American history; (5) historiography: relationship of topic to past scholarship; and (6) data and sources to be employed: location and availability. Fortunately, the topics ultimately selected by the students and approved by the instructor were ones that generated sufficient interest to sustain the class in the long hours of research and writing that lay ahead.

Several guest speakers lent their expertise to class sessions dealing with the research paper assignment. SUNY Oneonta reference librarian Nancy S. Cannon, the college's electronic resources coordinator, described and explained how to use the Web site that she designed specifically for Baseball and American Culture. The course Web site included several features: links to the National Baseball Hall of Fame Library Online Catalogue, the Major League Official Web Site, the Baseball Archive Database, the National Women's Baseball Hall of Fame, *The New York Times Archive*, and other online resources; a guide to relevant reference books available at the college library; detailed instructions on employing particular search engines to locate books, articles, videos, compact discs, and other materials; information about commercial sites maintained by the Society for American Baseball Research (SABR) and *Baseballlibrary*; commentary defining the distinctions between primary and secondary sources as well as information about the location of the *American Memory Collection* from the National Digital Library of the Library of Congress and other primary sources online and in print; an explanation of plagiarism and a warning about the draconian consequences of engaging in that practice; access to online and print manuals concerning writing research papers and the proper use of citations, including the *Manual for Writers of Terms Papers, Theses, and Dissertations* and the *Chicago Manual of Style*; and an overview of the steps in writing a research paper. Nancy Cannon's meeting with the class took place in the library's instructional resource room. With the students all sitting at their own computer stations, she made the Baseball and American Culture Web page come alive as she asked each student to identify topics that they were interested in and then taught the class how to call up specific materials. Soon students were examining and comparing contemporary primary materials on their computer screens about the Black Sox scandal, the game in which Babe Ruth allegedly called his shot, reaction to Jackie Robinson's major league baseball debut, and numerous other topics. To their surprise, students enjoyed their introduction to electronic resources and gave Nancy Cannon a loud ovation at the end of the session, shattering the quietude that typically cloaks the library. Throughout the semester, she and her SUNY Oneonta library colleagues generously made themselves available to the students, answering numerous questions and honing student research skills.

The staff and resources of the A. Bartlett Giamatti Research Center at the National Baseball Hall of Fame were also central to student research. During a class session, the Hall of Fame librarian, James Gates, employed PowerPoint to provide students with a virtual tour of the Giamatti Research Center, highlighting its vast holdings, including nearly every baseball book ever written, a complete run of most of the significant baseball magazines, all issues of *The Sporting News* and several other baseball newspapers, team publications, *Spalding's* and other baseball guides, players contract cards, extensive newspaper clipping files for any past or present player to appear on a major league roster as well as for numerous other figures associated with the game in diverse capacities, special collections of personal and institutional papers, radio and television broadcasts of games, commercial and documentary videotapes, photographs, and much more archival material. Gates explained how to access *Abner*, the Hall of Fame Library's catalogue, online. Moreover, Gates went around the room asking students about their specific research topics and identifying relevant sources at the Giamatti Research Center. Cooperstown, home to the Hall of Fame, is only twenty-two miles from SUNY Oneonta, and students were required to visit the Giamatti Research Center to gather information. In addition to the buses that run between Oneonta and Cooperstown, students with cars generously volunteered to transport their peers during expeditions to the Hall of Fame. Gates and his superb staff were most gracious to the students and of great assistance to them in locating germane materials. When scheduling appointments, students found that if they indicated what they were looking for the materials would be waiting when they arrived. Although the Giamatti Research Center is not a lending library, students took copious notes and photocopied much material.

Beyond the plethora of resources identified by the SUNY Oneonta and Hall of Fame librarians, students were required to conduct at least one original interview and to make some use of these oral history materials in their research papers. David Richards, an adjunct professor of history at the college, provided the class with an effective and informative program on the methodology of oral history, buttressing his formal remarks with detailed handouts. Drawing on his own extensive experience conducting interviews with participant observers concerning the American home front during World War II, Richards discussed recording the time, date and site of the interview, establishing rapport with subjects, crafting effective queries, the ordering of questions, means of encouraging the subject to expand upon a point, pacing the interview and keeping track of the allotted time, and bringing the session to closure. Pointing to the work of Studs Terkel, Richards noted that interviewees need not be celebrated individuals: senior citizens, family members, teachers, sportswriters, fans, and others might possess significant insights about baseball history or simply valuable perceptions about germane topics. Drawing upon his former career as a police detective, Richards suggested internal and external tests of validity concerning information received from interviewees. He counseled, however, that even when interviewee information is incorrect, it may reveal important insights about attitudes, opinions, values, and misconceptions, or provide evocative quotes and telling humor.

Following Richards' presentation, I discussed my own oral history ventures, stressing the need for research antecedent to the encounter, the protocols of setting up an appointment with an interviewee, offering the subject a copy of the interview or final paper sans any promise of censorship, careful designing and sequencing of questions, starting with basic factual questions, rewording and repeating questions later in the session, selecting appropriate recording equipment, focusing on etiquette and demeanor during the meeting, maintaining comfortable eye contact, interpreting tone and voice inflections, recognizing that a long silence may serve as a precursor to reflection rather than disengagement, taking note of body language and surroundings, using a counter, transcribing the session, evaluating and using the material obtained, and integrating the interview with other sources. Students then listened to and critiqued recordings of the interviews that I had conducted with former Red Sox pitchers Bill Monbouquette and Jim Lonborg. Subsequently, I met with students individually to discuss both preparation and results of the interviews they conducted. In varying degrees, oral history contributed to all of the student research papers.

In her presentation, Victoria Triola, an adjunct lecturer in the college's Writing Center, also provided students with tools that facilitated work on their research papers. Utilizing PowerPoint and handouts, she discussed note taking, organizing data, developing a thesis, constructing an outline, common research and writing problems, the attributes of good writing, diverse situations that call for specific forms of Chicago-style citations, composing a first draft, making revisions, and completing the final version of a research paper. Triola, like Cannon, identified online and print reference guides concerning writing style and source citations. Throughout the semester, students consulted with Triola and her colleagues at the Writing Center concerning problems and progress on research papers.

    I, too, scheduled opportunities for frequent feedback, requiring weekly office meetings, of variable length, with all students during the various phases of the course. Student outlines were critiqued, followed by discussions of five-page first drafts of research projects. A draft was due on the same evening that the student was scheduled to present the oral report on his or her research project. The content of the oral report and the draft were essentially the same: the purpose of both was to reflect on the direction of research projects. The formal oral presentations by students, approximately thirty minutes in duration, initially provoked some anxiety. During the last third of the semester, class sessions were organized around these oral reports, of which there were three per night. It was taken into account that oral reports given earlier would obviously reflect projects in a more preliminary phase of development. The oral reports gave students an opportunity to try out their theses, identify sources discovered, acknowledge problems locating and interpreting data, match generalizations to evidence, test the persuasiveness of their arguments, and experiment with synthesis. Oral reports were evaluated, and so, too, were peer comments. All students were expected to participate in discussions of the strengths and weaknesses of the oral reports. These discussions immediately followed the oral reports and, over time, sharpened analytical faculties, engendered respect for constructive criticism, and encouraged students to view themselves as part of a corporate enterprise. A number of the comments were laudatory, others suggested alternate approaches, and some questioned facts or evidence or interpretation. Students sometimes indicated that in their own research they had encountered sources that the presenter might find useful. Students came to realize that informed criticism was a form of support.

    Beyond my own notes, I recorded peer feedback to the oral reports and discussed both in depth during office meetings with students, making it clear that ultimately it was for them to decide which suggestions to incorporate into their work and which to reject. I also returned, with copious comments, preliminary drafts. Sometimes it was apparent that students needed to further narrow their topics or more overtly address historiographic context . As needed, students were reminded that secondary sources would gain nuance by use of primary materials, and conversely, employment of primary sources, though laudable, should not eliminate relevant monographic literature.

Papers were due at the end of the semester, as were anonymous student course evaluations. The latter suggested that respondents had learned much about historical research and writing as well as baseball's relationship to the American past. The most serious and common criticism was that the course entailed considerable work for three credits. Other History 394 seminar courses elicit similar comments about workload. To address this quite legitimate criticism, I and other members of the department advocate granting additional credits for the capstone seminar; it is to be hoped that this curriculum ameliorative will be realized. Aside from workload, however, students' statistical and free response evaluation of Baseball and American Culture was overwhelmingly positive.

I viewed all previous writing assignments and other exercises as preparatory to the research papers, believing that it was not where students began but where they ended that ultimately counted. By this criterion, the course was a success; it produced a set of research papers appropriate to a capstone seminar for undergraduate history majors. The papers varied in sophistication, but collectively represented notable achievement. Many of the papers created an effective amalgam of research, analysis, and good writing. Kevin Mason, for example, mastered the secondary literature and many primary sources on Moe Berg, offering new and significant insight about the relationship between catching, spying, and historiography. A gifted writer, Bryan Chambala thoughtfully examined the role of race, demographics, spatial relations, and economics as factors in the original Senators' abandonment of Washington, D.C., after the 1960 season. Synthesizing sources encompassing original interviews with participant observers, contemporary newspaper articles, the memoirs of Sparky Lyle and Jimmy Breslin, archival video from Court TV, Spike Lee's cinematography, and monographs on urban history, William Castro imaginatively related the tumultuous Reggie Jackson-Billy Martin-George Steinbrenner Yankees to the atmosphere that the Son of Sam serial murders created in New York City amid the scorching summer heat of 1977. Discovering new archival material, Diana Walling produced a seminal study of "How Trains Changed the Ball Games and Created Towns and Regional Identities in Central New York State in the Last Half of the Nineteenth Century." The correspondence of Walter O'Malley informed Tyler Rife's nuanced account of the Dodgers' departure from Brooklyn. A telling interview with gender and sports scholar Andi Stein, archival documents relating to player demeanor and obligations, and feminist literature shaped Stacey Huber's account of the contradictions inherent in the All-American Girls Professional Baseball League. And Chris Showens, passionate, informed, and revisionist, provided critical perspective on the relationship between the St. Louis Cardinals and rural America in his research paper, "The Hayseeds Fight Back." The evening that he, attired in a vintage Cardinals' uniform, delivered his formal oral report, Chris challenged himself and the class to regard the research paper as a significant milestone and opportunity. By and large, the class did.

Works Cited

Rader, Benjamin. *Baseball: A History of America's Game.* Urbana: University of Illinois Press, 2002.
Simons, William M., ed. *The Cooperstown Symposium on Baseball and American Culture, 2001.* Jefferson, NC: McFarland, 2002.

Labor Relations

As Many Strikes as It Takes—Using Baseball to Teach Labor Relations

(KAREN S. KOZIARA)

This essay provides ideas on how to use baseball to enhance student interest in and understanding of collective bargaining. Major league baseball is an excellent source of cases and illustrations to use in a labor relations course for several reasons. First, the bargaining relationship between the owners and the players is one of the most visible and dramatic in the United States. The bargaining relationship between the owners and the umpires has also been widely publicized. As a result, information about collective bargaining in baseball is widely available and easy for students to find.

Another benefit of using baseball examples in a labor relations course is that students are generally familiar with the industry. Students start out with an understanding of how the industry functions. Even international students and students who are not baseball fans are aware of the product being sold, the nature of the jobs involved, the operation of the labor market, and the employers' sources of income. That means aspects of baseball labor relations can provide insight into how collective bargaining functions without elaborate explanations about what goes on in the industry. This helps students understand abstract concepts by providing concrete illustrations from a familiar context.

Another advantage of using baseball labor relations is that something is always happening. It is a ready source of current topics to analyze and enliven class discussions. A recent case involving discipline is almost guaranteed every season. The existing drug policy agreed to by the Major League Players' Association and the owners also promises to be a fruitful source of labor and management interactions for class discussions. Finally, the existing Basic Agreement expires December 19, 2006, and that guarantees lots of lively topics for the 2006–07 academic year.

The National Labor Relations Act

Do you think major league umpires are supervisors? Clearly they make many decisions during a game that can affect the game's final outcome. Umpires have the power to eject players from games. Does this mean that they direct the players during the game or that umpires discipline and direct, hire and fire players? Is being a supervisor the essence of an umpire's job? If not, what is the essence of the job?

Why does it matter whether or not umpires are supervisors, and what does the answer have to do with teaching labor relations? The simple answer is that supervisors are not covered by the National Labor Relations Act (NLRA). The objective of the NLRA is to protect and encourage collective bargaining over the terms and conditions of employment. As a result, supervisors do not have the protected right to engage in collective bargaining. Without NLRA protections, it is very difficult for supervisory employees to form unions and get collective bargaining contracts.

The more complex answer is that the question uses two familiar concepts—what supervisors and umpires do—to introduce students to a conceptually challenging topic. Most of the enrollees in labor relations courses are business students. The possibility of sharing decision making power with a union is not a popular idea, and collective bargaining is seen by many students as an abstract idea that with any luck they will never have to grapple with in concrete terms. The case also introduces the NLRA and makes the point that NLRA protections are so important that employers can argue that their employees are supervisors, as did the American League when its umpires tried to organize (The American League of Professional Baseball Clubs and the Association of National Baseball League Umpires, Inc. 180 NLRB 30 [1969]). In the dance between labor and management, one move can involve defining who is a supervisor. Supervisors are legally wallflowers, and management may wish for all employees to be supervisors.

Such cases are extremely effective in helping students move from the abstract to the concrete. Useful cases illustrate both the labor and management positions, as well as general principles than can be used to analyze specific situations. As the above case illustrates, most students have a reasonable idea of what baseball umpires do. The case discussion does not have to focus on the umpire job. Instead the focus can be on who is a supervisor—and what difference it makes anyway. Baseball umpires oversee games by ensuring they are played according to the rules. Umpires do not coach players on how to play, or decide which players will play. They are not supervisors, and therefore the NLRA protects the right of umpires to engage in collective bargaining.

In the United States, the National Labor Relations Act regulates most private sector bargaining relationships. It holds elections to determine if nonsupervisory employees want union representation. Once a union is certified as a bargaining representative, the NLRA requires that the union and the employer bargain in good faith to reach an agreement. The law does not require, however, that the parties reach an agreement. Bargaining impasses are lawful, and so are strikes and lockouts.

Once a class is introduced to the NLRA, a few industries can be selected to discuss how the law affects those industries. Some interesting industries for this purpose might be public education, airlines, hospitals, janitorial services, and baseball. When students are asked which of these are covered by the NLRA, the one they choose first—and incorrectly—is airlines. (The airline industry is regulated by the Railway Labor Act.) The second one they choose—correctly—is baseball. The subsequent discussion reaches the conclusion that the NLRA covers hospitals and janitorial services, as well as industries such as manufacturing, mining, retail trade, and telecommunications

From there, the discussion can move to the concept of good faith bargaining. Do bargaining impasses show a failure to bargain in good faith, and does the NLRB settle bargaining impasses by imposing a contract? Undergraduate students are usually a little unsure about the answer to that question, so it is useful to ask whether strikes and lockouts are legal when a bargaining impasse occurs. Students are generally unsure about whether hospital workers can strike, think that the strikes and lockouts are legal in manufacturing and mining, and are unsure about janitorial services and telecommunications. They know with great certainty, however, that strikes and lockouts are legal in baseball—and hockey. Their familiarity with baseball then allows them to generalize the legality of strikes and lockouts to industries less in the public spotlight.

The External Environment and Negotiations Topics

The external environment affects the bargaining process and bargaining outcomes in all collective bargaining relationships. The external environment includes general economic conditions, the product market, the labor market, technology, public opinion, and, as discussed earlier, law. Baseball's external environment is similar to many employers with respect to economic conditions, competition with other products for consumer dollars, labor market competition, and the law. This allows baseball to provide the basis for student understanding of the external pressures that affect all bargaining relationships.

A particularly effective way to illustrate the link between the external environment and a particular bargaining relationship is to review the contract negotiated by a particular employer and union. Some parts of the contract will be similar to contracts in other industries. Other parts will be very industry specific, and they will provide interesting insight into how the forces in the external environment affect issues important to the parties.

In the past, one of my assignments for students was to "adopt" a bargaining relationship, do background reading on the industry, the employer and the union, and get access to the relevant collective bargaining agreement any way they could. On the day readings on the external environment were to be discussed, students handed in written examples of how the external environment was reflected in "their" contract. Their examples then became the basis for class discussion on the impact of the external environment on specific bargaining relationships.

This approach had two weaknesses. The first was that some students had an easier time than other students getting access to contracts. The students who had trouble finding contracts often came to class unprepared to take part in the class discussion. A second problem was that, because the industries and contracts varied widely, the discussion was fragmented and it was difficult to make good comparisons. A related issue was my difficulty in preparing for class without knowing in advance what contracts the students were reading. In some cases they came up with contract clauses that were difficult to understand and interpret without a careful reading of related provisions in the contract. Needless to say, confusing contract provisions were often a distraction rather than a good learning opportunity.

After some experimenting, it became clear that it was better to have students choose one of three specified bargaining relationships and the related contracts to review. The students continued to be responsible for doing background research on the industry, the employer and the union, but the collective bargaining contract was made available to them.

Focusing on a limited number of contracts facilitates discussion, and permits comparisons between the contracts because a number of students will have read each contract. From the standpoint of classroom management, this approach also ensures that the instructor will be prepared to lead the discussion, explain confusing provisions, and end the discussion by summarizing the lessons learned.

Most collective bargaining contracts are more than a hundred pages long. Their length makes it prohibitively expensive to provide students with photocopies. Therefore, the contracts chosen have to be available online. This limits the available contracts because not all contracts are posted online. Further, some of the posted contracts are only accessible to union members. Some contracts, however, can be found online. The Web site <http://www.mlbplayers.mlb.com/pa/pdf/cba_english.pdf> is the location for the 2003 to 2006 Basic Agreement between the major league clubs and the Major League Baseball Players Association.

Common Contract Provisions

The objective of having students review contracts is to identify which contract provisions are common to most industry, and which contract provisions are industry-specific reactions to the external environment. The students work from a scavenger hunt type of list. They are asked to find a number of items commonly found in contracts, including the wage and effort bargain, the steps of the grievance procedure, and the definition of the bargaining unit.

In the United States virtually all collective bargaining contracts focus on workplace issues rather than political or ideological issues. Baseball's Basic Agreement follows this model. The wage and effort bargain, as in most agreements, is a central part of the contract. The wage and effort bargain includes both salary and scheduling provisions, including minimum salaries, the length of the season, championship schedules, and rescheduled games.

Almost all collective bargaining contracts also identify the bargaining unit, or the specific jobs covered by the contract. Often students have difficulty distinguishing among the union, union members, and the bargaining unit. Baseball's Basic Agreement has an elegantly simple definition of the bargaining unit, which serves as a good basis for explaining to students how the bargaining unit differs from the union or union members. The contract identifies the bargaining unit as all major league baseball players and people who become major league players while the contract is in effect. (This is in marked contrast to the Philadelphia Federation of Teachers' contract that some students used several semesters ago. That contract's bargaining unit definition was several pages long and did little to clarify anything for the students.) Clearly people are in the bargaining unit while they are major league players, and are represented by the union, the Major League Baseball Players Association (MLBPA). The bargaining unit definition in the contract determines whom the union represents. The players are union members while they play in the major leagues. The players may come and go, but the union as an organization remains. The MLBPA contract does not contain a union shop clause. This means that players are not required to join the union. However, virtually all major league players become union members. One exception involved the replacement players used during the 1993–94 work stoppage. The union voted to deny them membership even if they became major league players at any point after the conclusion of the stoppage. This exception illustrates for students how strikers view striker replacements.

As with almost all labor contracts in the United States, the Basic Agreement provides for a grievance procedure with specific steps, and arbitration as the last step. The objective of a grievance procedure is to provide a mechanism to resolve questions about the parties' rights under the contract.

Questions about the interpretation of any contract provision are potentially topics for the grievance. Disciplinary issues, however, are among the most common grievance topics in baseball, as well as in other industries. Because discipline cases are common, over time the arbitration process has developed "just cause" principles to determine the fairness of discipline. Just cause discipline means that employees may be disciplined only for breaking consistently enforced and clearly communicated rules with known consequences, and that the punishment fit the crime. The exception to this is when, although the employer has no specific rule, an employee engages in conduct that clearly violates societal norms of acceptable behavior.

Fortunately for classroom purposes, baseball can be depended upon to provide at least one recent case involving the issue of just cause discipline. Baseball disciplinary cases are widely publicized, and students can get background information on the case from the sources of their choice. The assignment also requires students to identify the major arguments both management and the union will make, as well as the witnesses and documents they will use.

Having students get information from multiple sources increases both the amount of information they provide and their involvement in the class discussion of the case. Requiring students to identify the parties' major arguments, witnesses, and documents helps them learn how to prepare grievances. The essence of preparing a grievance case is to identify your side's best arguments and which witnesses and documents support those arguments. It is also important to have thought through the other side's best arguments and how those arguments are likely to be presented in order to be ready for them. This is important preparation for a major graded exercise later in the course when students work in opposing labor and management teams to present cases to an arbitration panel.

For example, in the summer of 2005 Texas Ranger pitcher Kenny Rogers shoved two cameramen who were on the field taking pictures. Commissioner Bud Selig thought Rogers' behavior was unacceptable and suspended him for twenty games (*Philadelphia Inquirer,* D7). The union filed a grievance over whether the discipline was justified. The arbitrator decided the penalty was excessive and reduced the suspension to thirteen days, the time already served. One useful lesson of this case is that it is not unusual for arbitrators to reduce disciplinary penalties.

Another interesting lesson came from Selig's reaction. He thought the decision sent a message that was inconsistent with the standard of behavior expected of players. He stated, "The arbitrator's decision diminishes that standard and is contrary to the collective bargaining agreement. In my opinion, the decision is seriously ill-conceived" (Brown D5). The real lesson is what did not happen next. Selig may not have liked the decision, but he did not appeal it. This is because courts are reluctant to overturn arbitrators' decisions except in very unusual circumstances.

As practice in preparing discipline cases, the students will be asked to research the case and then explain how they would present the case to an arbitrator—both as the union and major league baseball. The learning opportunity reaches far beyond baseball to include analysis of just cause discipline as well as how to prepare grievance cases.

Unique Contract Provisions

The contract provisions that set one industry apart from other industries are particularly useful in understanding the impact of the external environment on labor relations. The Basic Agreement states that it is a contract between the major league players and the thirty major league clubs, meaning that the contract is the result of multiple owners (or employers) bargaining together. Although multiemployer bargaining is not uncommon in the United States, baseball provides an easily understood example that is excellent for class analysis.

One question for students to answer is which characteristics of the industry result in baseball clubs bargaining together, rather than individually. In baseball the owners are dependent on each other to produce a joint product. As in other industries where multiemployer bargaining occurs, it makes sense for the employers to protect themselves from being individually picked off by the union. Another question involves difficulties that multiemployer bargaining faces. The baseball illustration shows clearly the stresses on multiemployer bargaining when employers have different organizational and financial structures, as well as personality differences.

The Basic Agreement includes a number of other unusual provisions that make sense only within the context of the industry. One of these is the Revenue Sharing Plan. The interesting questions for students to ponder are the objective of revenue sharing and whether revenue sharing would make sense in other multiemployer bargaining relationships. Two other unusual contract provisions are the reserve clause and its partner, free agency.

Never a Dull Moment

For collective bargaining classes, baseball is dependably unpredictable. Even during midcontract years something will happen that illustrates important labor relations issues. Baseball's recently developed drug policy required collective negotiations during the life of an existing contract, which generally shows that the parties have a sense of real urgency about the issue. One lesson to be learned is that midterm bargaining (rather than waiting for negotiations on a new contract) can be important to both parties.

This drug issue also invites analysis of why the parties found themselves in a reactive rather than proactive effort to resolve the matter. Although the union often is blamed for the delay in developing a drug policy, the owners were also slow to openly recognize its importance. It is critical for students to recognize that many employers do not have drug policies or require drug testing. An interesting topic for student discussion is whether all employers should have drug policies. The learning objective is for students to understand that whether to have or not to have a drug policy depends on the nature of the industry and whether its product could be fundamentally harmed by employee drug use. Of course, a major concern in baseball is why so little so late—and is the current drug policy likely to be effective?

The topic of guest speakers belongs in the "never a dull moment" category. The problem one faces is that most of the time classes are in session, players are working. When they are working, they are away half the time and busy when they are at home. Curt Schilling, however, graciously agreed to speak to my collective bargaining class when he was the Phillies' player representative. Everyone was excited about his visit. One young woman, apparently not a huge baseball fan, even asked if he was good-looking.

Unfortunately, the days on which he was scheduled to visit he was summoned away to work on collective bargaining. The lesson to be learned from that experience may be not to let the students know until the guest speaker is in the building. Or maybe not—maybe the students deserve the opportunity to be at their best, even when their instructor cannot protect them from disappointment.

A major lesson to be learned is that a person who understands collective bargaining in baseball will know a lot about labor relations in any industry. The cases, illustrations, and stories can be thought-provoking and entertaining. And, personally, I have a new idea for a guest speaker. No names will be named yet, but he is recently retired and also served as a Phillies player representative. If he is available, it is guaranteed the students will love him. Wish us luck!

Works Cited

Brown, Tim. "Around the Majors: Rogers Suspension Is Shortened." *Los Angeles Times.* 10 Aug. 2005: D5.
Selig, Bud. Quoted in *The Philadelphia Inquirer.* 28 July 2005: D7.

Law

Even the Best Lawyers Must Know Baseball
(ROGER I. ABRAMS)

If you get three strikes, even the best lawyer in the world can't get you off.
—Bill Veeck

Bill Veeck's aphorism about lawyers and baseball is not quite accurate. Although the standard through most of the 160 years of baseball in America has been "three strikes and you're out," for a brief time in the late 1880s it took four strikes to retire a batter. A good lawyer with a client who had only three strikes would get him off, assuming, of course, the player was at bat during the brief four-strike era.

Of more interest to my law school students are the strikes (and lockouts) of modern baseball. Between 1972 and 1995, Major League Baseball and the Major League Baseball Players Association engaged in eight work stoppages, causing enormous angst to the fans of the game. As a result of their remarkable solidarity, cohesiveness, and fortunate leadership, however, ballplayers became wealthy beyond their wildest dreams. Good lawyers trained in labor relations and the national pastime also made Major League Baseball live up to the terms of its collective bargaining agreements with the players union. It seems apparent that even the best lawyers must know baseball.

A legal education also appears to be a splendid preparation for sports management. Lawyers run the American sports enterprise that offers us such enjoyment (and heartache) year round. All the commissioners of our major team sports are lawyers: baseball (Bud Selig), basketball (David Stern), football (Paul Tagliabue), and hockey (Gary Bettman).

Lawyers have always played an important role in the National Game. Obviously, Judge Kenesaw Mountain Landis, baseball's first commissioner, comes to mind. His arch rival, Branch Rickey, was also a lawyer. John Montgomery Ward, a Hall of Fame pitcher from the nineteenth century and the organizer of the first players union and the 1890 Players League, graduated from Columbia Law School while pitching for the Giants and practiced law after retiring from the game. Yankees manager Miller Huggins and Tigers manager Hughie Jennings are also Hall of Fame lawyers. Tony LaRusso, current skipper of the Cardinals, was also trained as a lawyer, but he has declared that he would rather ride the buses in the minor leagues than practice law day-to-day.

For the past twenty years, I have taught a course or seminar in Sports Law at five different law schools (Case Western Reserve, Nova Southeastern, Rutgers, Northeastern, Harvard). We explore the legal, economic and social aspects of national and international, professional and amateur sports. While I cover issues that arise in football, basketball, hockey, boxing and track, the heart of the course is firmly fixed between the baselines on the diamond.

I have four goals in teaching baseball: (1) students should learn about the business structures of the game and the legal principles that control its operation; (2) students should appreciate the history of baseball and how private decisions drove legal and business issues; (3) students should be able to compare the legal treatment of baseball issues with the way the same concerns are addressed in other professional sports, for example, regarding antitrust law; and finally (4) students should see baseball as a mirror to American culture, a sport that reflects who and what we are as a society.

During the course of the semester, my students read state and federal court and administrative decisions, private arbitration awards, and contract provisions. The basic text helps reveal the principles used to resolve disputes involving athletes, clubs, leagues, unions and agents. The materials address a broad variety of legal issues, including antitrust, labor, torts, criminal, contract, agency, and constitutional law. The course focuses particularly on the business operation of the sports enterprise, the governance of sports, player reservation systems and player contracts, collective bargaining and salary arbitration, franchise free agency, violence, gender and handicapped discrimination, and the role of sports agents. I have always used my own materials, and the table of contents to them is included in an appendix to this paper. In 2006, I will be switching to the best casebook in the field, *Sports and the Law: Text, Cases, and Problems*, written by my friends Paul Weiler, Harvard Law School Henry J. Friendly Professor of Law, and Gary Roberts, Tulane Law School Vice Dean.

Baseball law is primarily embodied in privately negotiated contracts, both the individual uniform player contracts and the collective bargaining agreements that contain their own private judicial system, the labor arbitration process. Students parse portions of those contracts and try to determine why one party or the other might want those provisions included in the compacts. There is enough material to cover a two-semester course, but it must all be covered in one semester. It is a very full plate.

Baseball presents the perfect example of the unique position of sports in American society. To make that point at the outset, I start with Justice Blackmun's extraordinary introduction to *Curt Flood v. Bowie Kuhn* where he lists his all-time favorite baseball players (Ty Cobb, Babe Ruth, Tris Speaker, Walter Johnson, etc.). Justice Blackmun is extolling the virtues of Major League Baseball, the defendant in the suit. We return later to Curt Flood's case when we explore the antitrust exemption that baseball—and baseball alone—enjoys. It is the perfect example of judicial decision making stuck in the mud.

Napolean Lajoie's famous case from the turn of the twentieth century shows how and when courts enforce contracts. I use this opportunity to lecture on the origins of baseball—on the Elysian Fields cricket pitch in Hoboken, New Jersey, in 1846—the establishment of player-run amateur and professional leagues, and the creation of the magnate-operated National League cartel in 1876. The historically significant story of the success of Ban Johnson's rival American League in 1901 and 1902 leads right into Lajoie's tale. When that great (perhaps the greatest ever) second baseman jumped from the National League Philadelphia Phillies to the new crosstown rival American League Athletics in 1901, the Phillies sued for an injunction to get their player back. Lajoie was one of baseball's premier players, in that era second only to Honus Wagner, in my mind. When the trial court refused to issue an injunction because it concluded Lajoie was not unique (someone else could play second base), the "Big Frenchman" proceeded to have the best year any player has ever had in baseball. He led the new American League in every offensive category: batting average (.426), slugging average (.643), on-base percentage (.463), runs scored (145 in 131 games), hits (232), doubles (48), homers (14), and runs batted in (125). He also led the league's second basemen in every defensive category.

Following the 1901 season, the Pennsylvania Supreme Court reversed the lower court, but it still did not order Lajoie to return to the Phillies. It merely ordered that he not play for any other team. Courts have always been reluctant to affirmatively order the performance of a personal service contract. It edges close to involuntary servitude. The court's "negative injunction," however, would naturally have the effect of convincing Lajoie to return to the Phillies without ordering him to perform that personal service. However, Connie Mack, the Athletics' shrewd owner, traded Lajoie to the Cleveland franchise where he would prosper for twelve years. When the Cleveland nine came to Philadelphia to play ball in 1902, however, Lajoie faced the Pennsylvania court order. Instead of visiting the City of Brotherly Love, Lajoie went to Atlantic City on vacation.

Baseball's individual player contract is negotiated as part of the MLB-MLBPA's collective bargaining agreement. The students read the contract. I then role-play a baseball rookie who asks his agent to explain what all these strange provisions, written in legalese, actually mean. The students explain how I am paid, what obligations I have to the club, and how I can be "released" or "waived." (No players are ever "fired" in professional sports, although they do regularly lose their jobs.) We talk about bonus provisions, both real and "imaginary," like the clause that gives me lots of money when I am named the Most Valuable Player in the league.

The section on the powers of the commissioner uses classic cases, like Bowie Kuhn's battle with renegade owner Charlie Finley, and an article I wrote about the Commissioner's discipline of John Rocker that was modified in arbitration. Students study salary arbitration by using a simulation based on the cases I heard as an arbitrator starting in 1986. The key lesson here is to explain why almost 90 percent of all cases are settled before (or during) the arbitration hearing. It is the remarkable final-offer system that makes this operate so well. The panel of three arbitrators appointed to hear a case can select only the club's offer or the player's demand. The former is generally below market value and the latter is above market value. Clubs and player agents drive their final positions towards the middle to be the more reasonable option. That centripetal force fosters voluntary settlement.

We next look at the dramatic impact of grievance arbitration on baseball, starting with the Messersmith case in 1975, where Arbitrator Peter Seitz found in the language of the player contract only a one-year option rather than the career-long reserve system that baseball had followed for almost a century. It was the greatest victory any union has ever achieved in labor arbitration.

Faced with uncontrollable market forces under the new regime of free agency, the club owners naturally colluded to hold down the salaries they would pay for the players' services. The problem was that this cooperation among the clubs violated another provision of the collective bargaining agreement that prohibited collusion, as two labor arbitrators held in the mid-1980s. Here the object is to introduce students to the operation of private alternative dispute resolution systems. Law school curricula are heavily weighted towards judicial decisions. In baseball, decisions by private adjudicators jointly selected by the parties have proven far more important. We talk about how arbitration works.

Frustrated by their loss of dominance in the industry, baseball's magnates knew there was only one way to restore their unrestricted power, and that would require use of economic weapons. It would take a strike, and then replacing the strikers as football did in the 1980s. Students study carefully the 1994–95 baseball strike as an example of how collective bargaining negotiations do and do not work. This also serves as a paradigm for studying the use of established legal processes in baseball. The National Labor Relations Board under the chairmanship of Bill Gould took Major League Baseball to court, where the board obtained an injunction against the owners. (Gould was on leave from Stanford University where he was—and is—one of the nation's finest labor law and sports law professors.) Judge Sonia Sotomayor, then on the federal district court in New York City (and now on the Second Circuit Court of Appeals), thoughtfully reviewed the very difficult labor law precedents on point to find that the owners failed to bargain in good faith when they unilaterally altered important parts of the salary system without negotiating to an impasse with the union.

Teaching baseball in Boston—a town that lives and dies with its Red Sox—presents unique challenges and opportunities. There are always live issues involving the Old Town Team that may warrant a detour at any time. (Should the fan who allegedly touched Yankee right fielder Gary Sheffield in the spring of 2005 lose his season tickets? Can they do that?) There is no need to arrange a field trip to the park. My students have been there. Being less than a mile from Fenway does offer other advantages. Red Sox general counsel Lucinda Treat has visited my class to talk about the work of a club's lawyer, a dream job for all law students. Red Sox President Larry Lucchino and General Manager Theo Epstein are both attorneys. If there is anything better than being a baseball lawyer, it would be running a baseball team.

For most of my students, however, dreams of glory on or near the diamond are fantasies. Sports Law, however, is fantasy camp for lawyers, where I can play a sports lawyer without being one. It is important to support their dreams, however. It is the sugar that allows them to ingest some very difficult legal and business concepts. It even makes it possible to teach them the implied labor exemption to the antitrust laws, one of the law's great mysteries.

The basis for a student's grade in Sports Law is a research paper on a legal topic involving the sports enterprise or on a sports topic that has potential legal implications. My students receive a hundred or so possible topics to get them thinking about the possibilities. A handout of topics is also included in an appendix to this paper. They may also find some other topic that I must approve. The papers are twenty to twenty-five pages in length and must be well written and well researched. I always learn something from these papers, and each year I select the best papers to submit to sports law journals for publication.

I caution my students at the outset of the course that baseball is my field and I will be telling them stories about baseball history. If they cannot stand the game, then they can always take Wills and Trusts. They choose to stay in the game, however, and, in the process, learn a great deal about what a lawyer in a particular industry actually does. Every lawyer should learn about baseball. If litigation is the nation's real pastime, then baseball comes in a close second.

Appendices

Sports Law

Table of Contents

Preface	2
Chap. 1—The Nature of Sports and the Nature of Law	
Flood v. Kuhn (introduction)	3
Hackbart v. Bengals (tort law and sports)	4
Maddox v. City of New York et al. (assumption of risk)	10
Regina v. Bradshaw (1878)	13
Regina v. Green (criminal law and sports)	14
Chap. 2—The Structure of Professional Sports	
Philadelphia Base Ball Club, Ltd. v. Lajoie (negative injunction.)	18
National Basketball Association Uniform Player Contract	21
Boston Celtics v. Brian Shaw (enforcing contract)	32
Finley v. Kuhn (commissioner's power)	39
Peter Edward Rose and the Commissioner of Baseball	46
Chap. 3—The Reserve System, Antitrust Law and Baseball	
Flood v. Kuhn (antitrust exemption)	52

Catfish Hunter's Arbitration	58
K.C. Royals v. MLBPA ("liberation arbitration")	59

Chap. 4—The Rozelle Rule, Antitrust and Football

Mackey v. NFL (antitrust and sports)	73
Brown v. Pro Football (implied labor exemption expiration)	82
Los Angeles Coliseum (Raiders I) (franchise free agency)	88

Chap. 5—Sports Labor Law

MLB Players Association v. Steve Garvey (collusion)	97
1994–95 Baseball Strike	100
Silverman v. Major League Baseball Player Relations Committee	102
Salary Arbitration (Ron Darling—1986)	114
NBA Salary Cap	117
Union Royale Belge v. Bosman (transfer fee)	118
"Off His Rocker" (player discipline)	120
Latrell Sprewell (player discipline)	124

Chap. 6—Intercollegiate Sports

NCAA v. Tarkanian (state action)	127
Tai Kwan Cureton v. NCAA (1999) (Title VI)	134
NCAA v. Oklahoma and Georgia (collegiate antitrust)	142
Law v. NCAA (restricted earnings coaches ruling)	151
Cohen v. Brown University (Title IX)	160
Heather Sue Mercer v. Duke University (contact sports)	169

Chap. 7—The Right to Play

Ali v. State Athletic Commission (equal protection)	174
Me and Muhammed	180
Renee Richards v. USTA (gender identity discrimination)	187
PGA v. Casey Martin (disability discrimination)	194

Chap. 8—The Agents

Detroit Lions v. Argovitz (conflict of interest)	206
The Agent: The Most Hated Man in Baseball	210
Norby Walters and Lloyd Bloom	216

Chap. 9—International Sports Governance

Butch Reynolds v. IAFF (drugs, sports and civil procedure)	217
The Steve Howe Arbitration (history of regulation)	223

Suggested Paper Topics

1. Contractual rights
    a. The enforcement of the standard player contract: arbitration vs. court.
    b. Calculating damages for breach of contract in professional sports.
    c. Standards for granting injunctive relief in the sports context.
    d. Bonus provision calculation.
2. Constitutional rights of athletes
    a. The application of due process to the suspension of an athlete from a team.
    b. Equal protection in the regulation of professional and amateur sports.
    c. High school athletics and the Constitution.
    d. The impact of a state constitution's equal protection clause on amateur sports.
    e. Sex discrimination in amateur athletics.

3. Union Activity
   a. Organizing college athletes under state or federal labor statutes.
   b. Bargaining unit determinations in professional sports.
   c. Scope of bargaining in professional sports.
   d. Duty of fair representation by professional sports unions.
   e. Union regulation of sports agents.
   f. Unfair labor practice litigation in professional sports: the distinctive context.
4. Antitrust Law
   a. The legality of the player draft system after Clarett.
   b. Antitrust limitations on a league's prerogative to define the rules of competition.
   c. The legality of roster limitations and acquisition deadlines.
   d. Player discipline and antitrust law.
   e. The legality of league decisions on franchise ownership.
   f. The legality of league decisions on the location of sports franchises.
   g. The use of monopoly power by an established league against a rival league.
   h. The applicability of antitrust laws to international professional sports leagues.
   i. The legality of NCAA rules and regulations under the antitrust laws.
5. Miscellaneous
   a. Cause of action to overturn the decision of a referee, umpire, etc.
   b. The public regulation of sports licenses (e.g., boxing, racing).
   c. Unlawful sports activities.
   d. Federal taxation of professional sports teams.
   e. Federal taxation of professional athletes.
   f. State taxation of a visiting team's professional athletes.
   g. Gender discrimination in professional and amateur sports.
   h. Local use of eminent domain power over sports franchises.
   i. Criminal liability for sports activities.
   j. Should college athletes be paid? Be covered by Workers' Compensation?
   k. The validity of local laws prohibiting, e.g., installation of lights at Wrigley Field.
   l. Regulation of sports betting and gambling.
   m. Point-shaving scandals.
   n. The NCAA: Should it be reformed or abolished?
   o. Eligibility to compete in non-team pro sports, such as tennis, golf, etc.
   p. State and/or NCAA control over, and licensing of, sports agents.
   q. The NCAA "death penalty"—does it work?
   r. Payment of Olympic athletes as a perversion of the amateur ethos.
   s. Unionization of jai alai players: labor law and immigration law.
   t. Drug testing of professional and/or amateur athletes.
   u. Expert testimony in the proof of a sports tort case.
   v. Intellectual property issues in professional sports: copyright and trademark.
6. Tort liability
   a. Malpractice in the treatment of athletic injuries.
   b. Products liability for defective athletic equipment.
   c. The commercial exploitation of an athlete's name or likeness.
   d. Liability for injuries to spectators.
   e. Enjoining violent sports as a public nuisance.
   f. Vicarious and direct liability of coaches and owners.
   g. Should boxing be banned?
   h. Workers' Compensation for injured college athletes.
   i. State "skier responsibility" statutes.
   j. Liability of manufacturers of football helmets.

Actual Spring 2004 Sports Law Paper Topics
1. Trademark issues in sports and the new technologies.
2. Public financing of sports stadiums.
3. Federal regulation of boxing.
4. Artificial turf as an OSHA violation.
5. Salary caps in professional sports.
6. Title IX recent developments.
7. NCAA sanctions against "criminal athletes."
8. Formula One racing and the EU regulation of tobacco advertising.
9. Regulating sports ticket scalping.
10. Youth violence in sports.
11. Gender discrimination by Augusta National.
12. The use by athletes of performance-enhancing drugs.
13. Violence of professional football players off the field.
14. Regulating drug use in Olympic sports.
15. Eligibility of transgendered athletes in Olympic sports.
16. College recruiting scandals.
17. Who owns baseball statistics?
18. Are college athletes "employees" covered by the National Labor Relations Act?
19. How to increase graduation rates of college athletes.
20. Federal regulation of sports agents.
21. Why is the baseball players union more powerful than the football players union?
22. The extent of the baseball commissioner's power.
23. Player salaries and the uneven playing field.
24. Exploiting the commercial use of a college athlete's "persona."
25. Hockey violence.
26. Fighting back against Title IX.
27. Universities should be held responsible for the actions of their athletes under the doctrine of respondeat superior.
28. State-sponsored gender discrimination in sports.
29. Baseball in Montreal and the conspiracy that led to the demise of the franchise.
30. The realities of the Casey Martin case.
31. Gambling on college sports and focused on the importance of banning publication of point spreads.
32. Using Title IX to recover for damages caused by sexual harassment by college athletes.
33. The commercialization of college sports and the prevailing amateur model.
34. The lingering problems caused by baseball's antitrust exemption.
35. The merits of the NFL draft eligibility rule.
36. Competitive imbalance in baseball.
37. Player movement in international hockey, in particular the travails of Russian hockey stars moving to the NHL.
38. Online sports gambling and the risk to amateur athletics.
39. A suit against a school district for using an allegedly disparaging Indian nickname.
40. The immigration of Cuban baseball players and its impact on other Cubans refugees.
41. Public and community ownership of sports franchises as a way to stop franchise free agency, wasteful public subsidization and high player salaries.
42. How players are selected for baseball's all-star game.
43. The Celtics' termination of Vin Baker's contract.

Works Cited

Abrams, Roger. "Off His Rocker: Sports Discipline and Labor Arbitration." *Marquette Sports Law Review* 167 (2001): 167–74.

Weiler, Paul C., and Gary R. Roberts, eds. *Sports and the Law: Text, Cases, and Problems.* 3rd ed. St. Paul: West Group, 2004.

Law

"Legal Baseball" in the Law School Curriculum—The Contracts Example

(C. PAUL ROGERS III)

Baseball and the law go back a long way, 130 years or so. In recent times the intersection of the two has generated substantial commentary and study.[1] With the advent and expansion of sports law courses in most law schools, "legal" baseball's prominence as a subject for study has increased significantly. Sports law treatises and casebooks all consider baseball's reserve clause, its antitrust exemption, and its tumultuous labor relations history, among other topics.[2]

Further, a number of scholars have noted the developmental, operational, and functional relationships of baseball and the law—in other words the parallels between the two. Examples range from seemingly specious topics such as the development of the infield fly rule and the common law,[3] to heavier duty ones such as baseball rules and statutory construction,[4] baseball and the rule of law,[5] baseball and the interpretation of rules,[6] and baseball, legal theory, and jurisprudence.[7]

Obvious corollaries exist between baseball rules and statutory laws and perhaps even between reported cases, which describe what courts have done, and our sacrosanct baseball statistics, which detail what players have done. Further, litigators, who after all are managing a case against an opponent in our adversarial justice system, are supposed to be legal, procedural, and strategic experts, just as baseball managers are supposed to know baseball rules and strategy. The lawyer must understand the strengths and weaknesses of the facts of his case, while the manager must know the strengths and weaknesses of his personnel. Both should have some knowledge, understanding, and appreciation of their opponents and should try not to get too crosswise with the arbiter of the dispute/contest.

Baseball, however, can be used as a teaching tool rather than as a substantive or comparative topic in law school. Since baseball intersects with the law in so many areas, it can frequently be used as a substantive law example or illustration for law school study. One might term the concept as the illustrative use of legal baseball.

Contracts, a required first year course in virtually every U.S. law school, presents numerous opportunities for the illustrative use of baseball. For example, employment agreements are a category of contract that frequents the contracts course syllabus. The distinction between employment at will and employment for a fixed term is often confusing to first-year law students. Employees at will can be terminated at any time without cause while employees locked in for a fixed term cannot be dismissed at will.[8] An excellent illustration of the difference is a major league ballplayer's fixed term employment agreement.

For example, Alex Rodriquez, now of the New York Yankees, who signed his record-breaking ten-year, $250 million contract with the Texas Rangers before the 2001 season, is anything but an employee at will. A-Rod is guaranteed approximately $25 million a year salary through 2010 even if he hits .190, leads the league in errors, is injured and cannot play at all, or fails to drive in a run in the postseason.[9] An employee at will, in contrast, is guaranteed as a matter of contract law nothing but pay at the contract rate for work performed.[10]

Baseball's long-term guaranteed contracts also provide the basis for an important discussion about the economics of contract law and of our free market economy. Baseball is, of course, replete with bad deals where owners have entered into multimillion dollar guaranteed contracts for players who do not perform to the levels expected or who are chronically injured and cannot play.[11] These contracts illustrate the benefits and detriments of our right of freedom of contract, so important to our legal system and our society. Freedom of contract means the freedom to enter into unfavorable as well as favorable contracts. Tom Hicks, the owner of the Texas Rangers and a very successful businessman, has obviously entered into many advantageous agreements. But, virtually all would agree, he entered into a stinker when he paid well over market value to sign A-Rod to a ten year "personal services" contract.[12] The law enforces both good and bad agreements, as long as the contract requisites are present and there are no defenses to enforceability such as duress, mutual mistake, or fraud (temporary insanity in the A-Rod–Hicks deal?).

The A-Rod and baseball players' service contracts also illustrate the law of supply and demand, on several levels. Why do so many people work in employment-at-will jobs while others make more money in one year than most of us will make in a lifetime? It is because the free market dictates what employers are willing to pay for employees' services. If one has a special skill in an area where popular culture creates an extraordinary demand, salaries, endorsement contracts, and the like skyrocket upward. The highly competitive nature of major league baseball exacerbates the operation of the free market. Owners, like George Steinbrenner of the Yankees, literally striving to win at any cost, raise the salary market by outbidding rivals for the services of star ballplayers like Gary Sheffield, Randy Johnson, Mark Mussina, Roger Clemens, and Jason Giambi. The relatively short supply of "star" quality free agents (players who are no longer under contract to a team) each year, coupled with the desire of baseball owners to win (fueled by demanding, front-running fans who will not support a losing team) ensures that huge contract offers will be proffered. Demand sharply exceeds supply.

At the other end of the employment scale, labor supply far exceeds demand. Thus, for menial labor jobs, fast food restaurant employment, or part-time retail positions, we see the result: employment at will and minimum wage salaries with little or no benefits. The free market is at work, tempered by some government protections such as the minimum wage law to keep wages from dropping even lower for some jobs.

Team-player contract negotiations can also demonstrate the contract negotiation and formation issues encountered by every first-year contracts student, who quickly learns that an offer and an acceptance is required for a contract to be "formed." A player who is a free agent may be considering offers from several teams at once, although he can accept only one since the offer is for a personal services contract. If he waits too long he may find an offer effectively revoked, since, presumably, employment offers are freely revocable, lacking consideration to make them irrevocable. Questions of effective communication of the revocation (or the acceptance prior to revocation) may arise.

Indeed, since the first semester of contracts deals primarily with contract formation issues, one can effectively employ a baseball "free agent" problem for discussion, or even for use as a final examination question. (Law school final examination questions typically involve complicated fact patterns which require law students to identify the legal issues and apply their knowledge of the law in a coherent and concise manner. At least, that is the goal.) In such a problem, Zeke Barnes, a fictitious free agent pitcher, is negotiating with his current team, the Pirates, as well as three additional teams, the Yankees, Astros, and Rangers. The Pirates believe they have a valid option for another year at far below market value. In the meantime, Barnes, through his agent, Nora Norton, fails to strike a deal with any of the other three clubs, leaving, it would appear, no valid alternative but for Barnes to remain with the underpaying Pirates.

The problem requires the students to traipse through the negotiations and contract formation issues with each potential suitor and raises fundamental contract law concepts such as offer and acceptance, revocation, rejection, the mailbox rule, option contracts, consideration, and illusory contracts. In sum, it covers much of the contract law of the typical first semester contracts course.

Much of the second semester of contracts concerns defenses to the enforceability of contracts such as mistake, misrepresentation, fraud, duress, and commercial impracticability. A great example of unilateral mistake arises from the much publicized Nolan Ryan rookie card dispute of 1990. Thirteen-year-old Bryan Wrzesinski purchased a 1968 Ryan rookie card for $12.00 from an inexperienced clerk in an Itasca, Illinois, memorabilia store. The card was valued at between $800 and $1,200 and was marked at 1200, without a dollar sign, decimal point or comma. Even though the store had a sign stating "all sales final," the store owner sued to recover the card, claiming unilateral mistake and concealment.

The parties ultimately settled the case, agreeing to put the card up for auction and to split the proceeds for charities that each selected.[13] Even so, the dispute makes for great classroom discussion and highlights the difference between mutual mistake, when both parties are mistaken about that which is being contracted for, and unilateral mistake, where only one party is mistaken. Further, one can use the case to contrast the so-called assumption of the risk situation, where both parties are rolling the dice as to the value of that which is the subject of the contract.

Another important second-semester contracts subject is performance and breach. If one party breaches during the contractual period, the second party may seek to suspend its own performance, terminate the contract, and sue for damages. This course of action is fine if the breach is material but "fraught with peril" if the breach is deemed to be nonmaterial, as the suspension of performance by the second party will put that party in material breach and subject it to damages. Good breach examples arise in baseball from the recent termination of the contracts of Denny Neagle by the Colorado Rockies for soliciting a prostitute and Sidney Ponson by the Baltimore Orioles after two DWIs and an assault on a judge in his home country of Aruba.

To take the Ponson situation, the Orioles terminated his contract and thus the club's obligation to pay Ponson $10 million for 2006, the last year of his contract, after his second DWI, citing the clause in his player's contract that gives the team the right to terminate for conduct detrimental to baseball. The Players' Association, of course, immediately appealed the termination, and under the collective bargaining agreement the case will go to an arbitrator for decision.[14] If the arbitrator, for some unknown reason, decides that two DWIs and an eleven-day jail stint in Aruba for assaulting a judge (on Christmas Day, no less) does not meet the contract standard for termination, the contract would be reinstated. In contract terms, Ponson's breach would be deemed not material and the Orioles' action in terminating would in fact be a material breach.

The Orioles perhaps incur little risk by terminating Ponson's contract since the worst that can happen is a reversion to the status quo ante where the team has to honor a bad contract to a mediocre starting pitcher with off-field behavior problems. The instructor could create a "fraught with peril" situation by hypothetically inserting an acceleration clause in Ponson's contract for wrongful termination. In that case, if the arbitrator rules for the player that termination was not warranted, the acceleration clause would make all the money due Ponson under the contract immediately due and owing. The peril of the hypothetical would be enhanced if the contract had, say, four years and $50 million to go.

The New York Yankees' termination of World Series hero Aaron Boone's contract last year raises slightly different issues. Boone ruptured his Achilles tendon in January of 2004 playing basketball, an activity expressly forbidden in his player's contract. Boone was up front about the injury and its cause and the Yankees terminated his contract, costing Boone about $7 million for the 2004 season. The club understandably did not want to pay Boone, who would be lost for most or all the season, for an injury he incurred engaging in a contractually forbidden activity. The element of discretion was not present in the Boone contract term, in contrast to the "conduct detrimental to baseball" clause at issue in the Ponson case, so the Yankees undertook virtually no risk in terminating.

The instructor can put another spin on the issue by considering the Jeff Kent injury, which occurred in March of 2002. Kent first claimed he broke his left wrist when he slipped while washing his pickup truck. After considerable media speculation, Kent eventually admitted that the injury occurred while he was popping a wheelie on his motorcycle, an activity barred by the clause in his contract prohibiting dangerous activities. Kent missed only the first of the season and, although he had lied and breached his contract, the Giants did not act to terminate the agreement. His value to the team as a ballplayer and his availability for most of the season obviously impacted the manner in which the Giants responded contractually. If Kent was fined or penalized at all, it was handled privately. Thus, from a contracts perspective it appears that the Giants either waived the breach or treated it as nonmaterial.

A contracts teacher can use these various baseball examples to demonstrate how fact-specific issues of breach and performance in contract are.[15] And the larger point to be made is that this is appropriate since the law must be malleable to achieve its goal of a fair and just result in every case. That our common law system sometimes fails to reach this admirable goal is perhaps not surprising but, like democracy, no one has been able to come up with a better system.

Of course, the use of baseball in substantive law courses is not limited to contracts by any means. A couple of my colleagues who teach property have begun their course with the Barry Bonds 73rd home run ball dispute from 2001.[16] There, the individual who caught the record-setting home run, Alex Popov, sued Patrick Hayashi, the person who ended up with the ball after a mad scrum, for conversion, that is, appropriating another person's property. The case involved fundamental personal property concepts such as possession, conversion, and title in a very contemporary and high profile setting.[17] My colleagues, to accentuate the concept of possession, actually pass out soft rubber balls marked like baseballs to each student.

A caveat when using a baseball example, or one from any sport, as a teaching tool is that those students who are not sports fans may feel disadvantaged or even discriminated against. Those feelings may be particularly acute when an exam question features a baseball fact pattern. Female students in particular may complain since it is probably verifiable that a larger percentage of women have little interest in or knowledge of baseball than men.

Of course, one can properly argue that lawyers are frequently required to become conversant with and even master subjects about which they have little knowledge. It is inevitable that both litigators and transaction lawyers will represent clients engaged in businesses or activities totally foreign to them.[18] In those instances, it is up to the lawyer to get up to speed quickly or the client will go elsewhere just as speedily.

While that argument sounds good and is certainly accurate, it is not likely to appease baseball-ignorant students who will be concerned about the mere appearance of unfairness. They may still feel discriminated against and may argue that in handling a baseball (or sports) fact pattern the advantage, at least inherently, goes to those knowledgeable about the sport. Since first-year law exams are graded on the curve, it will be impossible to convince those students otherwise.[19]

Further, in my law school we traditionally attract a number of foreign students who are studying for a master of laws in international and comparative law. Those students are typically already law graduates in countries with civil law, rather than common law, heritages. They seek to study our common-law system and earn an American law degree, which can enhance their career opportunities in their home countries. As a result, most of them take at least a semester of contract law because it is foundational to our common-law system and is largely the product of appellate judicial decisions, what common-law lawyers call case law. Of course, while baseball abroad is growing in popularity (in spite of the recent International Olympic Committee decision to drop it from Olympic competition), to many foreign students our national pastime is as much a mystery as the game of cricket is to most Americans.

Thus, it is important to avoid the use of baseball jargon or to assume any knowledge of the rules of baseball or its structure and operation. And even though I have been careful to avoid those pitfalls, I have still heard grumbling when I have used a baseball- or sports-fact pattern on a final examination, so I do not use them very frequently. Using baseball examples or problems during class rather than on the final exam, however, significantly reduces the student grousing but, of course, even that can be carried to an extreme (the use of examples *and* the grousing).

As mentioned, law school exams invariably involve fictional fact patterns. While hardly instructional, I frequently use the names of old ballplayers for my fictional people in my fictional fact patterns. I believe it adds more realism to the question than writing "A agreed to sell Blackacre to B" or creating silly names like "Sally Seller agreed to sell Blackacre to Barry Buyer." Instead, I use interesting old baseball names like Van Lingo Mungo, Coaker Triplett, or Schoolboy Rowe, or older Hall of Famers who aren't household names like Tris Speaker (although he should be), Gabby Hartnett or Rube Waddell.[20] I will sometimes, to further amuse myself, incorporate a theme using only players from the 1950 Philadelphia Phillies (the Whiz Kids), the '34 Cardinals (the Gas House Gang), the early New York Giants of John McGraw and Christy Mathewson, or even some obscure team like the 1952 Pittsburgh Pirates, who finished in the cellar with a 42–112 win-loss record, 54 1/2 games out of first place.[21]

Usually these shenanigans elicit no response from the students. Occasionally, however, I do have someone write me a note after their answer, telling me, tongue in cheek, that he (or she) thought that Carl Hubbell used to pitch for the New York Giants rather than work as a commodities trader or that Pie Traynor played third for the Pirates rather than sold John Deere tractors. Needless to say, those occasional students fare well on the exam, irrespective of their knowledge of contract law.[22]

The use of baseball as a teaching tool in first-year law classes such as contracts is certainly appealing and useful pedagogically. Baseball can provide valuable real-life examples to illustrate and help differentiate important legal concepts. The caveat is that while use of baseball examples in class may stimulate and animate some it may annoy or even intimidate others. If that occurs, the pedagogy certainly suffers and one may get nasty comments on his or her student evaluations, to be considered if one is not so jaded as to no longer care about teaching evaluations. Thus, some caution is warranted to potentially overenthusiastic baseball aficionados who happen to teach first-year law school courses. The same caveat applies to the use of baseball fact patterns for the final examination, as tempting as doing so may be.

For those of us who need more of an outlet than an occasional baseball reference in class, I urge you to consider the more subtle approach of just pleasing yourself by using old ballplayers' names in examinations and the like. Sometimes what the students do not know cannot hurt them, and if it helps make the drudgery of exam writing, to say nothing of exam grading, a little less onerous, why not?

Notes

1. See, e.g., Roger I. Abrams, *Legal Bases: Baseball and the Law*; G. Edward White, *Creating the National Pastime: Baseball Transforms Itself, 1903–1953*; Spencer Weber Waller, Neil B. Cohen, and Paul Finkelman, eds., *Baseball and the American Legal Mind*.

2. See, e.g., John C. Weistart and Cym H. Lowell, *The Law of Sports*. For casebooks see, e.g., Paul C. Weiler and Gary R. Roberts, *Sports and the Law,* and Matthew J. Mitten, Timothy Davis, Rodney K. Smith, and Robert C. Berry, *Sports Law and Regulation*.

3. See Aside, "The Common Law Origins of the Infield Fly Rule," *U. Pa. L. Rev.* 123 (1975): 1474. See also Mark W. Cochran, "The Infield Fly Rule and the Internal Revenue Code: An Even Further Aside," *William & Mary L. Rev.* 29 (1988): 557.

4. See, e.g., Donald J. Rapson, "A Home Run Application of Established Principles of Statutory Construction: UCC Analogies," *Cardozo L. Rev.* 5 (1984): 441; Jared T. Finkelstein, "In re Brett: The Sticky Problem of Statutory Construction," *Fordham. L. Rev.* 52 (1983): 430; C. Paul Rogers III, "The Judicial Reinterpretation of Statutes: The Example of Baseball and the Antitrust Laws," *Houston L. Rev.* 14 (1977): 611.

5. See, e.g., Paul Finkelman, "Baseball and the Rule of Law," 46 *Cleveland State L. Rev* 46 (1998): 239.

6. See, e.g., "If You Write It, (S)He Will Come," *Conn. L. Rev.* 28(1996): 813, and Melvin A. Eisenberg, "Expression Rules in Contract Law and Problems of Offer and Acceptance," *Calif. L. Rev.* 82 (1994): 1127.

7. See, e.g., Charles Yablon, "On the Contribution of Baseball to American Legal Theory," *Yale L.J.* 104 (1995): 227, and Richard Lemper, "Error Behind the Plate and in the Law," *So. Cal. L. Rev.* 59 (1986): 407.

8. Often term employment contracts will identify behavior for which termination by cause can occur or, in the alternative, causes for termination will be listed in the employer's employee handbook, which is incorporated by reference into the employment agreement.

9. His contract probably does list certain activities which would cancel or void the contract, such as, perhaps, riding a motorcycle or other hazardous activities. With the events of the last year, presumably steroid use has become a basis for major league teams to cancel player contracts.

10. Of course, federal and state laws provide the at-will employee with some protections and some recourse for certain kinds of employment discrimination, for example because of race, age, or, in some cases, gender.

11. Kevin Brown's seven-year $105 million contract (the first $100 million deal in

baseball history) is a classic example of the latter. In 2005, he compiled a 4–7 record with a 6.50 ERA in 13 starts and three trips to the disabled list. At this writing, Brown's chronic back trouble has landed him on the disabled list ten times since signing the deal in late 1998, including a move to the Yankees' 60-day disabled list amid speculation that his career is effectively over.

12. Most Rangers fans would argue that Hicks's 2002 signing of pitcher Chan Ho Park to a five year, $65 million guaranteed contract was not too swift, either. Park was mostly ineffective or injured for three-plus years before the Rangers swapped him to the San Diego Padres in the middle of the 2005 season for Phil Nevin in what amounted to an exchange of bad player contracts.

13. The card, with the disputed price sticker intact, brought $5,000 at the auction because of the notoriety of the case (*USA Today*, June 24, 1991).

14. Denny Neagle's contract was terminated by the Colorado Rockies soon after his December 2004 arrest for solicitation. The Players' Association filed a grievance pursuant to its collective bargaining agreement and the parties reached an undisclosed settlement in May 2005.

15. The old contract jumping cases in which players broke contracts to play for another team, often in another league, raise performance and breach questions as well as issues of appropriate remedy. Earlier editions of the Dawson and Harvey contracts casebook included *Philadelphia Ball Club v. Lajoie*, 202 Pa. 210, 51 A. 973 (1902) as well as a large photo of the old Frenchman, Napoleon Lajoie. See John P. Dawson and William Burnett Harvey, *Contracts and Contract Remedies: Cases and Materials*, 573. The case does not appear in later editions, however. The *Lajoie* litigation arose when Lajoie, then the game's preeminent star, jumped to the Philadelphia Athletics in the fledgling American League, even though he had two more years on his contract with the Phillies. The Pennsylvania Supreme Court granted an injunction against Lajoie forbidding him from playing for any team but the Phillies. The Athletics thereupon traded him to the Cleveland Bronchos (who soon became known as the Naps in his honor), and an Ohio court refused to give full faith and credit to the Pennsylvania injunction, ruling that Pennsylvania exceeded its authority in issuing an injunction prohibiting conduct outside its borders. Thereafter, Lajoie played everywhere except Philadelphia, where the injunction still held. He managed to hit .378 despite all the turmoil. See C. Paul Rogers III, "Napoleon Lajoie, Breach of Contract and the Great Baseball War," *SMU L. Rev.* 55 (2002): 325. See also *American League Baseball Club of Chicago v. Chase*, 86 Misc. 441 (NY 1914) where the White Sox enjoined "Prince" Hal Chase from playing for the Buffalo Buffeds of the upstart Federal League in violation of his contract with the White Sox.

16. At least one property casebook includes the case in its materials. See James Charles Smith, Edward J. Larson, John Copeland Nagle, and John A. Kidwell, *Property: Cases and Materials*, 75.

17. The trial court ruled that both parties had equal and undivided one-half interests in the ball, ordering the ball to be sold, with the proceeds to be divided equally between the parties (*Popov v. Hayashi*, 2002 WL 3183373 [Cal. Superior]). The auction was held on January 25, 2003, and televised live on ESPN. The ball sold for $450,000, far less than the $3.2 million the same collector paid for Mark McGwire's seventieth home run ball in 1999. Popov was later sued by his attorney for $473,000 in attorney's fees.

18. The same is true for judges. For example, Federal District Court Judge John Jackson reportedly had no experience with computers before he presided over the Microsoft trial. See *United States v. Microsoft Corp.*, 87 F. Supp. 2d 30 (D.D.C. 2000) *and* 97 F. Supp. 2d 59 (D.D.C. 2000).

19. The emphasis on first-year grades by prospective legal employers exacerbates the problem.

20. Supreme Court Justice Harry Blackmun penned perhaps the most famous panegyric to baseball from the legal profession when writing the majority opinion in *Flood v. Kuhn*, 407 U.S. 258 (1972), upholding professional baseball's exemption from the antitrust laws. He quoted Grantland Rice and George Bernard Shaw, among others, and then provided a long list of baseball's legendary names like Nap Lajoie, Rogers Hornsby, Goose Goslin, and Rabbit Maranville. He was later heard to lament that he had neglected to include Van Lingo Mungo.

21. In the era of political correctness and, more importantly, because about one-half of current law students are women, I often alter names to make fictional fact-pattern people female. Thus, Joe Tinker becomes Josephine Tinker, or Frank Chance could become Frances Chance.

22. Just kidding, to see if the reader is paying attention.

Works Cited (Books)

Abrams, Roger I. *Legal Bases: Baseball and the Law*. Philadelphia: Temple University Press, 1998.

Dawson, John P., and William Burnett Harvey. *Contracts and Contract Remedies: Cases and Materials*. 2nd ed. Mineola, NY: Foundation, 1969.

Mitten, Matthew J., Timothy Davis, Rodney K. Smith, and Robert C. Berry. *Sports Law and Regulation: Cases, Materials, and Problems*. New York: Kluwer Law International, 2005.

Smith, James Charles, Edward J. Larson, John Copeland Nagle, and John A. Kidwell. *Property: Cases and Materials*. New York: Aspen, 2004.

Waller, Spencer Weber, Neil B. Cohen, and Paul Finkelman, eds. *Baseball and the American Legal Mind*. New York: Garland, 1995.

Weiler, Paul C., and Gary R. Roberts, eds. *Sports and the Law: Text, Cases, and Problems*. 3rd ed. St. Paul, MN: West Group, 2004.

Weistart, John C., and Cym H. Lowell. *The Law of Sports*. Indianapolis: Bobbs-Merrill, 1979.

White, G. Edward. *Creating the National Pastime: Baseball Transforms Itself, 1903–1953*. Princeton, NJ: Princeton University Press, 1996.

Literature

Baseball Literature for General Education

(Gary Gray and Gary Land)

Designing and teaching general education courses poses unique pedagogical difficulties. Many students take these courses only because they are required to and have little inherent interest or background in the subject. The teacher, therefore, must find means of gaining the interest of students, maintaining that attention, and encouraging students to commit themselves to high quality work, all without lowering academic standards. Baseball literature has proven to be an effective course that students at Andrews University may take to fulfill their general education literature requirement. Although not all students become equally engaged in the class, a variety of types of literature, interspersed with related but supplementary activities, has worked well both in attracting students and keeping their interest throughout what often seems a long semester.

Course Goals and Student Profile

Beginning in 1993, Gary Gray and Gary Land, teachers respectively in the English and history departments, have co-taught baseball literature five times, most recently in the spring semester of 2005. The course is one of several topical classes that are taught by a variety of teachers under a single, sophomore-level course number and title, ENGL255 Studies in Literature, which fulfills the general education literature requirement. Intended to attract students by appealing to a variety of interests, other course topics have included such subjects as biblical, women's, African-American, love, and Arthurian literature. Within this context, baseball literature offers something of potential interest to the sports-minded student.

The course has two major goals. First, organized around the subject of baseball, in which many students already have an interest, it seeks to awaken a desire to read and an appreciation of literature. A majority of students at Andrews University are either majoring in the sciences or are taking professionally oriented programs such as nursing, physical therapy, or business. Reading for pleasure seems to have little place in their lives. It is hoped that this course will encourage them to continue to read long after they have finished school. Second, the course attempts to increase the students' understanding of literature and how to approach it. It introduces several of the genres within which literature is written, including novels, short stories, essays, memoirs, and poems, explaining briefly the purposes and nature of each type of writing and various strategies for reading with understanding. Because this is a course for general education students rather than English majors, the teachers emphasize the text and give relatively little attention to theory, except in providing elementary tools for literary analysis such as identification of the plot and major themes, character development, images and metaphors, and use of language.

The number of students in the course has varied from about fifteen to thirty. The variety of backgrounds and interests, typical of students in general education courses, has presented a challenge. Some students are very interested in baseball and approach the course with enthusiasm, finding it almost too good to be true that they can take for credit a course involving the sport. Others are also baseball fans but think that a sports oriented class cannot be very academic and will therefore provide an easy way for them to fulfill a literature requirement in which they are otherwise uninterested. Each year there are also some students who have little interest in or knowledge of baseball and are taking the course simply because it happens to fill a requirement and fits into their schedule. Frequently among the latter are international students, some of whom have come from such baseball-barren regions as Africa and Eastern Europe and must learn some basics about the game in addition to coping with an alien literature.

Texts

Choosing works for the students to read has been both a pleasure and a trial, for there are always items that the teachers want to include but for which there is not enough time in the semester. The teachers have used a variety of criteria in making their decisions. These criteria include a potential pleasurable reading experience that might be used as a future model for a lifetime of quality reading; works that could be easily defended as good literature by a broad, general consensus (rather than a tight, technical definition or argument among English teachers); a variety of genres; an interdisciplinary approach, particularly the blending of history and literature; and writing by both women and men.

Within this context a few books have developed into a consistent core that the teachers supplement with a variety of other works. The course has always included Bernard Malamud's *The Natural* and W. P. Kinsella's *Shoeless Joe*. The second version of the course introduced Eric Rolfe Greenberg's *The Celebrant* and the third brought in Mark Harris's *Bang the Drum Slowly* and Doris Kearns Goodwin's *Wait Till Next Year*. The teachers used Lawrence Ritter's oral history, *The Glory of Their Times*, on the first three occasions but, although it was favorably received by the students, eventually discontinued it because of its length. Roger Kahn's *The Boys of Summer* was used in the second and third presentations of the course but was eventually dropped for the same reason. Donald Hall's *Fathers Playing Catch with Sons*, Thomas Boswell's *Time Begins on Opening Day*, and David Halberstam's *Summer of '49* and *The Teammates* have each been used once.

Finding resources for short stories, essays, and poems has sometimes proved to be difficult, for anthologies often do not stay in print very long. The first year's course used Jerome Holtzman's *Fielder's Choice* and Peter

C. Bjarkman's *Baseball and the Meaning of Life*, excellent short story collections that complemented one another but were not available the next time the course was taught. Elinor Nauen's *Diamonds Are a Girl's Best Friend* provided a wonderful collection of fiction, nonfiction, and poetry written from the female perspective, which was used in the third version of the course, but unfortunately also went out of print. Probably the best available anthology is Nicholas Dawidoff's *Baseball: A Literary Anthology*, a "special publication" of the Library of America, which was assigned the fourth time the course was taught. Despite its quality, however, after including other books that were regarded as essential, there was not enough time in the semester to use enough of the Dawidoff volume to justify the cost to the students. Also, selections from books such as *The Glory of Their Times* and *The Boys of Summer* included in the anthology, which it was initially hoped would substitute for the books themselves, proved to be too short for the purposes of the class. In 2005 the class also used selections from Gary Land's recently published *Growing Up with Baseball*, which offered an opportunity for the teacher to discuss with the students the process of publishing a book as well as the childhood experiences with baseball addressed in the volume.

Response of Students to Reading

In each of the five offerings of Baseball Literature, the teachers have surveyed the students in an attempt to determine their responses to the assigned works. The first time that the class was taught was clearly an experiment and the teachers were feeling their way, not sure that they would ever teach the course again. But, as in the first year, with each subsequent class the teachers formally surveyed the students at the end of the course, wanting some sense from them regarding which books seemed to resonate best. Of those works taught three or more times, students have ranked them as follows:

1993	1996	2000	2002	2005
The Natural / Shoeless Joe	Shoeless Joe	Wait 'Till Next Year	Shoeless Joe	Shoeless Joe
The Glory of Their Times	The Natural	The Natural	Bang the Drum Slowly / The Natural	The Natural
	The Glory of Their Times	Shoeless Joe	Wait 'Till Next Year	The Celebrant
	The Boys of Summer	The Glory of Their Times	The Celebrant	Bang the Drum Slowly
	The Celebrant	The Celebrant		Wait Till Next Year

1993	1996	2000	2002	2005
		The Boys of Summer		
		Bang the Drum Slowly		

Clearly, Kinsella's *Shoeless Joe* is the overall favorite, with Malamud's *The Natural* a close second. It should be noted that the films *Field of Dreams* and *The Natural* are shown in conjunction with discussion of these books. If one starts with the assumption that today's students are far more visually oriented than their counterparts from previous eras, then the most likely explanation for this choice is that both books spawned these popular movies that provide an appealing visual representation of a literary work. At least one student explicitly mentioned this factor. But that explanation does not speak to a literary evaluation and might not totally explain the popularity of these two works. *Shoeless Joe* is an "easy read" that presents an optimistic view of life, elements that one would expect to appeal to college general education students. But *The Natural* is more complex in its literary construction and expresses a much darker view of existence. The fact that students have responded with almost equal favor to both books defies simple explanation.

As the teachers did not want to discourage females from a class that on the surface might seem male oriented, they sought to include works by women. Goodwin's *Wait Till Next Year* has become a staple for this reason and also provides an opportunity to integrate social and political history into the class. Professor Land, a historian, usually teaches this work (typically, each teacher is responsible for leading the class discussions for about half of the assigned works) and uses the occasion to outline the historical context of the 1950s which the book recalls, thereby offering a way for the students to connect with the world of their parents and grandparents. Goodwin's book seemed generally quite popular with both men and women in the first two classes in which it was used. In 2005, for reasons unknown, Goodwin went to last place despite the fact that there were several women in the class.

The early popularity of *The Glory of Their Times*, an oral history, was a surprise, for the teachers thought that late nineteenth- and early twentieth-century baseball probably held little interest for present-day college students. Nonetheless, the volume was chosen because of its inherent quality and important influence in baseball writing. The book's popularity among the students might have been helped by use of audiovisual aids. Students listened to the actual voices from the book in an audio recording, comparing the original interviews with the written text, and saw historical photographs and film as well as heard the voices in a video based on the book. Because the class has not included *The Glory of Their Times* in recent years, it is not known how it might play with the current crop of college students.

In the second version, the teachers started with what some people consider the best baseball book, Roger Kahn's *The Boys of Summer*, requiring the students to read the entire work. Responding to student complaints about the length of the volume, in the next class the teachers decided to ask them to read all of Part I where Kahn describes his childhood and youth and his relationship to the Brooklyn Dodgers of the 1950s and only some of the portraits from the second half of the book, in which the author devotes chapters to describing what the passage of time had done to some of the players from that most famous of teams. A video of the same title, though only loosely based on the book, put a visual face on some of the players. The video seemed to help students understand the era, but the literary value of Kahn's effort seemed lost on most of them. The teachers have since dropped this book from the reading list but with mixed feelings, for they think that *Boys of Summer* is a great baseball book and has significant literary and philosophical value even apart from its baseball themes.

Eric Rolfe Greenberg's *The Celebrant*, a historical novel that interweaves the stories of Christy Mathewson, John McGraw, and the Jewish immigrant experience in America, has been a constant since the third time the course was taught. The teachers thought that the religious themes that emerge in the novel, including how baseball in essence becomes a religion itself, might have some resonance with students at a church-related university. But the students' reaction has been only lukewarm. Two factors may play a role in this response. First, focusing on interpersonal relations and psychological states, the novel has a slowly developing and subtle plotline that holds little immediate appeal to unsophisticated readers. Second, because much of the book can be understood only when the reader has some knowledge of the "new immigration" of the late nineteenth and early twentieth centuries, much of what occurs in the book may not seem significant to the general student despite the historical background explained in the class. Furthermore, the teachers have made *The Celebrant* the first assigned work in the class, largely because it is set in the earliest time period of any of the other texts. But the novel might work better if assigned later in the course, when—it is to be hoped—students have learned how to be better readers of literature.

The teachers have added Mark Harris's novel *Bang the Drum Slowly* in recent years, supplemented by a stage version in video. But again, the students' reaction has been only lukewarm. Perhaps the fact that the story is centered around a young ballplayer who is dying might be a rather negative element for young college students with their whole lives ahead of them. Some students have also expressed discomfort with the colloquial and ungrammatical writing style of the book, which contrasts dramatically with the writing they are required to do in college. General education students may have rather traditional standards when it comes to what constitutes good writing.

In the initial course, the teachers used David Halberstam's description of the torrid pennant race between the Yankees and the Red Sox entitled *The Summer of '49*. Again, like other works in this "rookie" season, it suffered from being too long for the students. Liking Halberstam's writing, however, the instructors included the same author's *The Teammates* in the spring 2005 class. Much shorter than *The Summer of '49*, it tells the story of the journey that Johnny Pesky, Dom DiMaggio, and Dick Flavin (a Boston media personality) take from Massachusetts to Florida to visit the ballplayers' teammate and longtime friend, Ted Williams. In his very effective storytelling style, Halberstam paints literary portraits of these major characters by tracing their individual histories, how they came to play for the Red Sox of the late '40s and '50s, how their friendship developed, and what kept them so close over the years. The story is poignant, of course, because Williams is dying, and the book ends with his death. But Halberstam wisely focuses on the history of these teammates, their human qualities (both good and bad), and the dynamics and depth of their friendships. Perhaps because young people are at the beginning of a lifetime of forming friendships, this book seemed to work with them, for it ranked third among the assigned texts, behind only *Shoeless Joe* and *The Natural*.

Although the teachers have taken these student reactions into account each time they plan the course they continue to use *The Celebrant* and *Bang the Drum Slowly* despite their low ratings relative to the other works, because of their literary quality and the questions they pose; the challenge is to find more effective ways to teach these apparently less accessible novels.

Writing Assignments and Examinations

In keeping with the course goals, when the teachers began they wanted the students to focus on the reading itself and have an enjoyable experience rather than be concerned with examinations. But obviously an evaluative instrument was needed. The instructors decided to assign a "thought quiz" that required the writing of a short essay at the beginning of the discussion of each work in order to provide an incentive for the students to read the material. In addition, students were required to submit three formal writing assignments. The first one focused on personal writing by having them relate an aspect of their background or experience with the game of baseball, and was intended as a transition into the next assignment, a more academic essay in which they analyzed one of the works read in the course. The third piece was a creative work in which the student wrote a poem, a short story, or a personal essay on some feature of the game. There were no examinations that first time around; later courses included examinations and dropped the creative writing assignment.

As the teachers read the three groups of papers, they realized that the essays in which the students focused on their personal history with the game were the most energetic and possessed the best writing. This assignment has therefore been carried over into each of the subsequent times the course has been taught, always coming as the first formal writing assignment. The instructors suggest that students focus on a particular game that was memorable, an individual coach they especially liked (or disliked), a funny (or sad) incident, a fellow player who stood out in their memory, or their overall experience in playing the game. For the most part, the students dive into this assignment with energy and creativity and come up with some very good writing. The course now requires two papers–one the personal history with the game and the other one something literary and more academic.

The academic papers have varied widely in quality. The English majors (usually there are a few in each class) naturally do the best, but the instructors believe there is value in having general education students try their hands at literary analysis even if it is their first effort. The process of thinking about and analyzing a text is a valuable skill, useful in many disciplines and vocations. Given the wide range of student abilities this assignment is best accompanied by careful instruction, including a limited focus ("don't try and cover everything") and specific suggestions ("pick and analyze a major character with whom you resonated—what actions shape this character and why, etc.").

Following the students' suggestions in their class evaluations, the teachers reduced the total number of works in the second and third versions of the course, spending more time on each individual text. As it was discovered that more structure was needed for general education students, rather than the instructors saying, "Please read this entire work for next week," as was done the first time the class was taught, each book is now broken down into reading increments of about fifty to seventy pages per class period. In addition, on most days each student receives a photocopied page with two or three study questions regarding the next period's assignment, which encourages them to think about their reading and interact with the text in ways that may be new to them; they are to write about one paragraph in response to each question. For example, regarding the Harris volume the students are asked to describe the characteristics of Henry Wiggins's "voice" as he tells the story, and to comment on what that voice contributes to the novel. The teachers collect these take-home quiz sheets at the beginning of the next class period and often begin the day's discussion by asking the students to tell how they answered these questions.

The pedagogical intention of these take-home quizzes is twofold. First, they provide an incentive for the students to actually read the text prior to class, a difficult-to-achieve objective among students for whom so much other media competes for their increasingly short attention spans. The act of reading itself, which might have been assumed in a previous time, cannot be taken for granted today, particularly for general education students. Second, these study questions and the subsequent classroom discussions are also intended to introduce students to increasingly sophisticated ways to think about and respond to texts without also burdening them with literary theory. The teachers believe strongly that there is value in teaching those universal elements of the interpretive process which are common to most reading situations and that many literate adults take for granted. Thus, they want students to see these questions as aids to deepen and enrich their reading experience, encouraging them to reflect on the text, including its structure, its clues in such elements as character and plot, its literary and historical allusions, and how these various elements work together to enhance the pleasure of the reading experience.

Despite an initial reluctance to incorporating examinations, the instructors soon discovered that the students needed this additional layer of structure to encourage them to consider the literary works in their entirety, rather than only in isolated segments. Therefore, midterm and final essay examinations are now included with such questions as the following:

1. Discuss how Doris Kearns Goodwin interweaves personal history, baseball history and national history into her book *Wait Till Next Year*. Show specific examples of each and note also how the totality of these experiences shaped the person that Goodwin was becoming.
2. Compare and contrast the two main characters, Matty and Eli, in *The Celebrant*. What qualities make each character into the kind of person they are? How are they similar? How are they different? What actions do they take that seem to be an outworking of who they are as persons?

From the beginning the instructors have included both the books *The Natural* and *Shoeless Joe* and their film versions. The obvious question was raised in both instances: how do the books and movies both differ and remain the same? In other words, how do the two mediums deal with the same subject? In the case of *The Natural*, there are the strikingly different endings to the book and the movie, which prompt the natural (no pun intended) question: why the difference and how does it change the meaning of the work? This question has appeared in a variety of ways: as an exam question, as the subject of a short paper, and as the basis of a classroom discussion, all with positive results. But the teachers try to go beyond the obvious differences to find other deeper, more subtle similarities and differences as the literary text is transformed into film.

With these various assignments, the grading breakdown is as follows: 20 percent—Paper #1 (personal history); 20 percent—Paper #2 (literary analysis); 30 percent—Homework (daily study questions, quizzes, and brief writing assignments); 15 percent—Midterm Exam; 15 percent—Final Exam.

Adding Sight and Sound

As noted at the outset of this essay, stimulating and maintaining student interest is a major challenge in general education courses. In addition to providing a variety of types of reading along with film versions of some of the works, the teachers have supplemented the literary texts with activities that not only provide periodic changes in the class focus but also link baseball and baseball literature to other aspects of American culture. Documentary videos offer both visual images and insightful commentary that stimulate student interest. For the first class period of the semester, before students have begun reading any assigned texts, American baseball is introduced through showing a portion of "Inning 1: Our Game" of Ken Burns's television documentary *Baseball*. This film has proved useful both in broadening the perspective of students already acquainted with the "national pastime" and introducing international students to the game's significance as a cultural phenomenon. *The Glory of Their Times*, a documentary based on the Ritter volume of the same name, is shown while the class is discussing *The Celebrant*, and provides not only pictures of Christy Mathewson and other players, but offers the students the opportunity to hear descriptions of early twentieth-century baseball through the voices of the players themselves. Later in the semester, during discussion of Goodwin's *Wait Till Next Year,* the teachers use a section of Burns's "Inning 5: Shadow Ball," which examines the Negro Leagues and Jackie Robinson's entrance into the major leagues, to provide perspective for Goodwin's memories about being a fan of the Brooklyn Dodgers of the late 1940s and 1950s. The photographs and film of Ebbets Field and such players as Robinson, Pee Wee Reese, and Roy Campanella, who figure significantly in Goodwin's book, as well as comments by Goodwin herself, also help bring the text alive for the students.

When Philip Bess, an architect with particular interest in baseball stadiums and author of *City Baseball Magic*, was a member of the university faculty (he now teaches at Notre Dame), he regularly made a presentation to the students on the development of baseball stadium architecture. With illustrating slides, he examined the evolution of the "green cathedrals" within which baseball is played, demonstrating the many influences–environmental, commercial, and artistic–that have shaped stadium design and how the resulting structures have influenced the fans' perspective on the game. While this lecture helped students see stadiums as works of architecture rather than just buildings for viewing a game, it also contributed to their understanding of the unique appeal of Ebbets Field and Fenway Park, which play significant roles in some of the literature they were reading.

Music has also provided an opportunity to link themes that appear in the literary texts with a medium familiar to students and it is included in two class periods. Although the teachers have used a variety of songs during the years they have taught this course, several selections, chosen for their relevance to the literature-based themes discussed in class, have emerged as "standards." Baseball's impact on individual fans and the shaping of their memories appears in Tom Russell's "Sunny's Diner," which deals with the Dodgers leaving Brooklyn, and John McCutcheon's childhood memories of "World Series 57." Paul Stookey's "Right Field," Christine Lavin's "Ballad of a Ball Game," and John Fogerty's "Centerfield" reveal the frustrations of individuals with limited athletic ability who still want to be part of the game. Childhood fascination with baseball cards and their more recent commercialization appear in Steve Vozzolo's "My Mother Threw Mine Away." Mostly ballads in the folk idiom, these songs offer opportunities to discuss themes such as coming of age, disappointment, and memory that also appear in the literature that students are reading. Because of its iconic status, students also listen to "Take Me Out to the Ballgame," with all the verses, as performed by Carly Simon. Although most American students are acquainted with this song, few have heard anything more than the chorus.

On the last day of class, the final activities include "Casey at the Bat." James Earl Jones's dramatic reading of this poem has proven to be an effective way of presenting this piece of Americana. Listening to the poem also provides an opportunity to talk briefly about the newspaper verse that was popular in the nineteenth century and its differences from the more self-consciously literary poetry examined in class. To show how this poem has taken on a life of its own in American culture, the teachers close the period with Garrison Keillor's parody. Although the course has dealt with many serious themes, these versions of "Casey" remind both teachers and students that ultimately baseball provides enjoyment to both participants and onlookers and thereby enriches the lives of all.

This course in baseball literature seems like a novelty to many students, a dream too good to be true. Yet, by emphasizing textual analysis and an interdisciplinary approach to the subject, it seems to have successfully met the goals for teaching literature to the general student. Experience has demonstrated, however, that these individuals need a structured series of reading and writing assignments, focused classroom discussions, and examinations. Periodic use of related films, musical recordings, and other activities helps maintain their interest throughout the semester. The many positive comments that students have written in their evaluations of the course suggest that they have benefited from it.

Works Cited (Books)

Bess, Philip. *City Baseball Magic: Plain Talk and Uncommon Sense about Cities and Baseball Parks.* Saint Paul, MN: Knothole, 1999.
Bjarkman, Peter C., ed. *Baseball & the Game of Life.* New York: Random House, Vintage, 1990.
Boswell, Thomas. *Why Time Begins on Opening Day.* New York: Penguin, 1984.
Dawidoff, Nicholas. *Baseball: A Literary Anthology.* New York: Library of America, 2002.
Goodwin, Doris Kearns. *Wait Till Next Year: A Memoir.* New York: Simon & Schuster, 1997.
Greenberg, Eric Rolfe. *The Celebrant.* Lincoln: University of Nebraska Press, 1983.
Halberstam, David. *Summer of '49.* New York: Perennial Classics, 1989.
____. *The Teammates.* New York: Hyperion, 2003.
Hall, Donald. *Fathers Playing Catch with Sons: Essays on Sport (Mostly Baseball).* San Francisco: North Point, 1985.
Harris, Mark. *Bang the Drum Slowly.* Lincoln, NE: University of Nebraska Press, 1956.
Holtzman, Jerome, ed. *Fielder's Choice: An Anthology of Baseball Fiction.* New York: Harcourt, Brace, Jovonovich, 1979.
Kahn, Roger. *The Boys of Summer.* New York: Perennial Classics, 1972.
Kinsella, W. P. *Shoeless Joe.* New York: Mariner, 1982.
Land, Gary, ed. *Growing Up with Baseball: How We Loved and Played the Game.* Lincoln: University of Nebraska Press, 2004.
Malamud, Bernard. *The Natural.* New York: Farrar, Straus & Giroux, 1952.
Nauen, Elinor. *Diamonds Are a Girl's Best Friend: Women Writers on Baseball.* Boston: Faber and Faber, 1994.
Ritter, Lawrence S. *The Glory of Their Times: The Story of Baseball Told by the Men Who Played It.* New York: Perennial Currents, 1984.

Recordings

Fogerty, John. "Centerfield." *Centerfield.* CD. Warner Brothers 25203–2, 1985.
The Glory of Their Times. CD. High Bridge Co., HBP 59237, 1998.
The Glory of Their Times. LP. Sonic Recording Products K-441, 1966.

Jones, James Earl, with Erich Kunzel and Cincinnati Pops Orchestra. "Casey at the Bat." *Play Ball!* CD. Telarc CD-80468, 1998.
Keillor, Garrison. "Casey at the Bat." *Diamond Cuts: Turning Two, Another Collection of Baseball Songs.* CD. Hungry for Music HFM 005, 1998.
Russell, Tom. "Sunny's Diner." Also John McCutcheon, "World Series 57"; Christine Lavin, "Ballad of a Ball Game." *Diamonds Cuts: Triple Play, a Third Compilation of Baseball Songs.* CD. Hungry for Music HFM007, 1999.
Simon, Carly. "Take Me Out to the Ball Game." *Baseball: A Film by Ken Burns*, Original Soundtrack Recording. CD. Electra Nonesuch 9 79340–2, 1994.
Stookey, Paul. "Right Field." *Peter, Paul and Mary: The Collection.* CD. Reader's Digest Music, OPCD-8505, Warner Special Products, 1998.
Vozzolo, Steve, and the Rookies. "My Mother Threw Mine Away." *I Love Baseball: Brand New Songs about the Grand Old Game.* CD. VOZZ-MAN Music/L & R Productions LVRMCD 100, 1994.

VHS/DVDs

Bang the Drum Slowly. Dir. John D. Hancock. VHS. Rhino Home Video RC 2062, 1956.
Baseball. Dir. Ken Burns. DVD. PBS Home Video 1415702438, 1994.
The Boys of Summer. VHS. VidAmerica 7017, 1983.
Field of Dreams. Dir. Phil Alden Robinson. DVD. Universal Home Video, 20166, 1998.
The Glory of Their Times. Dir. Bud Greenspan. VHS. Cappy Productions/*The Sporting News*, 1986.
The Natural. Dir. Barry Levinson. DVD. TriStar 0469, 1984.

Literature and Grammar

Baseball in the English Curriculum

(EDWARD J. RIELLY)

Several of my English courses involve baseball as a useful teaching tool, often as a significant part of the course content. The most extensive appearance of the sport in these courses occurs in Modern Literature, Baseball, and Society; but baseball also has its place in College Writing, the freshman composition course at Saint Joseph's College of Maine; The Nature and Application of English Grammar; and even occasionally in Creative Writing. The specific applications of America's national pastime in these courses include literature, grammar study, and composition.

Modern Literature, Baseball, and Society is a 300-level course open to English majors and other students who possess the interest and aptitude to take on an upper-level course. In reality, many students not especially fond of reading and not particularly skilled at interpreting literature do well in the course because of the high interest level of the material. Turning students onto reading is an important goal for English faculty, and baseball hits a home run with nonliterary students more often than virtually any other topic.

For example, a few years ago a senior taking the course stopped me in our cafeteria to let me know that he was enjoying reading the assigned books and, further, in one of those statements that tend to fluctuate between a compliment and a source of dismay, that this was the first time he had ever read the books required for a course. Every college certainly has its share of students who exhibit great ingenuity in avoiding assigned readings, but usually they keep the stratagem hidden from their professors. In this case, the young man, also a star slugger on the baseball team, seemed, however, to view his admission as a high compliment.

Several of the books and films in the course have been discussed by Professors Land and Gray in the essay immediately preceding this one— *The Celebrant, Bang the Drum Slowly, Shoeless Joe, The Natural* (novel and film), and the film *Field of Dreams*. Much of what they say about their experiences teaching these works parallels what occurs in my classroom, so attention here is better directed toward elements of this course not also present in theirs (or at least not discussed in their essay).

Modern Literature, Baseball, and Society is not envisioned as an introduction to literature. The assumption is that students either have the basics regarding plot, theme, symbolism, setting, character development, and other aspects of literature or can get up to speed in the early going. The primary focus is certainly on literature, but the course also emphasizes important aspects of American society, including race issues, immigration and cultural diversity, family relationships (especially parent and child), baseball as business, crime and the criminal justice system, and religion.

Each work, therefore, is approached as literature and as a reflection of one or more major aspects of American life. For example, *The Celebrant*, given its plot and characters, naturally leads to consideration of immigrants' responses to baseball and the sport as an agent of integration into American culture. The religious experience and parent-child relations are two important considerations for most students as well as major subjects in *Shoeless Joe* and *Field of Dreams*.

The film *Eight Men Out* has proved to be a successful addition to Modern Literature, Baseball, and Society. A well-acted, tightly constructed, and generally accurate depiction of the 1919 Black Sox scandal, the film is part of a 1919 unit in the course that includes *Shoeless Joe* and *Field of Dreams*. While Kinsella's novel *Field of Dreams* and the film version starring Kevin Costner, James Earl Jones, and Burt Lancaster present a similar approach to Shoeless Joe and his teammates, *Eight Men Out*, based on the book of the same title by Eliot Asinof, offers a firm grounding for students in what actually occurred.

Race relations is a major topic in the course, and the role of Jackie Robinson receives considerable discussion. Here and on other occasions during the semester, students watch segments from Ken Burns' documentary *Baseball*. The segment entitled "The National Pastime," also labeled the "6th Inning" of the documentary, depicts Robinson's integration of organized baseball. The "5th Inning," or "Shadow Ball," chronicles the history of the Negro Leagues. In the earliest versions of the course, students read the novel *The Bingo Long Traveling All-Stars and Motor Kings* by William Brashler. Although one of the better baseball novels, it gave way in more recent offerings of the course to August Wilson's play *Fences*. Adding one of the finest plays by one of America's greatest playwrights certainly did not lower the quality of the reading list, and it added another important dimension—drama. With its antagonistic relationship between father (Troy Maxson) and son (Cory), and Troy's betrayal of his wife (Rose), the story presents family situations well within the knowledge if not the personal experiences of current students. In addition, Troy's baseball background and his resentment of younger African-American players who received the major league opportunity he was denied invite consideration of the history of Negro league ball and the refusal of white organized baseball to admit African Americans into the sport. The play is the first literary selection that students read in the course because having students read the play aloud draws them into active participation before they can settle into a comfortable passivity.

However, the very first selections that students read are essays from *Baseball and American Culture: Across the Diamond*, a collection of essays on ways in which baseball interfaces with aspects of American culture. The book, edited by the author of this essay, consists of essays written by a distinguished group of individuals from across the United States, many of them college professors, and all of them highly knowledgeable about baseball's importance within American culture.

Students read two or three essays at a time at five points in the semester. Some of the essays yield classroom discussions, but all of them help to give students a broader context for baseball as America's national pastime. Quizzes over the essays undoubtedly help to encourage close reading, even of those essays not discussed in class.

Students read poetry from the collection *Line Drives: 100 Contemporary Baseball Poems*, edited by Brooke Horvath and Tim Wiles, the latter the director of research at the National Baseball Hall of Fame and Museum. Offering many excellent poems, the collection also includes a nice balance of men and women poets as well as both easily recognized and relatively unknown writers.

The approach to music has varied, from setting aside specific classes for songs to working them in from time to time. Whatever the approach used in a specific iteration of the course, the songs vary from the baseball standard "Take Me Out to the Ball Game" to modern baseball classics, including "Right Field," "It's a Beautiful Day for a Ball Game," "Centerfield," and "[You've Got to Have] Heart" (from the musical *Damn Yankees*). A variety of other songs also make their way into the course, such as Simon and Garfunkel's "Mrs. Robinson," with its reference to Joe DiMaggio; and the cowboy ballad "Streets of Laredo," whose lyrics supply the title to Mark Harris's novel *Bang the Drum Slowly*, which is on the students' reading list.

Perhaps the most unusual dimension of this course, among other courses that employ baseball, is the inclusion of service-learning. Students may select the service-learning option instead of two papers, the first an examination of a significant aspect of the life of someone important in the history of baseball, the second an imaginative dialogue between two people important in baseball (one from before 1950, the other after 1950).

Students who opt for service-learning work at least twenty hours in an after-school site run by the Portland (Maine) Housing Authority. They keep a journal and write a reflection essay at the conclusion of their service. These sites are established for students from elementary grades through high school to receive tutorial help or simply to do homework in a supervised setting. Many of the students (including a majority of students at some of the sites) are either immigrants or, more likely, the children of immigrants. Many of their parents came to Maine from Southeast Asia or Africa. The connection with Modern Literature, Baseball, and Society is the expanding globalization of baseball, including addition of the World Baseball Classic in March 2006. Students in the course have the opportunity to learn more about other cultures and share their own cultural interests, including baseball, through interaction with the youngsters that they assist.

Modern Literature, Baseball, and Society, however, is not the only course in which my students encounter baseball. In both College Writing and The Nature and Application of English Grammar (the latter a course developed for English majors in Secondary Education), a game that I devised, grammar baseball, proves an enjoyable and effective way to teach and learn grammar.

At both levels, the approach and rules are constant, with only the level of difficulty (one might say, the level of play) varying. The overall purpose of grammar baseball is to help students improve their grammar and writing. The game demands not only memorizing and understanding, but also applying. To translate grammar study into improved writing, students must consistently apply what they study, and this method fits nicely into that requirement.

The specific goals of the game depend on what the students are working on at the time: types of sentences, subject complements, diagramming, use of modifiers, or tenses, to cite a few possibilities. In The Nature and Application of English Grammar, we also have future-teacher-oriented goals in mind. The students know that they need a good grasp of grammar in order to teach it. The game also encourages the prospective teachers to realize the value of making learning more enjoyable for their future students.

If this is the first time for grammar baseball in the course, I go over the rules. If we have played it before, the students not only remember the rules but also probably have been asking me when they can play it again. That enthusiasm exists at each level, as pronounced, if not more so, in the upper-level grammar course as in the freshman College Writing.

Students are divided into two teams. Given the location of Saint Joseph's College in Southern Maine (Boston Red Sox country, with Boston's Double-A team, the Portland Sea Dogs, about thirty minutes away), the two teams become the Red Sox and the Yankees.

It is important to be sure that the two rosters are reasonably well balanced, a condition achieved by such basic approaches as counting off odd and even, rather than permitting students to choose their team. We may keep the same team rosters for a second game, often a "chance to get even," but we rearrange the rosters later in the semester. Then the two teams prepare their batting orders, and we are ready to begin, with my role being to present the question or problem (throwing the pitch, we might metaphorically say) and functioning as the umpire.

A homemade deck of cards created from index cards (each containing an annotation such as "single," "double," "triple," "home run," or "walk") is all the equipment needed except for a board on which students will write. The "pitches" are usually written out ahead of time on a sheet of paper. For example, if we are working on improving writing style and our knowledge of grammar through greater facility with different types of sentences, the pitches may be "simple sentence," "compound sentence," "complex sentence," and "compound-complex sentence." If the class is working on diagramming to understand objects and complements, the pitches will reflect concepts relevant to those structures.

The first batter goes to the board (in a high-tech classroom, students might use laptops with the sentence projecting on a screen), and I throw the first pitch: simple sentence. The student writes a simple sentence on the board. If the batter receives any help from a teammate, the batter is out. If the batter makes any error at all, he or she is out—so long as a member of the opposing team catches the error. This requirement keeps members of the other team sharply focused, which is to say, learning. Teammates of the batter are equally focused, watching and hoping for an error-free performance, which results in a hit or walk. When the batter performs the task correctly, or makes a mistake not recognized by the other team, I pull a card from the deck, the batter gaining whatever is pulled. As is normal with baseball, the team gets three outs.

As the inning progresses, base runners already on base advance at a uniform rate, e.g., two bases if a batter hits a double, one base with a single. There are no fielding errors in the deck of cards, errors being limited to mistakes at the board by the hitting team or by the other team's failure to note a mistake. The game thus remains simple, excluding many other aspects of baseball games, such as stolen bases and wild pitches.

A typical one-period game in College Writing lasts about two or three innings. Students in The Nature and Application of English Grammar usually know grammar better and make fewer mistakes, thus prolonging innings. The students therefore may not get beyond two innings, although it is possible, of course, to extend the game over more than one class meeting.

Finally, baseball often appears in the Creative Writing course that I teach. Students are given types of compositions to write—such as a short story, sonnet, free-verse poem, children's picture-book manuscript—but the subject is always open, with students encouraged to write about what they know well. For many, that includes baseball.

Submitting material for possible publication is one of the assignments in Creative Writing, and my students become acquainted with some fine magazines that publish baseball literature, such as *Spitball* and *Elysian Fields Quarterly*. Sharing my writing with my writing students helps to create a useful bond as well as adding a bit of additional credibility to what they hear from me. Along with other writing of mine, they thus get to hear some of my baseball poetry.

So baseball has a prominent place in the English curriculum at Saint Joseph's College, at least in this instructor's courses. Baseball, carefully presented, can be effective pedagogy. It also has inspired a great amount of excellent literature in a wide array of genres. To incorporate baseball into the curriculum, therefore, is far from trying to fit a square peg into a round hole. Instead, it fits, one might say, like a glove—like a baseball glove, worn, comfortable, and highly useful.

Works Cited

Asinof, Eliot. *Eight Men Out: The Black Sox and the 1919 World Series.* New York: Holt, 1963.
Baseball. Dir Ken Burns. PBS, 1994.

Brashler, William. *The Bingo Long Traveling All-Stars and Motor Kings.* 1973. Urbana: University of Illinois Press, 1993.
Cash, Johnny. "Streets of Laredo." *American IV: The Man Comes Around.* American Recordings, 2003.
"Centerfield" and "Take Me Out to the Ball Game." *Play Ball!* Telarc, 1998.
Eight Men Out. Dir. John Sayles. Orion, 1988.
Field of Dreams. Dir. Phil Alden Robinson. Universal, 1989.
Greenberg, Eric Rolfe. *The Celebrant.* 1983. New York: Penguin Books, 1986.
Harris, Mark. *Bang the Drum Slowly.* 1956. Lincoln: University of Nebraska Press, 1984.
"Heart." *Damn Yankees.* RCA Victor, 1988.
Horvath, Brooke, and Tim Wiles, eds. *Line Drives: 100 Contemporary Baseball Poems.* Carbondale: Southern Illinois University Press, 2002.
"It's a Beautiful Day for a Ball Game" and "Right Field." *Baseball's Greatest Hits: Let's Play II.* Rhino, 1990.
Kinsella, W. P. *Shoeless Joe.* 1982. New York: Ballantine, 1996.
Malamud, Bernard. *The Natural.* 1952. New York: HarperCollins, 2000.
The Natural. Dir. Barry Levinson. Tri-Star Pictures, 1984.
Rielly, Edward J., ed. *Baseball and American Culture: Across the Diamond.* New York: Haworth, 2003.
Simon, Paul, and Art Garfunkel. "Mrs. Robinson." *The Concert in Central Park.* Warner Bros., 1982.
Wilson, August. *Fences.* New York: Plume/Penguin, 1986.

Native American History

More than a Game—Teaching American Indian History through Baseball

(C. RICHARD KING)

I don't like to say this, but in those days, when I was young, I was considered a foreigner. I didn't belong. I was an Indian.
—John Tortes "Chief" Meyers (Ritter, 172)

To many students and citizens alike, Native American history unfolds as either a romantic drama in which once proud people defend a homeland and way of life against the fateful forces of progress or a tragic tale of the inevitable demise and destruction of primitive cultures by modern America, at once more technologically advanced and culturally sophisticated. These narratives are familiar from countless movies, television programs, and history textbooks, not to mention childhood games like cowboys and Indians, sundry celebrations of local, regional and national identity, and the symbols and spectacles associated with American Indian sport mascots. Unfortunately, such stories are stereotypical at best, patently false and racist at worst. In fact, far from being exotic curiosities trapped in the past or defined by their spiritual wisdom, Native Americans have always actively engaged modern life, most often negotiating its promises and problems from disadvantaged and marginalized positions (Deloria). In fact, over the past half-century, indigenous peoples in North America have experienced a cultural and political renaissance, regularly drawing upon their encounters with modernity to reclaim territory and tradition and reassert rights and identities (Nagel).

Clearly, teachers of American Indian studies face a daunting task: determining how one can simultaneously expose the injustices and traumas that have shaped the Native American experience while also clearing a space in which the enduring vibrance of indigenous peoples might shine. Baseball, I have found, offers a unique opportunity to offer a complex and unexpected account of American Indian cultures and histories. At the same time, it inspires many students, a number of whom would be inclined to resist, to care about the triumphs and tragedies of Native Americans and to seriously engage difficult issues like racism, cultural survival, and social change.

In this essay, I want to discuss some of the ways that teaching about American Indians and baseball at once illuminates the Native American experience and the sport and its unique history. Specifically, I review how I have taught about indigenous peoples and sport. First, I describe in a broader course on Native American history the role baseball has played. Next, I briefly consider how American Indian baseball might fit into a course on the historical and cultural significance of America's pastime. Finally, I present a module designed to foreground the past and present forms of racism encountered by indigenous peoples in baseball.

American Indian History

I routinely incorporate baseball into my introduction to the Native American Studies course. In this section, I describe the class and then detail the place of baseball in it. The course explores the cultures and histories of Native America. It cannot offer an exhaustive account, but seeks to present an array of perspectives on key issues. It concentrates on the identities and experiences of Native Americans during the nineteenth and twentieth centuries, examining the historical practices and sociocultural contexts central to the Euro-American colonization of North America and germane to Indian-White relations. It emphasizes a set of overlapping themes, including social identity, domination and resistance, and cultural change. It discusses these themes within an interdisciplinary framework, integrating anthropological, historical, and indigenous perspectives. At the same time, it offers a range of theoretical approaches. An effort has been made to address the complex, common, and occasionally contradictory experiences of Native Americans. To this end, illustrative examples have been drawn from throughout North America.

The course begins by working through stereotypes about American Indians while introducing basic concepts. On this foundation, by looking at baseball we endeavor to understand the complex and unexpected worlds in which indigenous peoples have sought to live meaningful lives. With a greater appreciation of the complexities of social contexts and cultural analyses, we turn to ask whether the (Native) American history is best understood in terms of genocide. Here, we will be particularly interested in dispossession and displacement, extermination and assimilation. We close the semester with the resurgence of Native America, especially the reassertion of sovereignty, the emergence of activism, and the crystallization of a pan-Indian identity.

The initial two weeks lay a foundation for critical thinking by challenging misconceptions and stereotypes and then offering a comparative discussion of indigenous life (in all of its diversity) in 1492 and in the present. Against this background, we turn to baseball and questions of modernity, identity, and assimilation. We devote two weeks to the life and career of Pawnee ballplayer Mose Yellowhorse. The key text during this period is Todd Fuller's *60 feet 6 Inches and Other Distances from Home: The Baseball Life of Mose Yellowhorse*, a quirky, nonlinear biography filled with care and insight that mixes poetry with prose, recollections of Pawnee elders with more conventional history, and local narratives about the pitcher with national media accounts. I typically ask students to write a review of Fuller's text, reminding them to think critically about its content and composition.

Few remember Yellowhorse, who pitched for the Arkansas Travelers, the Pittsburgh Pirates (1921–1922), and later Sacramento, but his triumphs and travails prove instructive, and Fuller's text is engaging and approachable. I like to use this book about baseball to tease out difficult issues: acculturation (boarding schools, going pro, succeeding and failing, and late-life alcoholism), biased media coverage, the popular fascination with Indians (Yellowhorse performed in a Wild West show as a kid and later in life was featured in a Dick Tracy comic), and Pawnee pride in themselves reflected through a local hero (palpable in remembrances and stories entrusted to Fuller). What truly distinguishes Fuller's work, however, is his sensitive incorporation of Pawnee storytelling structures. In the end, he crafts a wonderfully dynamic mixed-genre text that challenges students to rethink what they think they know about American Indians. Indeed, Yellowhorse is an unexpected Indian, out of place, doing things not part of common knowledge, and living in and out and against the modern world.

I like to incorporate baseball for a number of reasons. First, Yellowhorse, as Fuller renders him, insists that students recognize Native Americans as people—people who struggle, who love, who succeed, who lose. Second, in *60 feet 6 Inches and Other Distances from Home*, baseball emerges as a gateway to opportunity, as a battlefield upon which minor race wars were routinely fought, as means to craft oneself, and as a source of pride. Finally, teaching about American Indians and baseball forces students to begin to grasp the complexities of the Native American experience. Together, these elements allow me to ground and amplify subsequent discussions about the violence of cultural change and the survival and revival of native nations in North America.

Indian Baseball

Baseball is not simply America's pastime, it has also become an indigenous sport. Over the past century, American Indians have excelled in the big leagues and perhaps more importantly have brought the game into their communities and homes. Indeed, Native Americans have taken the game and made it their own. The following module would work well in a survey of baseball and society or a course on indigenous sport in North America. In the former, it might usefully follow discussions of the pastoral ethos and modern life, spiritual beliefs in mainstream baseball, or cultural imperialism in the history of the sport. In the latter, a type of course that I teach, it is a nice bridge between a consideration of native games like lacrosse and the participation of American Indians in contemporary athletics.

At center of this one-day exercise stands J.R. Fox's "Pueblo Baseball: A New Use for Old Witchcraft." Written in 1961, this brief ethnographic case study asserts that far from being a marker of assimilation, acquiescence, or imperialism, the play of baseball among the Pueblo is better understood as an instance of appropriation, adaptation, and reinvention. In this context, cultural creativity and the insistence of convention trumps change and conformity. Specifically, Fox demonstrates that Pueblo peoples have incorporated baseball into an existing cosmology and that the game actually encourages the retention of spiritual beliefs and behaviors, a set of magical practices and precepts he labels witchcraft.

Typically, I ask students to write brief answers to a set of questions before reading: What does it mean for Native Americans to play baseball? What are the implications for retaining and reproducing their cultures?

What does this incorporation tell us about baseball? (Obviously, these would be modified if the lesson were meant to foreground spirituality or cultural imperialism.) After completing the reading, I ask them to return to these questions, reflecting on their previous assumptions and emerging understanding.

Anti-Indian Racism

Baseball has also proven useful to work through past and present forms of racism experienced by Native Americans. In introductory courses devoted to sport and society, no less than those on ethnic studies, I have found the juxtaposition of the experiences of American Indian ballplayers with the current controversy over mascots, particularly its prominence in professional baseball, to be especially fecund.

I have designed this module to take up three class periods, or a week, in the courses in which I have used it. The content moves from past to present but remains focused on anti-Indian racism and how it has (or has not) changed over the past century (Cook-Lynn).

For the first class session, I have students read primary documents by two renowned native ballplayers: Lawrence S. Ritter's interview with Chief Meyers and Rudy York's "Letter to MY Son." Both Meyers and York talk about the prejudice and discrimination they experienced on and off the field. These are short and accessible readings and nicely facilitate good discussions. For more historically minded instructors, these works might be paired with articles by Thompson and Powers-Beck. I endeavor to stress common elements: being seen as a foreigner, having to work twice as hard, enduring racial slurs, and being demeaned by fans. I push students to consider context, contrasting the experiences of Native American and African American ballplayers.

The second class period focuses attention on Louis Sockalexis and the Cleveland Indians' Chief Wahoo. After reading essays by Feldman and Staurowsky, class discussion probes first the career of the Penobscot player, stressing his achievements as well as how mainstream society treated him. Against this backdrop, students explore recent doubt cast upon whether Sockalexis was in fact the inspiration for the team's name change. Finally, students interrogate the meaning of Chief Wahoo and the possibility that he (dis)honors the memory of Sockalexis or at the very least runs counter to the professed intention of the Cleveland baseball team.

The final class session of this module centers directly on the controversy over Native American mascots, seeking to make sense of the various arguments advanced by critics and defenders of the use of America Indian names and symbols in sport. Students concentrate on responses to a survey conducted by *USA Today*: Should the Cleveland Indians change their mascot if Native Americans are offended? In class, students read an analysis of the survey, "Arguing Over Images: Native Americans and Race," and work through its claims about race, culture, and history. The students are given the following instructions:

> Before reading this essay, write down every word, image, or sentiment that comes to mind when thinking about Native American mascots, such as the Cleveland Indians' Chief Wahoo, Chief Illiniwek of the University of Illinois, or the Washington Redskins. Then, after reading the essay, individually analyze your earlier responses. As a class, we will identify and interpret themes and patterns that emerged from this exercise.

At the conclusion of the third class period, an effort is made through discussion to draw out the key components of anti-Indian racism and how these have changed and remained the same over time.

Conclusion

I have tried to suggest some ways to teach about Native Americans and baseball. I have outlined three different ways to incorporate America's pastime into courses dealing with American Indians. First, I discussed a historic approach concerned with the indigenous athletes in the early years of American baseball, illuminating the promises and pitfalls of modern life. Second, I described an anthropological approach attentive to cultural change and adaptation. Third, I emphasized that baseball, particularly the ongoing controversy over the use of American Indian imagery, provides a powerful means to examine anti-Indian racism.

Understanding baseball to be a contact zone, borderland, or middle ground, teachers can offer unexpected understandings of American Indians and America's pastime. In doing so, they afford an opportunity to dispel popular stereotypes. Perhaps more importantly, faculty can offer a unique occasion to interrogate heritage and tradition, exchanges and appropriations, assimilation and resistance, race relations and ethnic identity. Integrating these issues into more courses promises to expand student appreciation of the means and meanings of sport and of the place of indigenous peoples in multicultural America.

Works Cited

Cook-Lynn, Elizabeth. *Anti-Indianism in North America: A Voice from Tatekeya's Earth.* Urbana: University of Illinois Press, 2001.

Deloria, Philip J. *Indians in Unexpected Places.* Lawrence: University Press of Kansas, 2004.

Feldman, Jay. "The Rise and Fall of Louis Sockalexis." *Baseball Research Journal* 15 (1986): 39–42.
Fox, J. R. "Pueblo Baseball: A New Use for Old Witchcraft." *American Journal of Folklore* 74 (1961): 9–16
Fuller, M. Todd. *60 feet 6 Inches and Other Distances from Home: The Baseball life of Mose Yellowhorse*. Duluth: Holy Cow Press, 2002.
King, C. Richard. "Arguing over Images: Native American Mascots and Race." *Race/Gender/Media: Considering Diversity Across Audiences, Content, and Producers*. Ed. Rebecca Ann Lind. Boston: AB-Longman, 2003. 68–76.
King, C. Richard, and Charles F. Springwood, eds. *Team Spirits: The Native American Mascot Controversy*. Lincoln: University of Nebraska Press, 2001.
Nagel, Joane. *American Indian Ethnic Renewal: Red Power and the Resurgence of Identity and Culture*. Oxford: Oxford University Press, 1996.
Powers-Beck, Jeffrey. "'Chief': The American Indian Integration of Baseball, 1897–1945." *American Indian Quarterly* 25:4 (Fall 2001): 508–538.
Ritter, Lawrence S. "Chief Meyers." *The Glory of Their Times: The Story of the Early Days of Baseball Told by the Men Who Played It*. New, enlarged edition. New York: William Morrow, 1984.
Staurowsky, Ellen J. "An Act of Honor or Exploitation? The Cleveland Indians' Use of the Louis Francis Sockalexis Story." *Sociology of Sport Journal* 15:4 (1998): 299–316.
Thompson, Stephen I. "The American Indian in the Major Leagues." *Baseball Research Journal* 12: 1–7.
York, Rudy. "A Letter to My Son." *The Fireside Book of Baseball*. Ed. Charles Einstein. New York: Simon and Schuster, 1956.

Philosophy

Baseball and Philosophy?
"Let's Go to the Video Tape!"

(ERIC BRONSON)

"What are they speeding?" Marina asked curiously.

"*Speeding?*"

Marina pointed to her mouth and mimed a projectile coming from her mouth.

"Oh, spitting," I corrected her. "They're spitting *semechki*. All baseball players do."

The class broke up in laughter. Most of the laughter was no doubt due to my poor pronunciation of *semechki*, the Russian word for sunflower seeds. But also, I am sure, there was a genuinely giddy feeling pervading the classroom at the realization that this seemingly exotic American game shared something indisputably in common with their own culture. Russians love sunflower seeds, too, though they are a lot more careful about disposing of their shells.

This scene played out in a political philosophy class at Barnaul's Altai State University, a large Siberian university near the edge of the Altai Mountains, just north of Mongolia. A tape of game five of the 2000 subway series between the Yankees and Mets was showing on the television. In truth, it was hard to see which players were spitting out sunflower seeds, and which players were just plain spitting.

As a visiting professor I was teaching two courses in political philosophy, one on the Cold War that largely focused on politicians and strategic policies, and this second class that leaned more toward cultural and sociological differences between capitalist and communist societies of the twentieth century. The argument was a standard one: capitalist societies like the United States tend to emphasize the individual over the family or community structure, in contrast to the former communist Russian and Chinese cultures. To prove the point, we went over the Bill of Rights and discussed popular issues like gun control, abortion, and police brutality, all issues that centered on individual rights. We read short stories like John Updike's "A&P" and Ernest Hemingway's "A Clean Well-Lighted Place" that touch on the alienation of lone individuals confronting their meaningless futures. To the literature we added some of the poetry of Robert Frost, where again the individual is placed on a large and lonely landscape with only his own wistful reflections able to see him through. Finally, we ended with baseball.

Many wiser commentators have noted baseball's individualistic slant. Yes, it is a team game, and team chemistry does sometimes play a role, but it is the individual that always seems to stand out most. Is that at least part of our attraction to the 2004 World Series Red Sox championship team? They could not play defense and hardly ever moved runners over. They were known endearingly as the "idiots" because individuals like Manny Ramirez and Pedro Martinez were unpredictable and unsteady, interrupting their stellar play with emotional breakdowns and concentration lapses that frequently cost their team. Boston's inspirational phrase of 2003, "cowboy up," evoked the lawlessness of the American Old West, when individuals had to arm themselves and stand up for their own beliefs, unmindful of the whims of their fragmented community.

More so than soccer, football, or hockey, baseball is a game that breaks itself down into individual parts. The 2000 World Series was about the Yankees and Mets, but it was also about Mike Piazza vs. Roger Clemens, Joe Torre vs. Bobby Valentine, the 7 train vs. the 4 train. Television close-ups of individual players appearing nervous or just spitting sunflower seeds helped drive this point home. When Mike Piazza hit his game-four home run blast, the class watched how the whole game stopped so that one person could jog around the bases while all the Queens faithful cheered him on. No other sport stops play so often to applaud particular individuals, and few other countries are as attracted to such sports.

Baseball, then, can be used as one example among many of how America's capitalist culture goes well with the individualism imbedded in its national pastime, and it is well worth a week's discussion in a political philosophy course that focuses on the Western world. It is a point that should not be overstated, though. We need to remember that baseball also enjoys widespread popularity in socialist Cuba. Japan, too, loves baseball but has rules in place to make it more of a team game. If rain prevents the team from coming out and stretching together, the entire game is cancelled. Sadaharu Oh, the great Japanese home run king, had Zen training to help him learn the value of selflessness. As philosopher Michael Brannigan writes, "In his autobiography, *A Zen Way of Baseball*, Oh attributes his swing and his ensuing success" to his batting coach, who "introduced Oh to the martial art forms of kendo and aikido, forms that clearly embody the spirit of Zen Buddhism" (224). Contrast Oh with American home run king Barry Bonds, who has his personal mini-lounge in the locker room and announces updates on his injured knee on his personal Web site before notifying the team. So perhaps we should say not baseball but *American* baseball is as individualistic as amassing wealth in the stock market, voting someone off reality shows like *Survivor* or *American Idol*, or simply shouting your "barbaric yawp over the rooftops of the world" *a la* American poet Walt Whitman (73).

And while America loves to see the selfless teams like the 2002 Anaheim Angels or 2003 Florida Marlins win championships without the inflated salaries and egos of bigger market teams, the higher ratings will always go to a more dysfunctional team like the Yankees or the Red Sox. Behind this attraction is a distinctly American ambivalence about following rules. The United States has a long history of establishing rules to make sense of the surrounding chaos. Many political scientists have pointed to the American Constitution, and the political philosophers who created it, as one reason for the quick ascension of American power in the world. Unlike the French and Russian Revolutions, the American Revolution did not immediately break down into a system of terror and intimidation. Instead, the rule of law saw the country through the early, uneasy days. As political philosophers like Alexis de Toqueville noted in the early nineteenth century, the rampant voluntary rule following in the East, and later in the Midwest, was highly unique in the world and worthy of much commendation. But such a precision to rules also carries a more negative side.

Our world gets dull. In the twentieth century, the rise of large American bureaucracies replaced the factory life and drew more middle class citizens into the nine-to-five (and later the eight to six) workday. More people trudge off to work and come back tired, ending the working day by watching the latest crime dramas on the couch or mindlessly firing darts in their local bar. In response to this dulling down of America is a genuine appreciation of the artists and athletes who break the rules. Standing side by side with the tradition of obedient rule-following is the love affair with the individualist. "Whoso would be a man must be a non-conformist," Ralph Waldo Emerson stated, warning against the rise of the modern bureaucrat (123).

To highlight this important philosophical point, I often turn to baseball. From Bernard Malamud's drunk, immoral protagonist in *The Natural* to the gleefully moronic individualists of Hollywood movies like *Major League* and *Bull Durham*, baseball fiction provides Americans with an outlet for rooting on outrageous characters who flout some of the very rules to which the rest of us feel bound. But while such movies help make an important point in the classroom, we in the teaching profession don't really need to rely on Hollywood. Whether they are real-life examples like Shoeless Joe Jackson dealing dangerously with the underworld, Babe Ruth insulting the power structure every chance he had, or Ted Williams spitting toward the sheltered media high above Fenway Park, the baseball athletes that best leave their mark on the American experience are the ones who flout the rules. Roger Kahn's *October Men* and Jeff Pearlman's *The Bad Boys Won!* are good books to use to showcase New Yorkers' fascination with people who break the rules and win despite, or because of, such public displays of nonconformity. Whether they are spitting, cursing, or taunting the opponents from the dugouts or the bleachers, baseball examples are great ways of getting students to think deeper about core American values like individualism and its equally American counterpoint, rule-following.

Back home in my Ethics classes at Berkeley College in New York City, we continuously return to the question of rule-following, and baseball examples can help students think through when it is ethical to break the rules. The classic case in Ethics is that of lying. Ask a class of college students how many of them follow the moral rule never to lie, and nearly all of them will raise their hands. But as we get deeper into it, more and more exceptions to the rule develop. If, for example, you are at a wake out of respect for the widow, and she asks you tearfully what you remember best of her husband, it is simply not ethical to tell her you thought he was cheap and conniving. If that is the truth, then clearly you should lie. Similarly, if a known terrorist asks where the nearest explosive store is, one would hope the person would again think up a convincing lie. The first two issues concern utilitarianism, a theory that endorses lying when it is for the greater good.

But I also like to give my Ethics class baseball examples and then the plot thickens. A pitcher will deceive the hitter about the upcoming pitch, and if asked directly, it seems reasonable to assume the pitcher will lie. The old hidden-ball trick works only when a fielder effectively lies to a runner about whether he threw the ball back or is still holding on to it. And yet, when Mark McGwire and Jason Giambi are asked about whether they have taken steroids, we expect them to tell the truth and judge them harshly when they lie. What is the difference between these lies? Baseball provides good fodder for getting Ethics students involved in a high-level discussion on the principles of lying.

Philosopher Mark Hamilton has a good essay on this theme which I sometimes use for the class. He writes that the first two kinds of lies (a pitcher's deception and the hidden-ball trick) "should be excused if they are told as part of strategy in a game.... This type of lying is expected and acting is part of the game. The participants, or those duped, have agreed in advance to be a part of a contest which could involve deception" (136). What students invariably conclude is that the expectations are what matter most. When one is expected to lie, then it usually is morally permissible. In the parameters of a baseball game, deception and lying are oftentimes part of the game and therefore not at all immoral. An umpire does not ask the hitter to call his own balls and strikes because he knows the batter will frequently lie. So if the batter says the ball grazed his bat, the umpire is not likely to be offended by the lie. On the other hand, in the context of a press conference, or a Senate hearing, it is neither morally permissible nor expected to lie. Therefore, when Giambi tells the world he never took steroids, and then later apologizes ambiguously, it becomes clear that he lied to the fans when they were expecting him to tell the truth. And though McGwire did not outright lie about his steroids use, he chose not to tell the whole truth when he was expected to come clean. It is through baseball examples that this important exception to the no lying rule best comes across. If you are a tired pitcher and the opposing manager asks how you are feeling, you should say you are doing great. If your own manager asks you the same question, you are expected to tell the truth.

Toward the end of my Ethics classes, I like to make the students defend unpopular arguments and thereby practice their skills in ethical reasoning. In 2004 and 2005, the issue of baseball players using steroids became particularly contentious. Everybody from *Sports Illustrated* reporters to the highest reaches of the American Congress said it was terrible for role models to gain such unfair advantages through steroid use. But why? The topic assigned to two opposing debate groups was to argue whether or not baseball players should be allowed to take steroids. The topic was chosen by the students but I made them switch sides, so the team defending the athletes secretly thought the steroid use was immoral. I made this switch to keep the students focused on the argument and so they would not simply fall back on emotional appeals or past experiences. There were three students per group and each group was given ten minutes, uninterrupted, to make its case. After the twenty minutes, the groups were allowed five minutes to argue back and forth before the entire class was allowed to sound off on both groups. Groups were also expected to use traditional ethical theories that were discussed in class.

Utilitarianism was one of two theories used in the debate. With utilitarian theories, one looks to see how the consequences affect everyone involved. Simply put, if the good consequences outweigh the bad consequences for the greatest number of people, it is a morally good act. If the bad consequences outweigh the good consequences, then one should avoid doing it. The argument for the students centered around who was being hurt by the consequences. Did the players who took steroids damage themselves physically? Perhaps, but as the students argued, this point is still largely disputed in the medical profession. Most negative effects seem likely to come after one stops taking the drugs and the body goes through a withdrawal period, not always necessarily severe. Were the fans hurt by the steroids? Certainly before the breaking of the balco scandal [that involved steroid use by professional athletes], more fans were drawn to the game, thanks in no small measure to McGwire's home run contest with Sammy Sosa in 1998. Taken then from a utilitarian perspective, the steroids issue is much less clear than we are accustomed to reading in the media.

In the debate, students also made Kantian arguments. Immanuel Kant is covered at some length in most college Ethics classes. For Kant an act is moral only if it is done from the motivation of duty, and not from self-interest. In other words, the important ethical question is not what a person *wants* to do, but what she *ought* to do. Kant's most famous development of following duty, the categorical imperative, states that an action is morally permissible only if one can universalize the rule that authorizes the action in question. It is a duty to act in a way that can be universalized, regardless of one's inclination or the benefits that may come as a consequence. Take a car thief, for example. Can the act of stealing cars be universalized? Of course not, for even the thief does not want anyone else stealing his car. Because the act cannot be universalized, it is the thief's duty not to steal. Back to baseball, the Kantian question that the students rightly ask is what would happen if everyone were allowed to take steroids. Can steroids be universalized? There would be more home runs, most likely. So many that perhaps the ballpark walls would need to be extended, much the same way the pitcher's mound was raised years ago. According to Kant's categorical imperative then, the biggest problem with a select few athletes taking steroids is that it gives them an unfair advantage. Were everyone allowed to take and have access to the steroids, the advantage would no longer be unfair. In fact, taking steroids would not give a ballplayer any advantage over any other athlete also able to take the drugs. Therefore, they argued, the taking of steroids could in fact be universalized without doing serious harm to the game itself.

The debate group opposed to steroid use, however, also articulated Kant's practical imperative, which is another formulation of Kantian duty. Kant also argues that it is an ethical duty to treat others as ends in themselves, and not as means to further an end. Once again, consequences are not relevant. In other words, killing one unwilling, innocent person to save twenty is not morally permissible. Unlike utilitarianism, Kant's ethics have little to do with causing the greatest amount of happiness to the greatest number of people. Instead, no person may be used as a means, even as a means to a greater good. While discussing suicide, Kant invoked the practical imperative, claiming that we should not use any bodies as a means to an end, not even our own bodies. When athletes take drugs to strengthen their muscles so they can hit more home runs, they are using their bodies for money and glory. Similar to a supermodel starving herself, a person's body is objectified as a thing that can be used. For Kant, such little regard for the human body could never be universalized and should therefore never be accepted morally. At least, that is how the argument went.

To tell you the truth, I do not know which side won the debate in our Ethics class. But the point was not really to come up with conclusive answers. Ultimately, bringing up baseball's steroids issue was meant only to get students working through utilitarianism and Kant's duty ethics (his categorical and practical imperatives). Utilitarian and Kantian arguments were used to argue both sides, and that helps the students understand the theories and how they can be applied in the world around them. The more entertaining the examples are, the more likely the class will take a lively interest in the theories discussed.

Of course, there are also pitfalls with using baseball examples in Political Philosophy and Ethics classes. The biggest concern is that baseball fans in the classroom will get too "into" the examples and ready themselves to make the same arguments they hear on ESPN, or at their local watering hole. For example, very quickly the class can break down into statistical arguments over particular players or tangentially related arguments on athletes' salaries and the interests of particular teams. But getting off the topic is a problem that professors have to deal with anytime they use real-life examples or show movies in the classroom. It is up to the particular professor to gently lead the discussion back to the philosophical issues at hand. When it comes to American values, or ethical issues like lying or steroid use, students can still be judged or graded on how well they apply these issues to the age-old philosophical ideals.

In the end, there is no good reason why baseball examples should not be used to make important philosophical points. In his great book on American Zen, Sean Murphy writes of a Zen teacher's visit to the Zen Mountain Monastery in upstate New York (194–95). The teacher, a great baseball fan, asked to be driven to the Baseball Hall of Fame in Cooperstown. The eager student who agreed to drive came back disappointed. He had hoped to learn about the profound mysteries of the world. When asked what he learned the driver replied, "Nothing!" Obviously he still had a long way to go on the path to enlightenment. He missed the point: "All they talked about was baseball!"

Works Cited

Brannigan, Michael. "Japanese Baseball and Its Warrior Ways." *Baseball and Philosophy*. Ed. Eric Bronson. Chicago: Open Court, 2004. 217–28.
Emerson, Ralph Waldo. "Self-Reliance." *Essays, Poems, and Addresses*. New York: Walter J. Black, 1941. 119–146.
Hamilton, Mark. "There's No Lying in Baseball (Wink, Wink)." *Baseball and Philosophy*. Ed. Eric Bronson. Chicago: Open Court, 2004. 126–38.
Kant, Immanuel. *Groundwork of the Metaphysics of Morals*. Trans. H.J. Patton. New York: Harper & Row, 1964. 65–99.
Kahn, Roger. *October Men*. Orlando: Harcourt, 2003.
Murphy, Sean. *One Bird, One Stone: 108 American Zen Stories*. New York: Renaissance, 2002. 194–195.
Pearlman, Jeff. *The Bad Guys Won! A Season of Brawling, Boozing, Bimbo-chasing, and Championship Baseball with Straw, Doc, Mookie, Nails, The Kid, and the Rest of the 1986 Mets, the Rowdiest Team Ever to Put on a New York Uniform—and Maybe the Best*. New York: HarperCollins, 2004.
Toqueville, Alexis de. *Democracy in America*. Trans. George Lawrence. New York: Harper & Row, 1969. 435–614.
Whitman, Walt. "Song of Myself." *Leaves of Grass*. New York: Bantam Books, 1983. 22–73.

Public Speaking

The Rhetoric of Baseball—Citizenship and the Public Speaking Classroom
(MICHAEL L. BUTTERWORTH)

Most introductory speech courses are designed around a core set of principles loosely borrowed from antiquity and modified to meet the demands of the modern world and market economy. While there is value in this approach, too often it reduces oratory to a highly formalized exercise in which technical skills are emphasized over creative and critical thinking. In our increasingly complex world, public speaking courses can benefit from a more complex engagement with their ancient tradition. Namely, understanding speech as rhetoric affords instructors the opportunity to think about public speaking as a performance of political awareness and citizenship. There are various cultural resources from which instructors can draw to examine the practices of rhetoric, not the least of which is baseball.

That baseball has long been regarded as the "national pastime" speaks directly to the game as a rhetorical construction. As early as the mid-nineteenth century, baseball proponents have touted it as a uniquely American invention. This is encapsulated, of course, in the Cooperstown myth that claims Abner Doubleday as the game's creator. When Albert Spalding published his *America's National Game* in 1911, it was evident that baseball was held as the ultimate display of nationalism and patriotism. Throughout the twentieth century the national pastime was deployed as a metaphor for democracy and the American Dream. Perhaps best symbolized by Jackie Robinson's inclusion on the Brooklyn Dodgers in 1947, this narrative views baseball as the ideal level playing field, transcending the political and social ills that have befallen the nation.

Yet if baseball has characterized the best hopes of a democratic nation, it has also symbolized the failure of the United States to embrace the democracy it so vigorously defends. Racism, sexism, and homophobia have plagued the game at various levels, and too often baseball, along with motherhood and apple pie, has been equated to an idealized America that exists only in mythology. This is the America that is celebrated in sporting rituals that baseball pioneered. Performing the national anthem prior to a game, for example, first occurred at ballparks during World War I. When President Franklin D. Roosevelt affirmed the role of baseball in

American culture during World War II, the anthem became standard. More recently, baseball games have become sites for elaborate patriotic displays in the wake of the September 11, 2001, terrorist attacks. Given the prominence of baseball as a cultural institution, and the extent to which the game responded to 9/11, it has become a rich text for understanding American attitudes toward terrorism, war, and citizenship. Moreover, it provides a compelling instructional site for illustrating the principles and practices of rhetoric.

At first glance, it may appear that baseball's response to 9/11 merits little attention in a public speaking classroom. However, the ancient tradition of rhetoric insists that oratory be seen as an exercise in citizenship. How we, as citizens, deliberate about politics yields important answers to the questions we face as a nation. As Aristotle was perhaps the first to tell us, rhetoric is ultimately about judgments. If public speaking, therefore, becomes a means for exercising judgment and performing citizenship, then rhetoric is a vehicle for accessing, evaluating, and responding to arguments made in public culture. A rhetorical approach asks students to engage with their communities, consume politics critically, and envision themselves as active citizens. It recasts the mission of the public speaking classroom, measuring success less by the standards of organization and delivery, and more by a speaker's ability to invent new worlds and shape them through language. It demands and rewards creativity, critical thinking, and responsibility. In short, rhetoric is a means for drawing important connections between the classroom and the world outside it.

How is it, then, that baseball can become a rhetorical resource for public speaking teachers? While many specific examples could apply, one text in particular illustrates the rhetorical articulations of patriotism found in baseball after 9/11. As many readers will recall, Major League Baseball (MLB) offered multiple ceremonies in tribute to the victims of the terrorist attacks, both in the fall of 2001 and on subsequent anniversaries and national holidays. On September 11, 2002, MLB organized a league-wide effort to memorialize the previous year's events. Each stadium was decorated with logos declaring "We Shall Not Forget," and ushers handed out miniature U.S. flags to fans attending games. President George W. Bush sent a letter to each ballpark reminding everyone that baseball had played an important role in healing the nation a year earlier. The most dynamic aspect of these ceremonies, however, was the MLB video, also titled *We Shall Not Forget*.

Stadium officials presented the video during the seventh-inning stretch at day games, and at precisely 9:11 p.m. at night games. It began with the terrifying images of September 11, 2001, with accompanying text that read,

"One year ago ... a nation mourned ... and then ... the healing began." The last line appeared at the top of the image of an empty Yankee Stadium as the camera then moved to open blue sky. A series of images followed that included Cardinals announcer Jack Buck, the sounds of fans chanting, "USA! USA!" and President Bush throwing the ceremonial first pitch during game three of the 2001 World Series in New York. Next, Chicago Cubs outfielder Sammy Sosa ran onto the screen with a miniature American flag, and the final text appeared: "We play.... But ... we shall not forget." The final line overlapped an image of the New York City skyline, with the World Trade Center towers intact. The video then closed with an image of the American flag.

Using this text as a primary resource, students are asked to consider what kind of messages are constructed and communicated through MLB's video. The lesson is composed of three parts: an introduction to rhetoric, a discussion of baseball's historical role as the national pastime, and an analysis of the anniversary tribute. There are at least two conditions that must be present in the classroom for this exercise to be effective. First, an environment must be established that demonstrates that students are encouraged to voice their opinions and that, even when they are at odds with the instructor, those opinions will be treated seriously and respectfully. Second, politics cannot be seen as a dirty word. In the early twenty-first century, colleges and universities face multiple criticisms from both outside and within higher education alleging that teachers use classrooms for political purposes. There is a distinct difference, however, between opening the classroom as a political space and attempting to manipulate students. In a course where public deliberation and citizenship are a central focus, politics must command our attention. Simply put, the classroom may be one of the few places where students are exposed to and challenged to think about different or multiple perspectives on a given issue.

As mentioned earlier, public speaking classes already draw from the tradition of rhetoric. Too often, however, this is done through a narrow and limited appropriation of Aristotelian principles. This perspective manifests itself through the focus on rhetoric as "the available means to persuasion" in the given case (Aristotle, 1355a), with an emphasis on Aristotle's proofs: *ethos*, *logos*, and *pathos*. And while students are encouraged to analyze their audiences, they do so with the implicit understanding that rhetoric is an instrument, a simple means to an end. This lesson begins, therefore, with a discussion about this orientation to public speaking, especially since many undergraduates will have taken a version of the course in high school. Most of them will understand rhetoric in these instrumental terms, assuming that public speaking represents a transaction of information from speaker to audience. Despite contemporary scholarship to the contrary, public speaking pedagogy remains driven by interpreting communication through the sender-message-receiver-feedback cycle. Rhetoric offers a challenge to such rigid modeling.

Asking students to define rhetoric represents another obstacle. There may be a considerable silence. When an answer is offered, it generally regards rhetoric with distrust or cynicism. Rhetoric, for most students, equates with "hot air." They hear the word thrown about in political campaigns, when one candidate insists that the other needs to "dial down the rhetoric." It is synonymous with empty promises, oratorical flourishes, or "mere words." It is not surprising that students treat rhetoric with suspicion. As early as Plato, it was seen as a powerful tool of deceit. In his dialogue *Gorgias*, Plato famously equated rhetoric with "cookery," suggesting there was something concocted about the art (462b-466a). There is, to be sure, something inventional about rhetoric, for it responds to a world of inconsistency and contingency. It is, then, a creative art, one in which new worlds and ways of living can be imagined.

The inventional quality of rhetoric is on full display when we think of baseball as the national pastime. The game's American origin is, itself, an invention of a patriotic spirit that sought to distinguish American sport from its supposedly less masculine British counterpart. Throughout baseball's history, it has been claimed as a symbol of an evolving nation. Its pastoral imagery evokes a nostalgic escape from technology and industrialization. The baseball calendar invites romantic comparisons to the cycles of life. Its multiethnic composition promises the idealization of the melting pot. All of this reveals baseball's capacity to function rhetorically, to provide a means for understanding the world around us. In the words of literary and rhetorical critic Kenneth Burke, baseball has always been a kind of equipment for living.

It takes little work for students to imagine the various ways that popular culture has turned to baseball as the essence of American mythology. They have heard John Fogerty's "Centerfield" at ballparks their entire lives, and may have heard Paul Simon's famous line from "Mrs. Robinson." Popular 1990s television shows like the *Simpsons* and *Seinfeld* frequently used baseball as a backdrop for plotlines. But perhaps most familiar to undergraduates will be the movies that feature baseball. Most of them will have seen *Field of Dreams*, for example, and can isolate the many fragments that compose the film's mythology. Here, it is important to deconstruct the narrative, recognizing that Ray Kinsella's quest speaks to a nostalgic longing symbolized appropriately by baseball. This is not to suggest that students should become cynical about the movie, but rather that they should recognize that its story works on multiple levels. Using fiction to demonstrate that a critical attitude need not lead to a dismissive attitude builds an important bridge to the MLB video.

Any discussion that is connected to September 11, 2001, is likely to arouse emotional responses from students. They all will have memories of that day, and some will have been tragically connected to the people and places directly affected by the attacks. It is important to be sensitive to these issues, but it is equally important to be willing to discuss the rhetorical responses to terrorism that have been a part of American culture since 9/11. Specifically, President George W. Bush and his administration provided a narrow definition of what constituted appropriate patriotic behavior. Americans were encouraged to be strong and resolute, to defend a "way of life," to not let the "terrorists win," and to support the administration's foreign policy with blind faith. His press secretary warned that Americans had better watch what they do and say, and his attorney general suggested that any form of dissent was tantamount to aiding and abetting terrorism. In the first year after the attacks, American public opinion rallied around the president and offered little resistance or argument against his words or deeds.

The connection between these political realities and the national pastime will not be immediately apparent to most students. They have come to view politics and sport as entirely separate affairs. Sport, in fact, provides an important escape from the social and political issues that we all face on a daily basis. For this reason, many fans will insist that games occur on neutral terms and that athletes should remain apolitical. Too often, athletes echo this sentiment. It was Michael Jordan, after all, who famously explained that the reason he could not endorse a Democrat in North Carolina was because "Republicans buy sneakers, too." Yet, the sporting arena has always been a political space, even if it is enacted in subtle ways. It is important, then, to invite students to consider the moments when politics and sport articulate with one another. They are likely to mention the myriad displays of nationalism that pervade the Olympic Games. Perhaps they will recall the ubiquitous red, white, and blue that characterized Fox television's coverage of Super Bowl XXXVI in 2002. Some will be aware of vocal athletes like Muhammad Ali or Billie Jean King who challenged the status quo. Making the connections between politics and sport more obvious is a crucial step before turning the attention to MLB's video.

The discussion about the video can be provocative. Many students are moved by the message of memorialization. Self-proclaimed patriots identify with the nationalistic sentiments. Baseball fans wonder why MLB would stray so far from the action on the field. Opponents of the war on terror lament the presence of President Bush in Yankee Stadium. It is helpful to begin with general reactions to the video. Students should be encouraged to acknowledge any emotions it may have evoked. Once this initial discussion has concluded, however, they should be asked to look at the video more critically. After the instructor points out various elements of the production, a second viewing often yields different responses. They begin to see new connections: there is religious symbolism in the images of Yankee Stadium as a sort of cathedral looking toward the heavens; the footage of the president makes clear that baseball and the nation's identity are inextricably linked; Sammy Sosa's sprint across Wrigley Field with U.S. flag in hand embodies the American Dream of a nonnative finding wealth and stardom in America. There are, of course, multiple ways to read the video, and the more interpretations the better.

The purpose of this exercise is not to persuade students that the video is necessarily bad or good. It is to insist that it cannot be viewed as a simple, disengaged text. Rather, it is a rhetorical response to a particular time and place in the nation's history. Whether or not that response is judged to be appropriate is a measure of its rhetorical effectivity. Although the video is not a public speech, it is a form of public communication that attempts to shape the way its viewers interpret the world and live in it. Moreover, it asks its viewers to consider the political landscape and perform patriotically as citizens. In other words, it claims that to be a good American in the aftermath of 9/11, one cannot forget the events of that tragic day. To forget, above all else, is to dishonor the memory of those who lost their lives. Yet, while presumably casting its view in the past the video provides much more of a focus on the present, featuring the solidarity between the president and baseball that symbolizes the strength of the nation. In this way, appropriate citizenship is measured not only by respecting and remembering the victims of 9/11 but also by affirming and assenting to the political aims of the current administration. Whether Americans should accept these terms of citizenship is open to rhetorical contestation.

In order to do justice to the MLB video, instructors should allow at least one full class session—preferably in a 75-minute period—for discussion. By the time students have considered the tradition of rhetoric, the history of the national pastime, the relationship between politics and sport, and the particulars of *We Shall Not Forget*, it should be apparent that baseball's response to 9/11 must be considered from a rhetorical standpoint. Most importantly, the connections between the national pastime, presidential leadership, and citizenship merit the critical attention of educators and students alike. The judgments that students will make about the video will be as varied as the political perspectives they bring with them into the classroom. Some will be moved, others enraged, and, yes, others will be uninterested. The significant lesson they can draw from the exercise is to recognize that rhetorical performances—be they speeches, videos, or songs—are constituted by political realities, and that they in turn constitute how we can accept, challenge, shape, and reinvent those realities. A rhetorical approach, therefore, offers a way to connect the course content with the critical issues of our time. Provided that the public speaking classroom is seen as a vital space for enacting citizenship and engaging with public culture, using baseball to introduce students to rhetoric can yield a class of students willing to critique productively the world in which they live and offer new possibilities for their futures.

Works Cited

Aristotle. *On Rhetoric: A Theory of Civic Discourse.* Trans. George A. Kennedy. Oxford: Oxford University Press, 1991.
Burke, Kenneth. "Literature as Equipment for Living." *The Philosophy of Literary Form.* 3rd ed. Berkeley: University of California Press, 1973. 293–304.
Field of Dreams. Dir. Phil Alden Robinson. Universal, 1989.
Fogerty, John. "Centerfield." *Centerfield.* Warner Brothers, 1985.
Plato. *Gorgias.* Trans. Terence Irwin. Oxford: Clarendon Press, 1979.
Simon, Paul. "Mrs. Robinson." *The Graduate Soundtrack.* Sony, 1967.
Spalding, Albert G. *America's National Game.* Intro. Benjamin G. Rader. Lincoln: University of Nebraska Press, 1992.

Race Studies

Redefining the Narrative—Effa Manley, Jackie Robinson, and the Integration of Baseball

(ROBERT CVORNYEK)

The intersection of race and sports in the Civil Rights era offers several important lessons for secondary and postsecondary students examining modern American or World history. The integration of American professional athletics, principally baseball, has become an integral part of a broader historical narrative that examines the struggle for racial freedom and equality following World War II. Freedom, especially, has always been an elusive and contested ideal for African Americans. As students more closely examine baseball's "Great Experiment" to desegregate the white major leagues, they confront opposing interpretations of the national pastime's significance in advancing the social and economic interests of African Americans. The collision of race and baseball encourages students to confront the pivotal question of the era; namely, did the black community surrender a sense of cultural identity and economic self-determination in its bargain for integration? In 1948, a dynamic public debate between Jackie Robinson, who had recently shattered the color line in modern major league baseball, and Effa Manley, who served as the successful co-owner of the Negro League's Newark Eagles provides one indication of the contested history of baseball's integration.

Historical Context

Approximately one year after Jackie Robinson debuted with the Brooklyn Dodgers, he penned an article for *Ebony* magazine, a popular black publication that endeavored "to mirror the happier side of Negro life—the positive, everyday achievements from Harlem to Hollywood" (Hall, 207). Robinson extolled the virtues of integration and, in the process, criticized the all-black Negro Leagues as an unprofessional operation that compromised the integrity of its ballplayers and fans. Robinson wrote that he never possessed a contract while he played for the Kansas City Monarchs and that salaries were too "low for good ballplayers in days of high living costs" (Robinson, 17). He complained that players traveled from city to city in uncomfortable buses and usually stayed in cheap, dingy, and dirty hotels. Owners rarely enforced team rules, leaving players to drink and carouse whenever they pleased. "The indifference of the owners towards the players' welfare and the laxity of the rules," Robinson argued, placed black athletes and fans in a "bad situation" (Robinson, 18). For Robinson, the only alternative was to leave the Negro Leagues.

Soon after Robinson's article appeared in *Ebony,* Effa Manley engaged Robinson in a public debate on the past importance and credibility of black baseball. Manley was the perfect person to respond to Robinson's charges. She had an impeccable record as a civil rights advocate and consistently demonstrated a genuine appreciation of black baseball's historical importance and vital role within the African-American community. As co-owner of the Newark Eagles, she managed the team's payroll, purchased the team's equipment, and arranged for lodging and other accommodations. She also handled the team's publicity as supervisor of its public relations department. Although Effa never served in an official capacity in the Negro National League's front office, she attended meetings, voiced her concerns, and assisted her husband in his role as league secretary (Manley and Hardwick, 54). Robinson's recollection of black baseball was ill-timed for Manley, given her efforts to keep the league alive in the post-integration era, and it clearly clashed with her own experience as a thirteen-year owner and promoter of the black game. Robinson's criticism angered and hurt

Manley. She forcefully responded in her own article published in *Our World—Ebony* magazine's main competitor. Manley stated that all her ballplayers held contracts and were paid promptly and diligently on the first and fifteenth of each month. She explained that the average player received $100 a week and the only reason the owners could not pay more was because they could not afford it. Manley reported that the Eagles owned a new and comfortable bus, but that the reality of Jim Crow America severely limited hotel and travel accommodations. Effa reminded Robinson that the Negro Leagues helped place him "where he is today" and scolded Robinson that he "wittingly or unwittingly ... lent his powerful name to the destruction of Negro baseball" (Manley, 28). According to journalist Leon Herbert Hardwick, "The Manley-owned Newark club holds the dubious distinction of being among the first to have to suffer from the pangs of racial integration" (Manley and Hardwick, 8).

For Manley and the rest of the league owners, integration was devastating. Local fans and the black press deserted the Eagles to follow Robinson and the Dodgers. Moreover, once baseball's "Great Experiment" succeeded, Branch Rickey, the general manager of the Dodgers, and other white major league officials began raiding the Negro Leagues for talent. Manley would eventually lose profitable gate attractions like pitcher Don Newcombe and future Hall-of-Fame stars Monte Irvin and Larry Doby to venturesome white owners for little or no monetary compensation. When asked about Rickey's raids on black teams for potential major leaguers, Manley responded that "Mr. Rickey didn't even answer our letters when we wrote him about Newcombe, let alone give us anything. He knew we were in no position to challenge him. The fans would never have forgiven us" (Holway, 317).

The impact of integration on the exploitation and demise of the Negro Leagues establishes the framework for this classroom lesson. On a theoretical level, the controversy over baseball's integration mirrors an historic and ongoing debate in the African-American community over the "ambivalence of integration." Cultural critic Gerald Early has made a strong case that Manley's concern over the viability of important black organizations in the aftermath of integration was probably shared by many blacks in a range of different professions (Early, 218–219). Manley's belief that integration cost the black community an important economic and cultural institution offers an alternative viewpoint, one that has not received adequate attention.

As historians unravel the story of the Negro Leagues, they begin to see baseball as part of the "expressive culture" of black life in the 1930s and 1940s. Manley perceived black baseball as an important cultural institution that gave expression to a black aesthetic similar to music and literature. She also believed that the baseball diamond occupied an important social "space" that provided blacks with important lessons on the construction of race, identity, and gender. This approach has the potential for expanding our student's definition of the freedom struggle beyond politics and the courts and into popular culture.

The Writing Assignment(s)

The assignment consists of two separate, but related, activities designed to introduce and analyze multiple perspectives on baseball's integration. Instructors may choose either assignment, as each provides the information required to assess the impact of integration on the Negro Leagues. Students in my Race and Sports in Modern America class have completed both of these assignments and students in my Black Experience course have completed Assignment I, reading and analyzing the Effa Manley and Jackie Robinson primary documents.

Assignment I. The Effa Manley/ Jackie Robinson Controversy

In this assignment, students read two primary source handouts that offer conflicting interpretations of the Negro Leagues and the impact of baseball's desegregation on black ballplayers. Students see the importance of primary sources for historians as they create their own secondary source based on the material gleaned from the writings of Manley and Robinson. I found it necessary to discuss the difference between primary and secondary sources as a prerequisite to this assignment, often with the help of a handout provided by the National Archives and Record Administration titled "History in the Raw," easily located at http://www.nara.gov. The assignment requires that students carefully read the documents and answer the following questions in a five-to-seven-page essay.

1. Discuss the criticisms that Jackie Robinson directed against the Negro Leagues. Why do you think he made these accusations?
2. How did Effa Manley refute Robinson's charges? Was she convincing?
3. Given your understanding of the Negro Leagues, what important economic, social, and cultural impact did the all-black leagues have on African-American communities?
4. Do you agree that Effa Manley offers an alternative viewpoint on the integration of the white major leagues? Does she cite reliable sources for her interpretation? What is Manley's perception of the role that Branch Rickey played in ending baseball's "Gentlemen's Agreement"?

Required Reading: Primary Sources

Manley, Effa. "Negro Baseball Isn't Dead." *Our World*, August 1948, 26–28.
Robinson, Jackie. "What's Wrong with Negro Baseball?" *Ebony*, June 1948, 16–19.

Instructors may wish to supplement these sources with Manley's memoir on the Negro Leagues titled *Negro Baseball: Before Integration*, published in 1976. She examines the "gathering storm cloud of integration" and Rickey's raids on the Negro Leagues in much greater detail. This book is currently out of print and available in only a handful of repositories from interlibrary loan.

Suggested Reading: Secondary Sources

In order to provide students with biographical information on Robinson and Manley and historical background on the people and events mentioned in their articles, I offer students the following list of suggested books and articles. The list is not exhaustive; it merely represents the most recent and easily accessible scholarship on the topic.

Manley Sources

Berlage, Gai Ingham. "Effa Manley, A Major Force in Negro Baseball in the 1930s and 1940s." *Nine* (Spring 1993): 163–184.
Burley, Dan. "The Mother of Negro Baseball." *Sepia* (August 1959): 51–54.
Hecht, Harry. "Woman with a Mission." *New York Post* 15 September 1975.
Holway, John. "Mrs. Effa Manley." In *Voices from the Great Black Baseball Leagues*. New York: Dodd, Mead, and Company, 1975.
Kisner, Ronald E. "White Widow of Baseball League Pioneer Writes Book about Saga." *Jet* (March 1977): 46–48.
Manley, Effa. "Baseball Leagues Spend Half Million." *Baltimore Afro-American* 26 (July 1941).
_____. File. Research Library. National Baseball Hall of Fame and Museum. Cooperstown, New York.
_____. Interview by Bill Marshall. 19 October 1977. Interview 770H79 Chan 41, transcript. A.B. Chandler Oral History Project. University of Kentucky Library. Lexington, Kentucky.
_____. Interview by John Holway. n.d. transcript. National Baseball Hall of Fame and Museum. Cooperstown, New York.
_____. "Negro Baseball Isn't Dead." *Our World* (August 1948): 26–28.
Nutt, Amy Ellis. "Baseball's 'Black' Trailblazer." *The Newark Star-Ledger* 13 February 2001: 37,41.
Overmyer, James. *Queen of the Negro Leagues: Effa Manley and the Newark Eagles*. Metuchen: Scarecrow Press, 1993.
Rogosin, Donn. "Queen of the Negro Leagues." *Sportscape* (Summer 1981).
Spink, C.C. "A Furious Woman." *The Sporting News* 20 June 1977.
Young, A.S. "The Fair Lady of Baseball Decides to Call It Quits." *Cleveland Call* 23 February 1948.

ROBINSON SOURCES

Falkner, David. *Great Time Coming: The Life of Jackie Robinson from Baseball to Birmingham*. New York: Simon and Schuster, 1995.
Frommer, Harvey. *Rickey & Robinson: The Men Who Broke Baseball's Color Barrier*. New York: Macmillan, 1982.
Rampersad, Arnold. *Jackie Robinson: A Biography*. New York: Knopf, 1997.
Robinson, Jackie. *Baseball Has Done It*. New York: Lippincott, 1964.
Robinson, Jackie, and Alfred Duckett. *Breakthrough to the Big Leagues*. New York: Harper and Row, 1965.
Tygiel, Jules. *Baseball's Great Experiment: Jackie Robinson and His Legacy*. New York: Oxford University Press, 1997.

Assignment II. Mr. Rickey Calls a Meeting

This assignment combines biographical sketches with historical fiction in a two-part activity that examines the integration of major league baseball from multiple perspectives. Ed Schmidt's play *Mr. Rickey Calls a Meeting* re-creates a meeting that hypothetically takes place between Rickey and Robinson just prior to the official announcement that Robinson would join the Dodgers for the 1947 season. Without informing Robinson, Rickey also invites Joe Louis, the heavyweight boxing champion; Bill "Bojangles" Robinson, Harlem's celebrated tap dancer and owner of the New York Black Yankees; and Paul Robeson, the internationally known singer, actor, and political activist. Rickey's intention is to gain the public support of these three popular and representative figures before he advances Robinson to the major leagues. During the meeting, Robeson, a communist supporter, argues that Rickey has little interest in African Americans except as cheap labor for his Brooklyn plantation. He cites Rickey's dismissal of the Negro Leagues as further evidence that Rickey cares less for the advancement of black Americans than he does for his own selfish interests.

PART I. BIOGRAPHICAL SKETCHES.

Before listening to the play on tape, students research and write five separate biographical essays (required length, 650 words each) on the lives of five important historical figures who participated in the successful effort to integrate baseball following World War II: Jackie Robinson, Branch Rickey, Bill "Bojangles" Robinson, Paul Robeson, and Joe Louis. Students must concisely capture the significant aspects of each participant's life, but particular emphasis should be placed on the relationship between race and the sport that each man embodied. Students consult model essays found on the Web site of the African American National Biography as examples of the scope, content and writing conventions required in this assignment.

The Web site is located at http://www.fas.harvard.edu/~aanb/SHTML/aanbFormat.shtml.

Students used a variety of Web-based and print sources to construct substantive biographies on the historical characters involved in the play, but two important connections were often overlooked. For the Bill "Bojangles" Robinson essay, students did not discuss his involvement as an owner of the Negro League's New York Black Yankees. This is partially explained by the fact that much of the scholarship on Robinson does not include his role as an owner and promoter of the black game. Less understandable is the fact that several students missed the opportunity to discuss the uproar surrounding Paul Robeson's controversial testimony before the House Un-American Activities Committee and Jackie Robinson's response to Robeson.[1]

PART II. THE PLAY: DISCUSSION AND RESPONSE

After students submitted their biographical essays, I had them listen to the play. An audio version of *Mr. Rickey Calls a Meeting* is available on cassette from the drama company L.A. Theatre Works. The play has a running time of ninety-nine minutes. Since my class met for two-hour blocks, students listened to the entire performance. My sense is that most instructors will break the lesson into two classes for either pedagogical or scheduling reasons. Student response to the play was guided, in part, by a number of critical questions that I asked students to consider as they listened to the performance. As part of a grant from the National Endowment for the Arts, L.A. Theatre Works published a teacher's guide to complement use of the play in the classroom. The guide includes a biography of Jackie Robinson, an essay on the premise of the play, and several reading and writing assignments that assess listening comprehension, encourage critical thinking, and strengthen the student's ability to organize and express thoughts and ideas clearly in writing and discussion. The guide is available online at http://www.latw.org/acrobat/rickey.pdf. The guide's critical questions helped my students understand the complexity of baseball's integration from multiple perspectives. A sample of some of its questions includes:

1. At the center of the fictional meeting in this play is a great struggle. What are the basic issues in this struggle?
2. Most of those present at the meeting are ready to give Mr. Rickey what he wants as long as Robinson is accepted into the major leagues. What are the reasons Robeson does not want to give Mr. Rickey his vote?
3. What are Robeson's objections to Jackie Robinson joining the Dodgers?

Robeson is suspicious of white bosses having control over African-American athletes and artists. What do you think of this concern?
4. Robeson wants Mr. Rickey and the owners of the Dodgers to pay the Negro League owners for the recruitment of Jackie Robinson. Do you think this is a fair request? (Alive and Aloud, 13).

Conclusion

The story of baseball's integration introduces students to significant historical concepts and reinforces important research skills. The debate over the meaning and consequences of the sport's integration, for both blacks and whites, permits students to grapple with the idea of conflicting interpretations and contested history. The central role of primary sources in the Manley/Robinson debate requires that students carefully analyze historical documents in light of such factors as bias and intended audience. Likewise, *Mr. Rickey Calls a Meeting* sheds considerable light on the diversity of black opinion regarding baseball's integration and, most importantly, humanizes the story with historical characters who led real lives. The use of historical fiction and the aural nature of this lesson also provide alternate ways of delivering content to students who possess different learning styles. As students consider the tentative nature of historical interpretation and use sources that encourage them to think differently about the past, they engage the discipline of history in its truest form.

Notes

1. Most historians agree that World War II and the ensuing Cold War served as significant turning points in the modern Civil Rights Movement. The integration of American professional baseball occurred within the broader international context of the Cold War. Following World War II, the United States and the Soviet Union sought to advance and safeguard their interests throughout Europe. Both superpowers, however, clearly understood the strategic importance of courting the favor of former colonial nations, especially the "colored" countries in Asia and Africa. These newly emerging postcolonial states became intense battlegrounds in the ideological conflict between capitalism and communism. America's betrayal of its own minority population through racial segregation, disfranchisement, and inequality posed significant problems for foreign policy initiatives designed to win the hearts and minds of those living in the developing world. Consequently, when Jackie Robinson signed with the Dodgers, it placed him squarely on the world stage and the Iron Curtin and the Color Line were inextricably linked.

America's interest in Cold War civil rights struck some African-Americans as being a bit disingenuous. Black leaders like W.E.B. DuBois and Paul Robeson drew sharp distinctions between symbolic and substantive changes in race relations and concluded that the government's official tale of racial progress was exaggerated for political reasons. Recently, scholars such as Brenda Plummer, Mary Dudziak, and Thomas Borstelman have examined the complex relationship between the Cold War and the Civil Rights Movement, but their work has focused on the political, not the cultural, aspects of the story. The integration of baseball and the resulting demise of the organized Negro Leagues add a much needed cultural dimension to the subject.

Works Cited

Alive and Aloud. *Mr. Rickey Calls a Meeting: Teacher's Study Guide.* Venice, CA: L.A. Theatre Works, 1999.
Early, Gerald. "American Integration, Black Heroism, and the Meaning of Jackie Robinson." *The Unlevel Playing Field: A Documentary History of the African American Experience in Sport.* Eds. David K. Wiggins and Patrick B. Miller. Urbana: University of Illinois Press, 2003. 215–221.
Hall, James. "Photographs Taken in Everyday Life: *Ebony's* Photojournalistic Discourse." *The Black Press: New Literary and Historical Essays.* Ed. Todd Vogel. New Brunswick, NJ: Rutgers University Press, 2001. 207–227
Holway, John. *Voices from the Great Black Baseball Leagues.* New York: Dodd, Meade, 1975.
Manley, Effa. "Negro Baseball Isn't Dead." *Our World* (August 1948): 26–28.
Manley, Effa, and Leon Herbert Hardwick. *Negro Baseball ... Before Integration.* Chicago: Adams Press, 1976,
Robinson, Jackie. "What's Wrong with Negro Baseball?" *Ebony* (June 1948): 16–19.

Race Studies

Teaching Social Justice by Examining the Desegregation of Baseball

(JOE MARREN)

Baseball used to own this country. It was everywhere: from college and village greens to rickety parks in mill and company towns, from the streets of the biggest cities to the "green cathedrals" of those same metropolises. And everyone played. It was the one great introduction to American society for immigrants and a chance for men who toiled their days away in the factories and fields to play. In the late nineteenth century, and for much of the twentieth, America grabbed hold of baseball and held it dear to its heart, like a child with a fistful of pennies in a candy store. We went out to the ball game, out with the crowd, bought some peanuts and Cracker Jacks, rooted for the home team and loved it so much we almost didn't care if we ever got back to the realities of daily life.

Or so the story goes. But those sweet dreams don't talk about players cursing, drinking and carousing before or after (sometimes during) the games. Or sweating through flannel uniforms in the summer heat; it's said that major leaguers played with lettuce leaves under their caps in St. Louis to try and keep cool. Ahh, St. Louis, at one time both the westernmost and southernmost big league city and a place with two teams, the proud Cardinals and the seemingly hapless Browns. Certainly not the most bigoted city—truth be told, almost every city is somewhat guilty—but a city with an all-white organization as late as 1953 when August Busch bought the Cardinals (Tygiel, 293). To be fair, it should be noted that the Browns were early leaders in desegregating baseball (Tygiel, 220). And a city whose beloved Cardinals allegedly were the ringleaders in what historians said was a threatened strike if Jackie Robinson played in the majors (Tygiel, 189).

So a study of baseball is a study of America. And not a study of an America found in stuffy tomes on dusty shelves, but a study of the lives and loves and fears of men and women who can talk with pleasure about playing the bounce off the Green Monster, or who measure greatness by comparison with a bunch of guys in pinstripes from 1927.

The advantage Buffalo State College offered me in the fall semester of 2005 was to teach baseball in a context of what the game and the aura meant to America, to define baseball's place in the dream. Another advantage it offered was to teach it as a humanities course in a learning community.

If the goal of a learning community is to help students learn together, to foster a sense of shared scholarship, then what and how we teach must be open to our own interpretation. Another goal of learning communities is to help keep students in school (Mitchell and Renaud, 75). If that premise is also accepted, then a humanities course must provide a shared experience around a central theme to get students interested, to spark their creative impulses, and to keep them in college to continue developing the life of the mind. To that end, one of the benefits of teaching in a learning community is connecting with colleagues in other disciplines, in my particular case with sociology, criminal justice, English, and library science.

I used to teach in a learning community that used the Matrix trilogy of films—*The Matrix* (1999), *The Matrix Reloaded* (2003), *The Matrix Revolutions* (2003)—as a base to explore social beliefs and assumptions. Our aim was to get students to stretch their imaginations and examine their world and the constraints we place on ourselves, or that we let society place on us. Perhaps some of the students weren't familiar with the words epistemology and metaphysics, but we introduced the concepts in class discussions to get students to think about what they believe and why they believe it. That particular learning community has evolved into one that now explores social justice. We no longer use the Matrix films because twenty-first century American reality provides ample sources; in short, social injustice is all around.

In the United States, we are taught that our canonical documents espouse liberty and equality as our most cherished values. Yet not everyone in this country has always been free and equal when measured against the political and economic status of middle class white men. Two events from about the middle of the twentieth century began to change that, and baseball, whether accidentally or purposefully, played a leading role. The second event, about seven years after the first, was the Supreme Court ruling in *Brown v. Board of Education* that struck down so-called separate but equal laws. It wasn't the death knell for Jim Crow, nor was the first event, but taken together they led the United States down the path toward greater social justice. There is still much work to be done, but baseball has a role in the evolution toward social justice.

The first event alluded to above was the signing of Jackie Robinson to play baseball. If life were fair and asterisks were banned, then Roger Maris would have been better appreciated in his time, the Dodgers would still be in Brooklyn, and Jackie Robinson would have settled into a career and life that judged him on his all-star, Hall of Fame abilities and didn't expect him to be ballplayer/pioneer/saint rolled into one package.

But life is not fair and so much was expected of Robinson that some civil rights crusaders argue that, in the long run, Robinson's days as a Dodger in the late 1940s shortened his life. That argument will not be taken up in this essay; it will simply be noted that Robinson's life ended at age fifty-three in 1972.

Rather, this essay is about how to use baseball as a means of studying social justice in modern America. At the end of the course students should:

- know the relevant facts about baseball in U.S. society and how it acquiesced to racism;
- be familiar with baseball literature and the journalistic approach to the game; students should be able to analyze feature stories for bias and meaning;
- know some of the legal and political aspects of the fight for social justice within the confines of Frank Chance's diamond;
- gain experience in literary criticism and descriptive writing;
- understand the basis of civic and ethical responsibilities.

As shown, a learning community course is ideally suited to a study of the social aspects of baseball in relation to the life and times of the

United States in the nineteenth and twentieth centuries. This course shows students how an academic study of a subject can relate directly to life. The other learning-community classes reinforce key social justice concepts, such as the fight for civil rights.

Specifically, the course examines the American Dream in relation to baseball and how the press played a role in integrating modern baseball. Professor Jules Tygiel's *Baseball's Great Experiment; Jackie Robinson and His Legacy,* Expanded Edition is the main text, supplanted with readings from anthologies and journals.

The first thing to do is introduce baseball in a social context and define it in relation to the American dream. Students are asked to contextualize some famous quotes about baseball. This is a nongraded exercise designed to get people thinking about—and discussing—the yin and yang of baseball in contemporary life. Some of the quotes are:

- "Whoever wants to know the heart and mind of America had better learn baseball," from Jacques Barzun.
- "[Baseball] breaks your heart, it is designed to break your heart," from the late commissioner A. Bartlett Giamatti.
- "The one constant through all the years has been baseball. America has been erased like a blackboard, only to be rebuilt and then erased again. But baseball has marked time with America, has rolled by like a procession of steamrollers," from W.P. Kinsella.
- "Scratch an intellectual and you'll scratch a baseball fan," from Roger Kahn.

These quotes both praise and damn baseball. The goal of using them is to have students realize the pull the game once had on this country's self-image. By discussing the authors, the context of the quotes, and the effect the words have on readers, students should gain a greater understanding of times and attitudes. Thus baseball can be seen as a barometer of American thought and life. As society has changed, so has baseball, but did baseball "lead the way," as some may say, or did it reflect the times? After all, Jack Johnson became the first black heavyweight champion in 1908; it can be argued that Joe Louis was the first black national sports hero after he knocked out Germany's Max Schmelling in 1938; Olympian Jesse Owens not only won several gold medals, but his actions also pointed out the inherent lies in Adolf Hitler's claims of Aryan supremacy during the 1936 Berlin Olympics; and outside the world of sports, the work of Frederick Douglass and W.E.B. DuBois stands out (Smith 2003). There are many others who contributed to the betterment of mankind, so what made baseball so special?

The answer has many facets. Part of the reason lies in social advancement, part in America's self-image, and part in the times that Jackie Robinson played in—just after a war to eradicate fascism and during a cold war waged to show the world that the United States was the shining city on the hill and the best hope for mankind. As such, discussing the quotes in a non-graded atmosphere will help students decide why Robinson's signing a major league contract was so important.

After the lecture-discussion class, students are asked to read the first chapter ("The Crucible of White Hot Competition") in Professor Tygiel's book as a background for the course's goals and pace. That is, they should get ready to recognize and be prepared to discuss historical developments and themes in U.S. and baseball history. By this time, the students are given their first writing assignment and told to submit it within a week. This immediately introduces them to research methods and forces them to incorporate concepts from the other courses in the learning community. The assignment is to write a brief paper (about two to three pages) arguing why someone not in the Hall of Fame should be in there, or why someone in there should be expelled. The argument should not be based on statistics alone, but should also include a call for social justice.

This exercise helps students determine who our heroes are and, indeed, makes them wonder if the person should be a hero. The goal is to make students determine how heroes are defined and consider whether they inspire us. The papers should attempt to answer whether we accept heroes with their faults and find a context for them in our own times. In short, must heroes be mythic figures? And how has the media built up, torn down and shored up our player/heroes? For example, there are plenty of former Negro Leagues stars not in the hall, and a few racists who are. The students' research must focus on biography and take into account the tenor of the nominee's times.

Some fans and scholars argue that Negro leaguers played ball against inferior competition and also contend that record-keeping and game coverage were spotty at best (Lanctot). However, it could also be argued that the Negro Leagues of the mid-twentieth century were a de facto third major league, or at least played as a high-level minor league because of future Hall of Famers such as Satchel Paige, Josh Gibson, Monte Irvin, James "Cool Papa" Bell, Oscar Charleston and Martin Dihigo (Smith, 366). Thus, the students' research will decide if the players deserve to be in the hall from a statistical and societal viewpoint, i.e., should those who played the forgotten innings of baseball be due a little more consideration now that there are only a few of them left? Or should blatant racists such as Cap Anson remain in the hall? What does his place in baseball immortality say about the game and the times? Or does it say nothing? Should it? Students have to show that a person can be judged on his or her thoughts and ideas, for example, that giving lip service to a cause is not enough, that a person has to be fully committed to an idea in action. For example, it is not good enough not to tell racist jokes. One must also not laugh at them when someone else tells them. A learning community, working across disciplines, can instill that philosophy perhaps better than a single class.

Students are also asked to define how baseball is part of the American Dream. For instance, is the American Dream just about owning a home in the country and golfing on weekends? Or is baseball's role in the American Dream something more? Where do freedom and equality enter into the definition? Is baseball part of social mobility? History tells us that baseball was not, so how and why did it change? In a democracy, can we posit that baseball reflects our own struggles to understand and appreciate diversity? How is that part of our ongoing quest for social justice?

A history lesson is needed here to help the students decide. The background includes references to Bud Fowler, Moses Fleetwood Walker and Cap Anson in the nineteenth century; and the role Andrew "Rube" Foster played in the rise of the Negro Leagues in the early part of the twentieth century. For each, race was a defining aspect of baseball, and the students must understand that to understand why a Jackie Robinson was necessary in 1947. To gain that understanding, students read Chapter 2 in Tygiel ("Twilight 'Ere the Noon") and Jerry Malloy's "Out at Home," in John Thorn's *The Armchair Book of Baseball II* (262–285). Of equal importance are links to original documents off the Society for American Baseball Research Web site (http://www.sabr.org) that show early segregation and grudging acceptance of inevitable integration.

A sequence on deciding whether integration was inevitable comes up a little later in the course. Before that, the class still has to absorb some historical background with the rise and fall and fall and fall of the Negro Leagues. In other words, most leagues failed. For example:

- the National Colored Base Ball League (the first of the Negro Leagues) lasted two weeks in 1887;
- the Negro National League lasted from 1920 to 1931, but the league's life was in jeopardy in 1930 when founder Rube Foster died and the Kansas City Monarchs withdrew to become an independent team;
- the Eastern Colored League lasted from 1923 to 1928;
- the American Negro League played one season in 1928;
- Gus Greenlee organized another Negro National League in 1933, which disbanded in 1948;
- the Negro American League was formed in 1937 and lasted until 1949.

Readings include John B. Holway's "Hilton Smith Remembers" in Thorn's anthology (165–176) and Richard Donovan's "The Fabulous Satchel Paige," (68–101) in Charles Einstein's *The Baseball Reader*.

It is important for students to understand that the Negro Leagues existed partly because of the intransigence of white team owners and players as well as the interpretative context of the Supreme Court's 1896 ruling in *Plessy v. Ferguson*, which upheld Louisiana's "separate but equal" statutes.

For their second brief paper, students are asked to evaluate Plessy in the wake of baseball and societal changes. For example, Michael Klarman, in his *From Jim Crow to Civil Rights: The Supreme Court and the Struggle for Racial Equality*, argues that the Plessy ruling reflected the view that white northerners and white southerners equally despised the Fifteenth Amendment (Gillman).

But those attitudes had seemingly changed by the mid-point of the twentieth century. The students' second paper requires writing about what they think is the sea change that allowed Jackie Robinson and Larry Doby to make their marks in 1947. Utilizing content from other courses in the learning community, and after reading Chapter 3 in Tygiel ("The Conspiracy of Silence"), students formulate a theory of civil rights progress from Plessy to the NAACP's Double V campaign of World War II. They take into account how baseball reflected the times—from the lynchings, disenfranchisement, and segregation of the Plessy era to the push for greater civil rights, along with the urbanization and industrialization of the New Deal era. One obvious example of pressure for progress was that the South came under increased media attention with spring training visits by more and more integrated teams. Klarman argues that such an increased media focus meant that the worst excesses of Jim Crow could not be contained and glossed over by a sympathetic southern community (Klarman, 188). In assessing this viewpoint, students are expected to factor the effect of *Brown v. Board of Education* into the equation. As a guide, students will be introduced to Klarman's theory and expected to find out more anecdotal or statistical evidence using content from other learning community courses and original research.

Briefly, Klarman argues that the Brown decision stirred up a conservative backlash in the southern white community and led to increased political suppression of African Americans. When southern police literally turned the dogs loose on African-American protesters, which was broadcast nationally, it partially transformed some northern racial opinions and this, in turn, led to the passage of the Civil Rights Act of 1964. In fact, Klarman says that many landmark Court rulings have produced more backlash than support since white supremacy in politics and economics depended on physical violence or the threat of violence. Therefore, he says, an assault on entrenched social mores requires patience and constant struggle, much like what the early pioneers of baseball endured and why Jackie Robinson and Larry Doby were much more successful than Fleetwood Walker.

Another anecdotal light on the topic is the Jake Powell incident of 1938. To summarize, Powell, a New York Yankee outfielder, told a radio interviewer on July 29 that he kept in shape in the off-season by working as a policeman in Dayton, Ohio, and cracking African Americans (though he did not use that term) over the head with his nightstick (Lamb 21). Powell was suspended for ten days, which *The Sporting News* reported was the first time a major league ballplayer was suspended for a racist remark. Professor Chris Lamb of the College of Charleston argues that Commissioner Kenesaw Mountain Landis would likely not have suspended Powell (after all, the irony of it is that baseball was segregated) if it had not been because of pressure brought by some mainstream dailies, African American journalists and *The Daily Worker*, a Communist Party daily in New York City.

Taken together, there is enough anecdotal evidence and theory to get students started on the research for the paper. Whether students agree or disagree with Klarman, Lamb, and Tygiel, they are expected to dissect the reasoning and persuasively argue their position on the evolution of attitudes to take their narrative up to the day that the Dodgers announced Robinson's signing on Oct. 23, 1945.

This brings up an interesting speculative argument that forms the backdrop for the rest of the course: was Robinson necessary in the modern integration of baseball? Was he the right man in the right place and time? Would the cause of integration have been set back a number of years without Robinson and Branch Rickey? (Given the elements already introduced it would be hard to argue that integration would never have occurred.) Would things have been different if Satchel Paige had been first? Josh Gibson (if he had lived long enough)? Larry Doby? The call for integration was there in the NAACP's Double V for Victory campaign during World War II—symbolizing victory overseas in the fight against fascism and victory at home in the fight for civil rights—but the answer lies in whether students subscribe to the "great man" theory of history or not. It is my job to get them to think about the question and challenge them to refine their thinking; it is not my duty to answer the question for them with my own view. Thus, the students are expected to show some originality and creativity in formulating and defending their answer. Chapters 3 and 4 in Tygiel and an excerpt from "Baseball Has Done It," by Jackie Robinson, edited by Charles Dexter, in Einstein's *The Baseball Reader,* serves as a jumping-off point for research and sources.

Since the media was alluded to several times in previous paragraphs, this is about the time in the semester when a discussion of the role of the press comes into play. Basically, the press section can be divided into three categories:

1. The African-American press had always called for greater social justice, whether by integrating the major leagues or in providing equal pay and opportunity. Most of the newspapers were weeklies, but a few daily sportswriters and columnists lent their voices to the struggle in the 1920s and 30s. Chief among them were Sam Lacy of *The Baltimore Afro-American*, Wendell Smith of *The Pittsburgh Courier*, and Joe Bostic of *The People's Voice of Harlem*.
2. The socialist *Daily Worker* began a campaign for baseball integration when sports editor Lester Rodney, and later Bill Mardo, started writing about the crusade in the 1930s.
3. The mainstream white press, in particular noted columnists such as Shirley Povich, Jimmy Powers, and others, would sometimes call for the abolishment of the so-called color barrier, but mostly the mainstream press followed the lead of people such as Lacy, Smith, Bostic and Rodney.

As the semester draws to a close, the main themes are refined and discussed and the remainder of Professor Tygiel's book is read. By the end of the semester, instead of writing a third analytical research paper, the students instead write a book review from one of the books mentioned in the works cited section in this essay, or from a bibliography provided at the start of the semester of post-1941 books. Students analyze the writer's main point and the evidence he or she cites in support of that thesis. It is expected that the report will show how much the students have gained from the course discussions and research.

The three papers should show a progression in the depth and understanding of course content rather than a rote memorization of facts and figures. It is essential not to get bogged down in baseball esoterica, but rather to show the clash of values from Anson to Robinson and Rickey and to explain the struggle over whose values emerged triumphant and why. Skirting along major themes, students may become more comfortable with class discussion and research because the goal is to become conversant with broad questions. Thus, a course in social justice and baseball is a course about conflict and cooperation, competition and individualism, as well as the overriding theme of justice and racism.

Along the same vein, as a final, open-book essay during what we prosaically call the critique and evaluation period at Buff State (it is known as finals week on other campuses that lack a flair for euphemism), students draw on their knowledge and write their opinion on whether baseball deserved to be called a national pastime during its most segregated years. Taken into account must be an explanation of how the game and its aura have evolved. For instance, some may say that baseball is too pastoral and is therefore an anachronism in a fast-paced, confrontational world (becoming the national "past time"). Regardless of whether we believe that or not, students are expected to evaluate how the "old school" sport showed other sports that equality and diversity were strengths and not weaknesses. In its way, baseball became the expression of democracy. In the learning community, students have the advantage of drawing upon research methods and content from other classes that also explore the concept of social justice.

Works Cited

Baldassaro, Lawrence, and Richard A. Johnson, eds. *The American Game; Baseball and Ethnicity*. Carbondale, IL: Southern Illinois University Press, 2002.
Berger, Jason. "Promoting Monarchs' Baseball Through Community-based Weekly Journalism: Quincy J. Gilmore, the Pitcher, and the Kansas City Call, the Catcher." *Grassroots Editor* 45.4 (2004): 1–8.
Dorinson, Joseph, and Joram Warmund, eds. *Jackie Robinson: Race, Sports, and the American Dream*. Armonk, NY: M.E. Sharpe, 1998.
Einstein, Charles, ed. *The Baseball Reade: Favorites from the Fireside Books of Baseball*. New York: Bonanza, 1989.
Gillman, Howard. Rev. of *From Jim Crow to Civil Rights: The Supreme Court and the Struggle for Racial Equality*, by Michael J. Klarman (New York: Oxford University Press, 2004). On the *Humanities and Social Sciences* Web site, 24 Dec. 2004. Retrieved 8 April 2005.
Heaphy, Leslie A. *The Negro Leagues, 1869–1960*. Jefferson, NC: McFarland, 2003.
Kessler, Lauren. *The Dissident Press: Alternative Journalism in American History*. SAGE CommText Series 13. Beverly Hills, CA: 1984.
Klarman, Michael J. *From Jim Crow to Civil Rights: The Supreme Court and the Struggle for Racial Equality*. New York: Oxford University Press, 2004.
Lamb, Chris. "L'Affaire Jake Powell: The Minority Press Goes to Bat Against Segregated Baseball." *Journalism & Mass Communication Quarterly* 76.1 (1999): 21–34.
_____. "'What's Wrong with Baseball': *The Pittsburgh Courier* and the Beginning of Its Campaign to Integrate the National Pastime." *The Western Journal of Black Studies* 26.4 (2002): 189–192.
Lamb, Chris, and Glen Bleske. "Democracy on the Field." *Journalism History* 24.2 (1998): 51–59.
Lanctot, Neil. *Negro League Baseball: The Rise and Ruin of a Black Institution*. Philadelphia: University of Pennsylvania Press, 2004.
Mitchell, Nancy, and Jerry Renaud. "Building a Learning Community for Journalism and Mass Communications: The Nebraska Experience." *Journalism & Mass Communication Educator* 56.3 (2001): 72–83.
Reisler, Jim. *Black Writers/Black Baseball: An Anthology from Black Sportswriters Who Covered the Negro Leagues*. Jefferson, NC: McFarland, 1994.
Silber, Irwin. *Press Box Red: The Story of Lester Rodney, the Communist Who Helped*

Break the Color Line in American Sports. Philadelphia: Temple University Press, 2003.

Smith, Jessie Carney, ed. *Black Firsts: 2,000 Years of Extraordinary Achievement.* Canton, MI: Visible Ink Press, 2003.

Thorn, John. *The Armchair Book of Baseball: An All-Star Lineup Celebrates America's National Pastime.* New York: Charles Scribner's Sons, 1987.

Tygiel, Jules. *Baseball's Great Experiment: Jackie Robinson and His Legacy.* Expanded edition. New York: Oxford University Press, 1997.

Social History

American Vice and Teaching Baseball History
(Kevin Grace)

I

As students take their seats for the first class meeting of the Social History of Baseball at the University of Cincinnati, they are hit with two questions: "Who invented baseball?" and "What is the biggest sin in baseball?" For those who answer "Abner Doubleday" to the first question, they are jokingly failed for the quarter. But for the second question, more serious attention is paid to the discussion. After some tentative stabs at "drug use" or "fighting with the fans," the class very quickly settles in on "gambling," the correct answer. In the view of Organized Baseball, gambling on the games in any way is the surest way to compromise the integrity of the sport. And the discussion of that topic leads the class into the content of the course: how has baseball throughout its history been affected by "vice" in society? How has gambling, the abuse of alcohol and tobacco, cheating, violence on and off the field, the use of performance-enhancing or recreational drugs, or the commitment of sex-related crimes been related to the National Pastime?

All of these topics, of course, are common issues in American society today, encountered by the students on a daily basis, whether through reports in the national media, in their local communities, or in their personal lives. But it is in sport and in entertainment where the sharpest scrutiny and publicity occur. And, since the class is one in social history, the emphasis is on the roles various groups have played in shaping baseball—immigrants, women, ethnic and racial groups, politicians, media, and children, for instance—while the course examines baseball in terms of American and global concerns from the nineteenth century to the present in war, economics, religion, health and recreation, and politics. In short, the course provides a historical and analytical study of a sport through social change and cultural assimilation. That the students sometimes refer to the course as "baseball through sex, drugs, and violence" allows them to relate historical processes to what they see in present-day sports.

One example of a causal relationship between baseball and social issues explored in the course is that of tobacco and its historical partnership with the game. In the September 2005 issue of *American Heritage* magazine, for instance, there appeared a full-page color advertisement for Macanudo, a cigar imported from the Dominican Republic. The focus of the ad was two gentlemen sitting in the stands at a ballpark. As the game is played out in the background, the male fans are enjoying "the best-selling premium cigar in America." The strong implication is that baseball and tobacco are linked together in an expression of manhood and national heritage.

The use of tobacco has always been viewed as being as much of a vice as it is a health risk. Billboard advertising is banned, smoking is prohibited in public places such as ballparks, and Major League Baseball has an active education campaign that warns of the dangers of smokeless tobacco. In fact, through its 1993 agreement with the minor leagues, the majors have prohibited tobacco use in the minors, resulting in a series of fines and suspensions for violations. The aim is that tobacco use in the major leagues will diminish over time as minor league players make their way up the professional ladder.

But the links between the two industries date to the mid-1800s, and they have always been characterized by both conflict and mutual advertising revenue, the latter extending from packaging to outfield billboard advertisements to baseball cards. In terms of the conflict, antitobacco activists such as industrialist Henry Ford, who used the testimonials of Ty Cobb and Connie Mack in his *The Case against the Little White Slaver,* have tried to eliminate tobacco from the game. Cigarettes in particular were seen as a vice of the lower classes, young working men, and immigrants. Considering the rosters of professional teams in the different eras of American history, there were strong links between who played baseball, who used tobacco, and who constituted the fan base.

In the early years of the twentieth century, evangelist Billy Sunday would hit the revival trail with a sermon about the evils of tobacco, especially in the way it was associated with the baseball players who were the idols of America's youth. Sunday was a former outfielder, having played for the Chicago White Stockings and the Pittsburgh Pirates from 1883 to

1890, and after he left the diamond for the pulpit he became one of the best-known preachers in the nation by using his baseball background to enliven his sermons, complete with pitching motions, bat-swinging, and sliding into home. The story he told was of his former teammate, John Clarkson. Clarkson is in the National Baseball Hall of Fame, and rightfully so, with 326 wins over a 10-year career. But Clarkson, Sunday said, actually ruined his career and his mental health because of his addiction to nicotine. As Billy Sunday put it, poor Clarkson died in a Massachusetts insane asylum. Cigarettes destroyed his health because he smoked eight to ten boxes of cigarettes every day. Sunday roomed with the pitcher and exclaimed that the bath water would be stained with nicotine whenever he bathed.

Perhaps the most famous historical example of the pairing of the two enterprises is, of course, the T-206 Honus Wagner card, withdrawn from a 1910 set because of Wagner's reluctance to use his celebrity to market tobacco to children, though he enjoyed cigars and chewing tobacco. Viewing historical examples of advertising and photographs, and reading relevant lectures and publications, the students can make a direct connection between baseball past and present.

II

With few exceptions, the students in the course are not hard-core fans of baseball, though they may have more than a passing interest because they either follow the progress of the season or attend a few games a year. For the most part, they are seeking to fulfill a social science segment as part of the general education requirements for every matriculating student. Some are also fulfilling electives to build toward the total number of academic credits for a degree, or are pairing the subject of baseball with other course work they are doing in architecture, marketing, management, sociology, education, or history. The result is a nicely diverse representation of the student body in terms of majors and by race, ethnicity, and gender.

The Social History of Baseball is offered twice per academic year, in the autumn and spring quarters. The nature of the class is defined in the syllabus with a note that it is not a course on sports trivia, nor does it involve glamorizing baseball and sport. Rather, the course approaches sport as an important aspect of American life and an integral part of human culture. It is a 300-level course, so the content is directed to junior and senior students, though it is open to underclassmen who have already fulfilled certain general education requirements. And because the class is an upper-division one, there are expectations that the students have achieved a suitable measure of skill in researching primary and secondary sources and are able to write cogent, thoughtful essays.

One of the most effective teaching and learning tools is the Blackboard software system used by the University of Cincinnati. A very flexible and adaptable system, Blackboard is available through the university's main student and faculty automation access points. The syllabus is loaded on Blackboard, along with all the assignments, study guides, and faculty contact information. In addition to that, however, I am able to link to selected Web sites that discuss the issues of drugs, cheating, and gambling in general, along with news articles on current events, whether the steroids scandal, a player caught with a corked bat or a scuffed ball, or even recent situations with drunken or violent fans at the ballpark attacking coaches and players.

In addition, hundreds of images of baseball history can be made available on Blackboard when previously they had to be shown to the class through slide presentations. Since slides are now a dying technology, this capability is important because it provides the students with a visual context to the course material. The images are batched for each lecture, so either in preparation for a particular class discussion or for study and review, students can see the images at their leisure. If they prefer, they can download the images to their own computers or to a disc. It is so much easier to learn history when there is a visual reference point to the names and events that are discussed in class. With this visual context available throughout the entire course, the students can view the images along with the assigned readings and the notes they have taken to gain a full presentation. Many of the university's classrooms are "electronic" in the full sense so that PowerPoint presentations, images, graphs, and charts can be easily presented in class.

A couple of additional uses of Blackboard have increased the interaction among students themselves and between the students and me. One of these uses involves the so-called hidden curriculum. With this instructional approach, each week an open-ended statement is posted on the course site's discussion board. For example, at the beginning of each week, the simple phrase "steroids and sports" or "baseball players and violence" might be listed. The students are then given until the following week to research and post a single fact about steroids and their relationship to sport, or about players who commit acts of violence on the field or in a domestic situation. These facts usually are a paragraph or two and include the students' own commentaries, but they must be written in essay form with the source of each fact given at the end of the brief essay.

Given the technological resources available to students, and their research inclinations, typically their facts are drawn from Internet sources. A couple of requirements, though, make this a more in-depth assignment than it appears to be. The posting of facts is done on a "first-come, first-served basis," that is, no one may post a fact that has already been discussed, and comments and critical assessments from other posters are encouraged, including from me, particularly regarding whether the source is a reputable one or not. This criticism requires the students to assess carefully the research much as they do for traditional printed sources. In this way, students are drawn into an active discussion with each other and with me. They also are drawn into the habit of writing coherent essays similar to what is expected on the exams. In addition, they feed each other with knowledge. On a typical topic, "alcohol and baseball," for instance, there will be thirty to thirty-five postings, each with a different fact about the subject. The students are expected to take notes on these postings, discuss them in class, and be able to incorporate them into questions on the exams. This hidden curriculum adds more substance to the lectures and debates in the classroom, and to the reading assignments. It fosters the creation of a class community of sorts, and makes the student an active learner rather than a passive one.

III

The course is divided into weekly lectures that follow the chronological history of baseball from the colonial period up to the current era, with an emphasis on concurrent development of patterns in socioeconomics, class and politics, and ethnicity and race. The standard text used is the second edition of Benjamin Rader's *Baseball: A History of America's Game*. Rader's book is the best single-volume history of the sport because, in addition to covering the particular events in baseball history, it also discusses the ethnic, class, and immigrant history of the United States. Supplementary required textbooks are typically Steven Riess's *City Games: The Evolution of American Urban Society and the Rise of Sports* and a topical book. In 2005, *The American Indian Integration of Baseball* by Jeffrey Powers-Beck was used because it provides a specific look at the subject of alcoholism in baseball. A general reading list of baseball books is also given to the students.

As part of the weekly lecture subject, an individual topic on vice and baseball is traced. Copies of primary source documents are distributed, for instance tobacco and alcohol ads with a baseball theme, or letters to Garry Herrmann, president of the Cincinnati Reds from 1902 to 1927 and chairman of the national commission from 1903 to 1920. Herrmann was the de facto commissioner of baseball before Kenesaw Mountain Landis was named as the sole head of baseball in 1920. As his papers in the library at the Baseball Hall of Fame show, Herrmann received thousands of letters, often concerned with the mundane operations of organized baseball, but many of them were personal or requested action on vice issues. For example, in a 1904 letter from Ban Johnson, president of the American League, Johnson was paying off a bet he lost to Herrmann on the outcome of a game. In another letter, Cora Stoddard, the famous temperance activist, wrote to Herrmann in 1911 asking him to ban the selling of hard liquor in ballparks. And correspondence from 1921 reveals Cincinnati's Juvenile Protective Association taking Herrmann and the Reds to task for allowing lewd dancing in the dark corners of the grandstand when Redland Field was leased for movies and dancing (Grace, 2004).

Or, for a discussion on baseball, ethnicity, and gambling in the nineteenth century, students are given a copy of "O'Toole's Ghost," an 1885 anonymous Cincinnati short story that lampoons the Irish, Jewish, and German element in baseball, and how they are supposedly given to cheating, gambling, gluttony, and greed (Grace, 2001). Even a popular song, Blanche Merrill and Irving Berlin's "Jake! Jake! The Yiddisher Ball-Player" (1913), lends texture to what they will read in Benjamin Rader's book when the 1919 World Series gambling scandal is discussed and Rader points out the media tried to foist baseball's betting woes onto Jewish gangsters and gamblers. The class discussion on gambling continues to the present era with the question: if the greatest sin in the major leagues is betting, why are casinos allowed to advertise in ballparks, in game programs, and in radio broadcasts? A deck of playing cards with baseball trivia questions, an officially licensed Major League Baseball product from 1996, is shown to the students. On the inside flap is printed the statement: "Major League Baseball does not approve of any form of gambling." On September 3, 2005, the Associated Press reported that the Baseball Hall of Fame rejected a gift of Barry Bonds' 700th home run ball because it was purchased at auction by an online gambling business that wanted to present it to the museum. How, they are asked, is this a reflection of American society and baseball history? We discuss the issue of Pete Rose's gambling, since it is an issue close to home, but his accomplishments are pointedly ignored. Instead, the focus is on what Rose represents to baseball fans and the general public, how his case may be different from other gambling circumstances in baseball and in other sports, and the implications of either his reinstatement in organized baseball or his continued banishment. Trial transcripts and other documents are examined as well.

A hands-on experience accompanies the topic of cheating. Students are asked, "In sports, when is it 'cheating' and when is it 'getting an edge'?" Their responses are typically enthusiastic and varied, and they are asked to apply their reasoning to everyday life in the business and academic worlds. Then, boxes of Thayer's Slippery Elm tablets are passed around the classroom. Each student is asked to take a tablet (spitball pitchers in the early twentieth century, such as Shufflin' Phil Douglas of the New York Giants, actually chewed pieces of the tree bark), wait until everyone has one in hand, and then put it in their mouths. The woody, musky taste of slippery elm gets their attention immediately, and almost everyone is put off by it. However, there is the desired effect: their mouths start salivating, and this leads into a discussion of the spitball. What have pitchers used to doctor the baseball? Why were doctored pitches banned in 1920? How was this ban not only a result of the alarm over cheating generated by the 1919 Black Sox series, but also influenced by sanitation concerns following the devastating 1918 Spanish Influenza pandemic, Progressive Era notions of urban hygiene, and the safety of the batter from an often unpredictable pitch? One or two of the students are given a vintage baseball mitt from the 1920s, along with an old baseball almost black from age and use, and shown the mechanics of throwing a spitter. Then, they are invited to lick the surface of the ball with the saliva generated by the slippery elm. No one has ever dared to do so, but the lesson hits home.

The same method is used when talking about drinking and alcoholism (minus the actual drinking, of course). Along with primary documents, students are shown packaging that carries the images of the heritage of baseball, such as beer cartons from Pete's Wicked Summer Brew, Cincinnati's former Oldenberg Beer (which featured a brew called "Crosley Red"), Cooperstown Brewing Company's "Old Slugger Ale," and even baseball bat-shaped bottles used by Coors in the early 1990s. Even as recently as the summer of 2005, the Helmar Brewing Company of Pleasant Ridge, Michigan, produced "Babe Ruth's Big League Brew" featuring bottle caps and labels with pictures of Ruth, Lefty Grove, Joe Jackson, Honus Wagner, Jimmy Foxx, Christy Mathewson, and Mordecai "Three-Finger" Brown. The students compare these materials to the issue of alcohol in sports throughout American history and with contemporary elements—such as campaigns for responsible drinking, designated drivers, alcohol-free zones in ballparks, a seventh-inning cut-off of concession sales, and team alcohol management—and then discuss the questions of revenue sources, social responsiveness, and fan enjoyment and expectations.

IV

Assessment and grading in the course varies somewhat from term to term, but in general the students are given midterm and final exams, along with a research project. The exam essays are grouped by subject, with a choice of one of two questions under each topic, and grading is based on creativity, logical progression of thought, specific details that support the argument, and quality of writing. Sometimes the questions are quite general: "Discuss the impact of gambling on baseball throughout its history," or very targeted: "Discuss the circumstances in both baseball and in society in the decade leading up to 1920 that threatened to harm the game, and which made citizens feel that American society was becoming unraveled. How did baseball address these circumstances in the 1920s?" In addition, the final exam includes a primary source document or photograph which the students have not previously seen, and they are asked to write an analysis of the content based on the nature of vice in baseball and American society.

For the research project, students are divided into groups of four or five, and told they are now in charge of a professional baseball team. They must select a real city, determine at what level their team will play (the four general levels of the minor leagues or as a major league team), explore the sports heritage of the city (along with ethnicity, economics, urban development, and tourism), and construct a ballpark in which they take into account surrounding entertainment, family-friendly policies within the park, and marketing. Additionally, they are presented with a series of scenarios they must address: a star player has been arrested for domestic battery—how do you handle it? Two players have been overheard gambling on football or basketball—how do you address it? A marginal player has tested positive for steroids, or has been charged with carrying a concealed weapon, or has been through alcohol rehabilitation programs more than once—how do you resolve this? The final written report is accompanied by the group's in-class PowerPoint presentation of their project.

V

Given the subject matter of a course like The Social History of Baseball, there will always be unavoidable questions by some students and parents, other faculty, and administrators regarding academic value, for example, whether the course is merely a filler or easy elective. And, given the size of the University of Cincinnati, with nearly 35,000 students, there always will be a changing stream of students who see the course's availability, enroll in it, and walk into class with this thinking. That's just the way it is. But the number of colleges and universities that offer a baseball-oriented course has skyrocketed, and baseball courses are becoming standard offerings in the curricula. The key in a baseball history course is to inject the colorful personalities of the game, and to relate the topics, research assignments, readings, and other elements of the class to what the students experience either in their own lives or in what they are learning in other courses, to integrate the subject matter—in this case, vice and baseball—with their own awareness of the sports world. As much as I would like them to realize that the triple is the most beautiful play in the game, it is more important that they are aware of how we moved from the Irish role in organized baseball in the nineteenth century to the Latino influence in the twenty-first, or how "sex, drugs, and violence" are factors in every element of sport and society in which we move. The aim of this course, as I tell the students during the first meeting of the term, is that at its conclusion they will never view a baseball game or read a sports page in the same way again, that they will see the interrelatedness of America's social parts, and that, concerning these changes, they will ask themselves, "Why is this so?" and be able to understand why.

Works Cited

Ford, Henry. *The Case against the Little White Slaver*. 4 vols. Detroit: Henry Ford, 1916.

Grace, Kevin. "*'O'Toole's Ghost': A Cincinnati Baseball Story from 1885*. Cincinnati: The Archives & Rare Books Department, University of Cincinnati, 2001.

———. "Sporting Man: Garry Herrmann and the 1909 Cincinnati *Turnfest*." *Cincinnati Occasional Papers in German-American Studies*. Cincinnati: No. 3, 2004.

Powers-Beck, Jeffrey. *The American Indian Integration of Baseball*. Lincoln: University of Nebraska Press, 2004.

Rader, Benjamin G. *Baseball: A History of America's Game*. 2nd ed. Urbana: University of Illinois Press, 2002.

Riess, Steven A. *City Games: The Evolution of American Urban Society and the Rise of Sports*. Urbana: University of Illinois Press, 1989.

About the Contributors

Roger I. Abrams, Richardson Professor of Law at Northeastern University School of Law, is former dean of the law schools at Northeastern University and Rutgers University. He has authored three books on the law, economics, and the history of baseball, all published by Temple University Press: *Legal Bases: Baseball and the Law* (1998), *The Money Pitch: Baseball, Free Agency and Salary Arbitration* (2000), and *The First World Series and the Baseball Fanatics of 1903* (2003). He has served as a baseball arbitrator and has written widely on labor arbitration, sports law, and other legal issues.

Gerald D. Bailey is professor of education at Kansas State University. He teaches graduate courses in technology leadership and staff development in the department of Educational Administration and Leadership. He is the author of many articles and books. Currently, he serves as the Negro Leagues Baseball Museum liaison for the College of Education, Kansas State University, Manhattan, Kansas.

E. Michael Brady is a professor of adult education at the University of Southern Maine where he teaches graduate courses in the history and philosophy of adult education, action research, facilitation of adult learning, and gerontology. He also serves as a senior research fellow at USM's Osher Lifelong Learning Institute, a noncredit college for learners over the age of 55. He has published articles about his sandlot baseball experiences as a child and created the travel course that is described in this essay.

Eric Bronson is a professor of philosophy and history at Berkeley College in New York City. He is a frequent contributor to Open Court's Popular Culture and Philosophy series, having edited *Poker and Philosophy* (2006), *Baseball and Philosophy* (2004), and *The Lord of the Rings and Philosophy* (with Greg Bassham, 2003). He has produced and edited the award-winning documentary *My Lazy White Friends* (with Dean Ishida) and cowritten the short film *Ruckus!*

Michael L. Butterworth is a Ph.D. candidate in the Department of Communication and Culture at Indiana University in Bloomington. He has taught public speaking at Indiana University, Northern Illinois University, the College of Lake County (IL), and Ivy Tech Community College (IN). His research focuses on the rhetorical constructions of citizenship and identity in and through sport, especially baseball. His work appears in *Communication and Critical/Cultural Studies*, *Journal of Sport and Social Issues*, and *Aethlon: The Journal of Sport Literature*.

Robert Cvornyek is an associate professor of history and secondary education at Rhode Island College. In addition to his teaching responsibilities, Professor

Cvornyek is the director of the college's Working Class Studies Program. He is the coeditor of *The Black Worker: A Documentary History from the AFL-CIO Merger to the Present* and author of *Baseball in Newark*. His work on Negro League baseball includes "Race, Memory, and Professional Baseball in Newark" and "Between Memory and History: Black Sportswriters and the (Re)Construction of Negro League Baseball (with Lawrence Hogan)," both in the *Cooperstown Symposium on Baseball and American Culture* (McFarland, 2001 and 2003–04). He is currently editing Effa Manley and Leon Hardwick's book *Negro Baseball ... Before Integration* for St. Johann Press.

Raymond Doswell has served as curator/education director for the Negro Leagues Baseball Museum in Kansas City, Missouri, since 1995. He also serves as a member of the Missouri State Historical Records Advisory Board and has been selected to serve on the National Baseball Hall of Fame special election committee for Negro Leagues players. He has taught high school in the St. Louis area.

Rob Edelman, who teaches film history at the University of Albany (SUNY), is the author of *Great Baseball Films* (Citadel Press, 1994) and *Baseball on the Web* (MIS Press, 1998), which Amazon.com cited as one of the top ten Internet books of 1998. He has lectured on the manner in which baseball films reflect America in the Speakers in the Humanities program, sponsored by the New York Council for the Humanities. With his wife, Audrey Kupferberg, he has authored *Meet the Mertzes* (Renaissance Books, 1999), a double biography of Vivian Vance and fabled baseball fan William Frawley, and *Matthau: A Life* (Taylor Trade Publishing, 2002), a biography of Walter Matthau. He has contributed essays to *Baseball and American Culture: Across the Diamond*; *A Political Companion to American Film*; *Total Baseball*; *The Total Baseball Catalog*; *International Dictionary of Films and Filmmakers*; and *Women Filmmakers and Their Films,* and is a long-time contributing editor of *Leonard Maltin's Movie & Video Guide* as well as a film commentator on WAMC (Northeast) Public Radio.

Kevin Grace is the university archivist and the head of the Archives and Rare Books Library at the University of Cincinnati, where he also teaches in the College of Education, Criminal Justice, and Human Services. In 1984 he created the Urban Sport Research Archive to document the historical place of sport and recreation in the urban environment. He has received various grants to study the politics of alcohol, urban ballparks, and the African American heritage in baseball. His current research centers on sport and education during the Progressive Era, bloodsports, sport and vice, and ethnic history and leisure. Currently he is editing, *German-Americans in Sports and Physical Recreation,* which will be published in 2007 by Peter Lang Publishers.

Lise Graham chairs the finance department at the University of Wisconsin at La Crosse. Her publications include articles on long-term care financing, predicting thrift closure by comparing book and market values, and capital budgeting, which have appeared in such journals as *Managerial Finance, Bank Accounting and Finance*, and *The Journal of Insurance Issues*. She has presented papers at conferences in the United States and Italy. Her papers include a study of financial aspects of the Babe Ruth trade, delivered at the annual meeting of the Financial Education Association in 2005.

Gary Gray is an assistant professor of English at Andrews University, Berrien Springs, Michigan. He is a doctoral candidate at Western Michigan University, where he is specializing in seventeenth-century American literature.

George Grella is a professor of English and film studies at the University of Rochester, where he specializes in American literature of the nineteenth and twentieth centuries and twentieth-century British literature. He publishes extensively on film, on detective, crime, and mystery fiction, and, of course, on baseball—his papers have been included in several editions of the *Cooperstown Symposium on Baseball and American Culture* published by McFarland. He serves as film critic for *City Newspaper*, an alternative newsweekly in Rochester, and for WXXI-FM, a local PRI affiliate.

Michael Haupert chairs the economics department at the University of Wisconsin at La Crosse. He has applied economic principles to baseball in a number of articles in such journals as *Nine: A Journal of Baseball History and Social Policy Perspectives* and *Essays in Economic and Business History*, as well as in articles for *The Economics of Sports* and *The Oxford Encyclopedia of Economic History*. He writes primarily about the New York Yankees because, as he says, he "knows where the money is."

C. Richard King, an associate professor of comparative ethnic studies at Washington State University, has written extensively on the changing position of Native Americans in post-Civil Rights America, the colonial legacies and postcolonial predicaments of American culture, and struggles over Indianness in public culture. His work has appeared in such journals as *American Indian Culture and Research Journal, Journal of Sport and Social Issues, Public Historian, and Qualitative Inquiry*. He is also the editor of several books, including *Team Spirits: The Native American Mascot Controversy* (with Charles Fruehling Springwood); University of Nebraska Press, 2001; (a CHOICE 2001 Outstanding Academic Title) and *Postcolonial America* (University of Illinois Press, 2001). He has recently completed *Native American Athletes in Sport and Society* (University of Nebraska Press, 2005) and *The Encyclopedia of Native Americans and Sport*.

Karen S. Koziara is a member of the Department of Human Resource Management and the Fox School of Business at Temple University. Her research focuses primarily on labor relations or public policy and labor market issues. She has published in a wide variety of journals, including the *Industrial and Labor Relations Review, Yale Journal of Regulation, Employee Relations Law Journal, Monthly Labor Review, Proceedings of the Industrial and Relations Research Association, Labor Law Journal*, and in several edited books, including a chapter entitled "Baseball Labor Relations: Is It Safe to Go Back to the Ballpark?" in *Baseball and American Culture*, edited by Edward J. Rielly (Haworth, 2004).

She has been a Woodrow Wilson Fellow, a Fulbright Fellow, and a German Marshall Fellow, along with receiving a Lindback Teaching Award, an Asher Outstanding Faculty Award, and School of Business Faculty Research Award.

Gary Land is a professor of history and chair of the Department of History and Political Science at Andrews University, Berrien Springs, Michigan. He has taught at Andrews University since 1970. In addition to writing and editing several works in American religious history, he has edited *Growing Up with Baseball* (University of Nebraska Press, 2004).

Alar Lipping is a professor in the Department of Educational Specialties at Northern Kentucky University. His teaching responsibilities include courses in sport history and sociology, educational research, and baseball history. He has presented papers at such conferences as the North American Society for Sport History, Popular Culture Association, American Culture Association, International Sport History and Physical Education Society, and Southwest Texas Popular Culture Association. His publications include contributions to the *Journal of Physical Education, Recreation and Dance*, *Physical Educator*, and the *Canadian Journal of History of Sport*. He served as chair of the Sport History Academy of the American Alliance for Health, Physical Education, Recreation, and Dance.

Dan Lumley is the director of curriculum and instruction in the Lee's Summit R-7 school district in Lee's Summit, Missouri. In addition to his public school career, he is an adjunct professor at Kansas State University. Together with Gerald D. Bailey from Kansas State University he has authored a number of books and journal articles. Bailey and Lumley's leadership books are used as resource books in school districts and universities throughout the country.

Joe Marren is an assistant professor in the communication department at Buffalo State College, where he teaches newswriting, news editing and news media courses. In his eighteen-year career in journalism, he worked for various western New York community dailies and niche newspapers, working as a reporter or editor in every editorial department, including cityside, features, sports, business, and the editorial page. He has won writing awards for his columns and has also written freelance articles on sports history and other topics. His first book, *Buffalo's Brush with the Arts: From Huck Finn to Murphy Brown* (Meyer Enterprises, 1998), was about the literary and artistic history of his hometown. With Tim O'Shei, he has written three presidential biographies for children. He also does commentaries for the National Public Radio affiliate station in Buffalo.

Edward J. Rielly chairs the English department at Saint Joseph's College of Maine, where he teaches a variety of writing and literature courses, including several courses involving baseball. In addition to ten volumes of poetry, he has published books on Jonathan Swift's *Gulliver's Travels*, F. Scott Fitzgerald, popular culture of the 1960s, and baseball and American culture. He currently is writing a biography of Sitting Bull and a book on football and American culture.

About the Contributors

Jerry Rodnitzky is professor of history at the University of Texas at Arlington, where he specializes in recent American cultural history. His four books include *Minstrels of the Dawn: The Folk-Protest Singer as a Cultural Hero* (Nelson-Hall 1976), and, more recently, *Jazz-Age Boomtown* (Texas A&M University Press 1997) and *Feminist Phoenix: The Rise and Fall of a Feminist Counterculture* (Praeger, 1999). He is a founding and continuing advisory editor of the journal *Popular Music and Society*.

C. Paul Rogers III is professor and former dean of the Southern Methodist University School of Law. He is the coauthor of three baseball books, including *The Whiz Kids and the 1950 Pennant* (Temple University Press, 1996), written with his boyhood hero, Robin Roberts. His baseball writings have appeared in *National Pastime*, *Elysian Fields Quarterly*, *NINE: A Journal of Baseball History and Culture*, and *Spitball*. He is president of the Hall-Ruggles Chapter (Dallas-Ft. Worth) of the Society of American Baseball Research (SABR) and series editor for a new Sport in American Life series for the SMU Press.

William M. Simons is a professor and former chair of history at SUNY Oneonta, and the recipient of the Chancellor's Award for Excellence in Teaching. His offerings include courses in sport and baseball history. Widely published in sport, ethnic, and social history, Simons, along with series editor Alvin L. Hall, has edited four volumes of McFarland's *Cooperstown Symposium on Baseball and American Culture* series (2000, 2001, 2002 and 2003–2004). As a speaker for the New York Council for the Humanities, he has lectured on baseball for public schools, colleges, libraries, museums, civic groups, and other sponsors. He is the former radio cohost of *SportsTalk* on WONY.

John A. Vernon has served the National Archives and Records Administration (NARA) in outreach capacities as archivist, historian, and teacher, and has directed courses for outside researchers and potential users as well as others for federal agency personnel. Before coming to the Archives he was a history professor at Tuskegee Institute (now Tuskegee University), where he gradually became interested in using archival records to advance classroom teaching. To that end, he has often worked in the holdings of the Library of Congress as well as those of the National Archives to develop black history and sports history–related educational articles, exhibit catalogs, and curriculum supplements. His most recent research interests have concentrated on Jackie Robinson's civil rights activities and advocacies, sports documentation issues, and the Negro Leagues.

Kenneth Winter chairs the accountancy department at the University of Wisconsin at La Crosse. He has presented papers on financial issues relating to the New York Yankees at the annual *Cooperstown Symposium on Baseball and American Culture* at Cooperstown and as part of the Indiana University Economic History Seminar Series at Bloomington. His articles include analyses of cash flow problems in *Accounting Instructors' Report* and of learning strategies with accounting students in the *Journal of Accounting and Finance Research*.

Index

Aaron, Henry 41, 46–47
Adams, Ansel 8
Alcohol problems 175
An American Dilemma: The Negro Problem and American Democracy 10
American Indian baseball 133–135
The American Indian Integration of Baseball 173
America's National Game 145
Angel in the Outfield 54, 64, 68
Anson, Cap 163, 164
Aparicio, Luis 13
Aristotle 147
The Armchair Book of Baseball II 164
Armetta, Henry 54–55

The Babe Ruth Story 63–64
The Bad Boys Won! 140
Baker, Home Run 71
Baker, Jesse 52
Bang the Drum Slowly 65, 75, 115, 118, 119
Barzun, Jacques 162
Baseball (Burns) 28, 122, 127
Baseball: An Encyclopedia of Popular Culture 1
Baseball: A History of America's Game 79, 173
Baseball: A Literary Anthology 116
Baseball and American Culture: Across the Diamond 41, 127
Baseball and the Meaning of Life 116
Baseball in '41 69–70
The Baseball Reader 165, 166
Baseball's Great Experiment: Jackie Robinson and His Legacy 70, 162
Basic Agreement 91, 93–94
Bavasi, Buzzie 15
Bearden, Gene 57
Bennett, Joe 52
Berg, Moe 52, 74, 86
Berkenstock, Nate 52
Bess, Philip 123
Beyond the Shadow of the Senators 12

Bingo Long's Traveling All-Stars and Motor Kings 68, 127
Bjarkman, Peter C. 116
Black Sox 20–21, 65, 66, 73, 83
Blackboard software system 172
Blomberg, Ron 52
Body and Soul 57
Bonds, Barry 13, 49, 139, 174
Boone, Aaron 108
Bostic, Joe 167
Boston Braves 22
Boston Red Sox 19, 22, 50, 99, 138
Boswell, Thomas 115
Boudreau, Lou 57
The Boys of Summer 115, 116, 117
Brashler, William 127
Brodsky, Chuck 74
Brooklyn Dodgers 12–13, 21, 32, 74, 145, 152–153
Broun, Heywood Hale 73
Brown v. Board of Education 165
Bull Durham 4, 55, 67, 75, 140
Burke, Kenneth 148
Burns, Ken 28, 73, 122, 127
Bush, George W. 146, 147, 149

Cagney, James 56
Cameron, Chris 42
Campanella, Roy 7, 9–10
Campanis, Al 16
Cannon, Nancy 82–83
Carnegie, Andrew 71
Carrasquel, Alfonso "Chico" 13
The Case Against the Little White Slaver 170
Case Study Method 22–26
Casey at the Bat 54, 123
The Celebrant 62, 115, 118, 119, 121, 126
Celebrity and baseball 71–71, 73
Chicago White Sox 21, 50
The Chosen 60–61
Cimarron 56
City Baseball Magic 123
The City Games: The Evolution of Ameri-

Index

can *Urban Society and the Rise of Sports* 173
Clarkson, John 171
Cleveland Indians 57, 67
Comiskey, Charles 71, 73
The Cooperstown Symposium on Baseball and American Culture: 2001 78
Coover, Robert 62
Costner, Kevin 66, 67
Counsellor-at-Law 55
Creamer, Robert 69
Cristall, Bill "Lefty" 52
The Curse of the Bambino 44
Curt Flood v. Bowie Kuhn 97

Dawidoff, Nicholas 116
Diamonds Are a Girl's Best Friend 116
Dimaggio, Dom 73, 119
Dimaggio, Joe 73
Dimaggio, Vince 73
Doby, Larry 41, 57, 153, 165
Documents, use of 11, 15–17
Douglass, Frederick 162
Dowling, Bill 43
Drug use 94, 141–142
DuBois, W.E.B. 162
Durham Bulls 45

Early, Gerald 153
Eight Men Out 64, 73, 126
Einstein, Charles 165
Elysian Fields 130
Epstein, Theo 99
Evers, Bill 45

Fathers Playing Catch with Sons 115
Feller, Bob 41, 57
Fences 127
Ferber, Edna 56
Field of Dreams 66, 67, 68, 73, 75–76, 117, 126, 148
Fielder's Choice 115
Films 53–61, 61–68, 148–149
Finley, Charlie 98
Flavin, Dick 119
Fleetwood, Mose 164
Force of Evil 57
Foster, Rube 164
Fowler, Bud 164
Fox, J.R. 134
From Jim Crow to Civil Rights: The Supreme Court and the Struggle for Racial Equality 165
Fuller, Todd 133

Gambling 169, 174–175
Gates, James 83
Gehrig, Lou 21–22
Giamatti, A. Bartlett 162
Gibson, Josh 12, 13, 15
The Glory of Their Times 115, 116, 117, 122
Goldstein, Izzy 53
Goodwin, Doris Kearns 115
Goosen, Greg 52
Grammar baseball 128–130
The Great Gatsby 62
Green, Shawn 52
"Green light letter" 11
Greenberg, Eric 62, 115
Greenberg, Hank 52, 53, 57, 58, 59, 61, 73
Griffith, Clark 71
Growing Up with Baseball 116
Guillen, Ozzie 13

Halberstam, David 115
Hall, Donald 115
Hall of Fame (National Baseball Hall of Fame and Museum) 15–16, 17, 32, 42, 50, 52, 83, 127, 144, 163, 174
Hamilton, Mark 141
Harris, Mark 62, 115
Hearst, William Randolph 71
Herrmann, Garry 173–174
Hicks, Tom 105
Holtz, Jerome 115
Holtzman, Ken 52
Home runs 20–21
Horvath, Brooke 127
Hot Curves 58–59
Huggins, Miller 96
Humoresque 57

I Had a Hammer 47
Ickes, Harold 9, 11
Idioms in baseball 76, 110
Iron Man 44
Irvin, Monte 153, 163
It Happens Every Spring 64
It's My Turn 60

The Jackie Robinson Story 63, 64
Jackson, Shoeless Joe 73, 140
James, Bill 24, 44
Japanese baseball 6–9, 74–75
Jennings, Hughie 96
Jewish Major Leagues, Inc. 52
Jewish players 55–61, 174
Johnson, Jack 162

Jones, James Earl 66, 76, 123
Journal of Sport History 29, 32
Journals, use in classroom 41
Joyce, Kenny 48

Kahn, Roger 115, 140, 162
Kansas City Monarchs 152
Kant, Immanuel 142–143
The Kid from Cleveland 57, 58
Kinsella, W.P. 66, 115, 162
Klarman, Michael 165, 166
Klepp, Eddie 74
Koufax, Sandy 52, 53, 61
Kuhn, Bowie 97, 98

Labor relations 87–95, 96, 105–109
Lacy, Sam 167
Lajoie, Napoleon 97–98
Lancaster, Burt 26
Landis, Kenesaw Mountain 9, 11, 96, 166, 173
LaRusso, Tony 96
Latin American baseball 13–14, 74–75
Law in baseball 95–100, 104–111
A League of Their Own 54, 65, 68
Lemon, Bob 57
Leonard, Buck 12
Levinson, Barry 52
Lewis, Michael 41, 46
Liberty Heights 52, 54, 60
Library of Congress 3–4, 17
Line Drives: 100 Contemporary Baseball Poems 127
Lonborg, Jim 84
Louis, Joe 156, 162
Lucchino, Larry 99

Mack, Connie 98
Major League 67, 140
Major League Baseball (MLB) 95, 99, 146
Major League Baseball Players Association 88, 91–92, 95, 107
Malamud, Bernard 62, 115
Manley, Effa 151–153, 155
Manzanar Relocation Center 7–8
Mardo, Bill 167
Mascots 135–136
Mathewson, Christy 71
Matrix trilogy 160
Mayer, Erskine 52
Mayor of Hell 56
McKee, Ron 48
Media 71–72, 167
The Mirror Has Two Faces 72

Mr. Rickey Calls a Meeting 156
Monbouquette, Bill 41, 84
Moneyball 41, 44, 46
Murakami, Masanori 8
Music 123, 128, 148, 174
Myer, Buddy 52
Myrdal, Gunnar 10

National Archives and Records Administration (NARA) 17–18, 154
National Labor Relations Act (NLRA) 88–89
National Labor Relations Board (NLRB) 99
The Natural 62, 65–66, 67, 75, 115, 116, 140
Nauen, Elinor 116
Negro Baseball: Before Integration 155
Negro Leagues 10, 12, 13, 33–34, 35, 70, 74, 127, 152–153, 156, 163, 164, 165
Negro Leagues Baseball Museum (NLBM) 34–35, 37–38
Negro Leagues Education Partnership 35
Nehf, Art 22
New York Giants 21, 22
New York Yankees 19, 20–21, 22
Newcombe, Don 153

October Men 140
Oh, Sadaharu 139
The Old Man and the Sea 62
Owens, Jesse 162

Paige, Satchel 15–16, 57, 163
Past Time: Baseball as History 70, 73
Patriotism 146–147, 149
Pearlman, Jeff 140
Pesky, Johnny 119
Philosophy 140–142
Photographs, use in classroom 4–5, 7–8, 10, 14
Pike, Lip 52
Plato 148
Plessy v. Ferguson 165
Ponson, Sidney 107–108
Portland Sea Dogs 42, 48–49
Powers-Beck, Jeffrey 173
The Pride of the Yankees 63
"Pueblo Baseball: A New Use for Old Witchcraft" 134

Race 9–13, 15–16, 29, 74, 127, 135–136, 145, 151–158, 161–162, 163, 165–166
Radar, Benjamin 79, 173, 174

Reel Baseball 62
Reserve clause 20
Revenue streams 21, 23–25, 94
Richards, David 84
Rickey, Branch 12, 18, 74, 96, 153, 156–157
Rielly, Edward J. 41, 42
Riess, Steven 28, 173
Ripken, Cal, Jr. 47
Ritter, Lawrence 115, 135
Ritterpusch, Dave 44
Rituals 145–146
Roberts, Gary 97
Robeson, Paul 156–157
Robinson, Bill "Bojangles" 156–157
Robinson, Jackie 12–13, 15–16, 28, 32, 74, 83, 127, 145, 152–153, 156–157, 162, 163, 166
Rockefeller, John 71
Rocker, John 98
Rodney, Lester 167
Rodriguez, Alex 105
Rogers, Kenny 93
Roosevelt, Franklin D. 11, 73, 145
Rose, Pete 42, 174
Rosen, Al 52
Ruth, Babe 19, 20, 22, 24, 52–53, 71, 73, 83, 140

Sanctuary 62
Sarandon, Susan 67, 68
Sayles, John 73
Schilling, Curt 94–95
Schmeling, Max 162
Schmidt, Ed 156
Selig, Bud 93, 96
The Shamrock Handicap 58
Shaughnessy, Dan 44
Sherry, Larry 52
Shoeless Joe 66, 115, 116
60 Feet 6 Inches and Other Distances from Home: The Baseball Life of Mose Yellowhorse 133–134
Smith, Chris 48
Smith, Wendell 167
Snyder, Brad 12
Society for American Baseball Research (SABR) 23, 82
Sockalexis, Louis 135
Solomon, Eric 61
Solomon, Mose 52

Sosa, Sammy 150
Spaulding, Albert 145
Speaker, Tris 57
Spitball 130
Sports and the Law: Text, Cases, and Problems 97
Statistics 72
Stereotypes in film 54–55
Stone, Steve 52
Summer of '49 115, 119
Sunday, Billy 170–171

Take Me Out to the Ball Game 59–60
Taxi 56
The Teammates 115, 119
Terkel, Studs 73
Thorn, John 164
Time Begins on Opening Day 115
Tobacco 170–171
Tokyo Giants 7, 9–10
Triola, Victoria 84–85
Tygiel, Jules 28, 61, 70, 76, 162, 163, 164, 165, 166, 167

Underworld 62
Universal Baseball Association, J. Henry Waugh, Prop. 62

Veeck, Bill 57, 95
Vernon, Mickey 57
Video, use in classroom 29, 36, 146–147, 149–150

Wait Till Next Year 115, 116, 121, 122
War Relocation Authority 8
Ward, Geoffrey 28
Ward, John Montgomery 96
We Shall Not Forget 146, 149–150
Weaver, Robert 11
Weiler, Paul 97
Wheeler, Lonnie 41, 47
Wiles, Tim 127
Williams, Ted 73, 119, 140
Wilson, August 127
Win shares 24, 44
Wolfe, Thomas 47

Yellowhorse, Mose 133–134
York, Rudy 135
You Know Me Al 44
The Younger Generation 55

www.ingramcontent.com/pod-product-compliance
Ingram Content Group UK Ltd.
Pitfield, Milton Keynes, MK11 3LW, UK
UKHW042012140426
5217IPUK00015B/1126